The Assessment of Emergent Bilinguals

Full details of all our publications can be found on http://www.multilingual-matters. com, or by writing to Multilingual Matters, St Nicholas House, 31-34 High Street, Bristol BS1 2AW, UK.

The Assessment of Emergent Bilinguals

Supporting English Language Learners

Kate Mahoney

MULTILINGUAL MATTERS
Bristol • Blue Ridge Summit

Library of Congress Cataloging in Publication Data
A catalog record for this book is available from the Library of Congress.
Mahoney, Kate (Professor) author.
The Assessment of Emergent Bilinguals: Supporting English Language Learners/Kate Mahoney.
Bristol: Multilingual Matters, [2017] | Includes bibliographical references and index.
LCCN 2016043805| ISBN 9781783097265 (hbk : alk. paper) | ISBN 9781783097258 (pbk : alk.
paper) | ISBN 9781783097272 (Pdf) | ISBN 9781783097289 (Epub) | ISBN 9781783097296 (Kindle)
LCSH: English language—Study and teaching (Elementary)—Foreign speakers. | English
language—Study and teaching (Secondary)—Foreign speakers. | Educational tests and
measurements. | Education, Bilingual—Evaluation.
LCC PE1128.A2 M313 2017 | DDC 428.0071--dc23 LC record available at https://lccn.loc.
gov/2016043805

British Library Cataloguing in Publication Data
A catalogue entry for this book is available from the British Library.

ISBN-13: 978-1-78309-726-5 (hbk)
ISBN-13: 978-1-78309-725-8 (pbk)

Multilingual Matters
UK: St Nicholas House, 31-34 High Street, Bristol BS1 2AW, UK.
USA: NBN, Blue Ridge Summit, PA, USA.

The policy of Multilingual Matters/Channel View Publications is to use papers that are natural,
renewable and recyclable products, made from wood grown in sustainable forests. In the manufac-
turing process of our books, and to further support our policy, preference is given to printers that
have FSC and PEFC Chain of Custody certification. The FSC and/or PEFC logos will appear on
those books where full certification has been granted to the printer concerned.

Typeset by Deanta Global Publishing Services Limited.
Printed and bound in the UK by the CPI Books Group Ltd.
Printed and bound in the US by Edwards Brothers Malloy, Inc.

Contents

Acknowledgments

My deepest gratitude is owed to my family (Jon Storm, Emma Kane-Mahoney Storm, Jack Mahoney Storm, and Eva Jean-Mahoney Storm) – and also to my loving parents Pat and Bill Mahoney, and siblings Mary Andres, Jim Mahoney, Amy Mahoney and Daniel Mahoney. I am so thankful for the many great colleagues who supported this work: colleagues from State University of New York (SUNY) at Fredonia, University of Maryland (UMD), Arizona State University (ASU), Caslon Publishing, and especially to colleagues from City University of New York-New York State Initiative on Emergent Bilinguals (CUNY-NYSIEB) and the staff at Multilingual Matters for valuing this work and supporting me to finish it. Finally, my warm thanks go to many TESOL students who read this manuscript and provided valuable feedback, and also to the creative teachers and administrators who provided examples contained in this book.

Introduction

This book is intended to be a comprehensive introduction to the topic of assessing students in schools who use two or more languages in their daily life: the foundations of assessment for emergent bilinguals (EB). The topic of assessment, measurement and bilingualism is a complicated one. The content of this book breaks down the complex issue of assessment in a digestible way by providing in-depth chapters on the following areas: a decision-making process called PUMI, history, validity, methods, content and language, psychometrics, accommodations, special education and accountability. These major topics within assessment are all connected by a decision-making framework called PUMI (Purpose, Use, Method, Instrument), a framework that allows practitioners to better inform assessment decisions for bilingual children. I have been teaching university-level assessment courses since 1999 and using the concept of PUMI in my courses to help teacher candidates understand and ask critical questions about assessment for bilingual children. Since teaching assessment to teachers for the first time in 1999, I have conducted research on these topics, designed assessment courses for Arizona State University and the State University of New York at Fredonia as well as given workshops and interacted with teachers in professional circles across New York State on the topic of assessment. This book is the outcome of these experiences. The following sections provide more information about the organization of the book.

Snapshots

Most chapters contain 'snapshots' of real case scenarios mainly drawing from my experiences in the field.

End of Chapter Activities

At the end of each chapter, there are activities that college instructors can use in assessment courses to practice some of the key points in assessing bilingual children. I also offer advice to instructors based on my own experience of implementing these activities in undergraduate and graduate university assessment courses. These activities are all designed to be interactive and to give students practice in digesting and processing some of the critical ideas in this book.

Themes in this Book

The following shows a breakdown of each chapter and the main themes presented in each chapter.

Chapter 1: A Decision-Making Process called PUMI

(1) Teachers have to compromise along a continuum of assessment practices leading to deficit or leading to promise.
(2) Good assessment practices for EB students are grounded in four guiding principles or assumptions.
(3) A useful tool called PUMI can assist teachers in making informed and appropriate decisions about assessment.

Chapter 2: History – How Did We Get Here?

(1) The history of testing EB students includes many examples of inappropriate testing and misuse of results.
(2) Despite more than a decade of warning from the measurement community, test scores from tests given in English, to students who don't know English, are still being used for important education decisions.
(3) The current political climate favors accountability over validity.

Chapter 3: Validity

(1) Tests aren't bad; it's how we are using them that may be bad.
(2) Viewing EB test scores through the unified view of validity puts due importance on how we use EB test scores. This includes social consequences.
(3) Construct irrelevant variance (CIV) is a major validity threat for test scores of EB students.
(4) The social consequences of using test scores or 'side effects' are having wide-range impact on the field of English as a new language (ENL) and bilingual education (BE).

Chapter 4: Methods

(1) Selecting an appropriate method of assessment is directly related to aligning with the purpose of the assessment.
(2) Rubrics and checklists can be made easily from standards and criteria (purpose).
(3) Main categories of methods are one-to-one communication, written response, selected response and performance.
(4) Interviews, portfolios, storytelling and teacher observation are all very popular methods of assessment with EBs. Which one you should use depends on your purpose.

Chapter 5: Content and Language

(1) When assessing content, minimize or simplify the language so you can focus on content (you can never completely eliminate language, but there are ways to reduce it, without reducing content).

(2) Language is best assessed in context and over time. Language is not assessed well out of context (decontextualized) and at one point in time.

Chapter 6: Psychometrics

(1) Criterion referenced tests (CRT) are more popular than norm referenced tests (NRT); however, both have drawbacks.

(2) There are many types of scores but they are all generated from the same raw score.

(3) Teachers and parents have grown to not trust test scores due to multiple public test item or scoring errors made by testing companies.

Chapter 7: Accommodations

(1) We don't need accommodations if we create better assessments for EB students.

(2) Many accommodations are permitted with EBs, but few of them have research to suggest that they work.

(3) Linguistic simplification is a promising accommodation.

Chapter 8: Special Education

(1) There is significant federal and state policy governing the assessment of students who may have special learning needs.

(2) Many challenges regarding the education of EBs with special needs hinge on assessment.

(3) It's difficult to disentangle speech or language impairment (SLI) from learning disabilities (LD) from second language acquisition (SLA).

(4) The dominant practice of assessment in special education supports a fractional view of EBs.

Chapter 9: Accountability

(1) Accountability related to assessment has come to the forefront of education in the last 10 years.

(2) Accountability based on student assessment results has never been more intense and directly tied to assessment.

(3) Accountability without validity isn't meaningful (see also accountability/validity discussion in Chapter 2).

Terminology

Despite the prevalence of the terms *English language learner (ELL)*, *English learner (EL)*, *multilingual learner (MLL)*, *dual language learner (DLL)*, etc., I have chosen to use the term *emergent bilingual (EB)* in this book. I'm happy to choose a term with the word 'bilingual' in it to represent the bilingual children this book is intended to serve.

1 A Decision-Making Process Called PUMI

Themes from Chapter 1

(1) Teachers have to compromise along a continuum of assessment practices leading to deficit or leading to promise.
(2) Good assessment practices for emergent bilingual (EB) students are grounded in four guiding principles or assumptions.
(3) A useful tool called PUMI can assist teachers in making informed and appropriate decisions about assessment.

Key Vocabulary

- Assessment or testing
- Assessment lens of promise
- Assessment lens of deficit
- Translanguaging
- PUMI (purpose, use, method and instrument)

PUMI Connection: Purpose, Use, Method, Instrument

This chapter introduces the concept of PUMI – 'purpose, use, method, instrument' – which will be used in each chapter for the remainder of the book. PUMI is a decision-making process to help stakeholders make better decisions about assessment for emergent bilingual (EB) students. The author recommends that when you are unsure about what questions to ask and what is important, start asking PUMI questions. What is the <u>purpose</u>? How will the results be <u>used</u>? What is the best <u>method</u>? What is the best <u>instrument</u>? Finding the answers and understanding PUMI help slow down the process of assessment and lead us to using fewer and better assessments.

This foundational textbook has three primary objectives. First, it helps teachers and administrators understand the challenges with assessment and accountability for EB students that dominate the field today. Second, it prepares teachers, administrators and leadership teams to make decisions about how to use and select appropriate assessments for EBs. Third, this book prepares educators to advocate on behalf of EBs in regard to appropriate test-use policies and practices.

It's a Continuum: Promise to Deficit

Valid assessment for EBs is a complex scientific challenge, especially in a monolingual schooling context. The various approaches to assessing EBs in the field today draw on contrasting views of assessment and bilingualism. This section briefly reviews a continuum of views, followed by guiding principles that teachers and administrators can draw on as they make practical decisions about assessing EBs.

There are many ways to view the assessment of EBs, and these can be best understood as a continuum – a wide range of approaches with extremes on either end – ranging from deficit to promise. Promising approaches to assessment highlight what the student knows and can do relative to multiple measures; on the other hand, deficit approaches highlight what the student doesn't know, usually relative to one measure. What is especially challenging is whether and how educators can look at EBs through a lens of promise within an accountability system focused on what children cannot do (Figure 1.1 and Table 1.1). Understanding this continuum will prepare the ground for better EB assessment policy, practice and advocacy.

The lens of promise is grounded in the ideas of dynamic bilingualism (García, 2009) and sociocultural assessment (Stefanakis, 1999), and is typically used in assessment courses and popular textbooks to guide educators in how to assess (and instruct) EBs within a meaningful and culturally relevant context. However, more often than not, and in contrast to a promising lens, deficit views of assessment dominate the policies and accountability system under which educators must perform. Deficit and promise are strikingly different, and educators are required to negotiate them in a public-school setting in order to maintain good evaluations of their own teaching and do what is best for students. These two views are presented here as a continuum; that is, one end of the continuum differs extremely from the

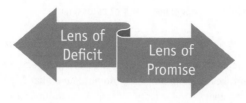

Figure 1.1 Assessment practices are on a continuum from deficit to promise

other end, but points near one another on the continuum may not be that noticeably different. These two views are not a dichotomy – mutually exclusive of one another, where educators must choose one view or the other. What is most common in schools today is a mix of both deficit and promising assessment approaches; state and district accountability systems are more often connected to looking for deficits or areas where children are lacking, whereas classroom assessment is more connected to the approach of promise. Usually, teachers negotiate both views. Table 1.1 illustrates in more detail both ends of the continuum.

Assessment vs. Testing

Oftentimes in conversations that take place in schools, the words assessment and testing are mistakenly used synonymously. Assessment is a much broader concept than testing and can be thought of generally as the use of information from various sources to make decisions about a student's future instruction/schooling. Testing, on the other hand, is a measuring instrument that produces information we use in assessment. A test can be thought of generally to be like a measuring instrument such as a measuring cup or a scale or a tape measure … used to measure ideas to help make decisions in schools. The example given above is a very simplified view, just to point out the difference between assessment and testing. Measuring flour in a measuring cup is much easier than measuring language in a child emerging as bilingual.

Support for EBs in Measurement Community

It is important to note that stand-alone tests themselves are not bad. However, with the increase of testing and the high-stakes decisions made from test scores, most educators have become very frustrated with the way that tests scores are used. The frustration is usually with the test-use, not the test, and especially for groups of students like EBs. Many times, policymakers, legislators, school boards, etc., *use* test scores for EBs in wrong – or invalid – ways. Examples of this from current practice include using achievement test scores to judge language ability (wrong construct), using one test score only to reclassify an EB (never use one score to make a big decision) or using test scores from a test that EBs cannot read very well (not a fair measure). It is important to point out that the educational measurement community does not support these types of test-use practices, and they do in fact support promising practices for EBs.

Table 1.1 Comparing deficit vs. promising views of assessment

Leading to Promise	*Leading to Deficit*
Students are active participants or agents in the evaluation, which takes place in an authentic learning environment.	Students are objects of evaluation – they do not know what is on the test; tests and responses to items are confidential.
• Example: Teacher shares rubric with students well ahead of assessment and students have the opportunity to ask questions and clarify what is expected.	• Example: Teacher announces a 'pop quiz' and students don't know what to expect. • Example: State achievement tests are kept in locked cabinets until a state-sanctioned time and day.
Assessments look for what students can do – assessing *ability*.	Assessments look for disability or deficit in the child – assessing *disability*.
• Example: Teacher uses a portfolio to show writing ability/strengths/potential.	• Example: Teacher highlights items that are wrong on a multiple-choice test and results are compiled to create an academic intervention plan.
Each child represents an example of difference and complexity.	The learning deficit is in the child/family.
• Students give an oral presentation of recent changes in their family with audio, visual, digital and artistic components.	• A very low test score in math leads the teacher to say 'the child is at a disadvantage. He would do better if he had more support at home'.
Assessments are authentic and contextualized.	The assessment is decontextualized from authentic situations.
• Unknown to the students, a teacher uses a checklist to observe and document use of English language during math problem-solving.	• During an oral language standardized assessment, the administrator reads each item and none of the items are connected or real. For example, 'How many hands do you have?' and scores the response.
Several measures are used to make a decision (similar to the idea of triangulation in research).	A single measure determines a decision – frequently a high-stakes decision like reclassification or graduation.
• A teacher uses results of a reading retell, role play and standardized reading assessment to make decisions about what level of reading the student should advance to.	• A student has to score 65 or better on a state test to graduate from high school.

Leading to Promise	*Leading to Deficit*
Instructional decisions are made on an individual basis.	If a child does not meet an expected norm, remediation is required.
• A student with high reading levels in the home language is selected to be the leader of a bilingual dictionary activity.	• All students below the 50th percentile on an English-only math achievement test are automatically assigned to a pull-out remedial math course.
The assessment occurs over many points in time and with conferences and feedback from teacher and peers.	The assessment occurs at one point in time.
	• Testing day is April 10 from 9am to 11am.
• Writing in the home language is assessed every five weeks of school to look for changes. Results are sent home to parents with a personal note from the student.	

The term 'measurement community' refers to measurement scientists who have studied educational measurement, topics such as fairness and validity, for several decades. The three organizations that dominate the science and use of test scores in the US are the American Educational Research Association (AERA), the American Psychological Association (APA) and the National Council on Measurement in Education (NCME). The study of (educational) measurement is basically the practice of assigning numbers to traits like achievement, language, interest, aptitude and intelligence. Oftentimes, measurement scientists design studies to try to validate whether those numbers really represent the trait and as a result, they make recommendations about how to use test scores; however, it is up to policymakers to write good policies about how to use test scores. This is usually where 'a disconnect' occurs, leading to deficit assessment practices.

A good example of the increased attention toward EBs from the measurement community is an important publication called *The New Standards for Educational and Psychological Testing* (AERA, APA, NCME, 2014) where standards for fair test-use are made explicit for the first time in a separate chapter on 'Fairness in Testing'. Fairness, especially with subgroups like 'individuals with disabilities' and examinees classified as 'limited English proficient' received increased attention by the measurement community (AERA, APA, NCME, 2014). In this important document, fairness in testing is considered a central idea, as those responsible for test development are held to the standard of designing all steps of the testing process to be accessible to the widest possible range of individuals, removing barriers, such as English proficiency, that may create unfair comparisons or interpretations of test scores (AERA, APA, NCME, 2014). Details about standards for fair testing are presented, especially on topics such as validity, test design and accommodations. Unlike previous versions of these standards, the importance of testing EBs (and other groups who have been marginalized from fair test development and interpretation) in a fair way has become a central idea.

Home language is typically undervalued or ignored

Although federal, state and most district accountability systems focus primarily on the assessment of English, this book emphasizes the importance of recognizing bilingualism. A fundamental assumption of research and practice in the education of EBs is that the students' home language(s) is a resource to develop, not a problem to overcome. Promising assessment practices focus on how students really use language, in authentic ways. If the purpose is to measure content knowledge in history, then the assessment can be conducted in English, Spanish or a combination of two or more languages that is meaningful to the student and can better show what the child knows (see Figures 1.2 and 1.3 for examples of translanguaging in a content-area assessment).

Why did the War of 1812 happen?

La Pelea de 1812 Paso porque Estados unidos robaron los cargo Gran Bretaña.

What was the most interesting thing about the War of 1812 that you learned?

The most interesting thing that happend in the war of 1812 Francis Scott Key because el escribio un Poema que se conritio hinno.

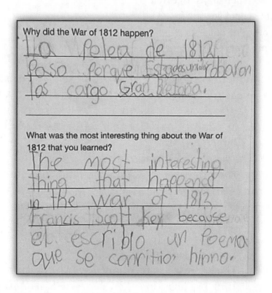

Figure 1.2 Example 1 of translanguaging in assessment

How did the Native Americans feel about westward expansion?

The Native Americans felt that westward expansion ___ estaba hevando y las personas se fueron pal west and they Was sad because the americans take oway ther land because ther Was farmers,

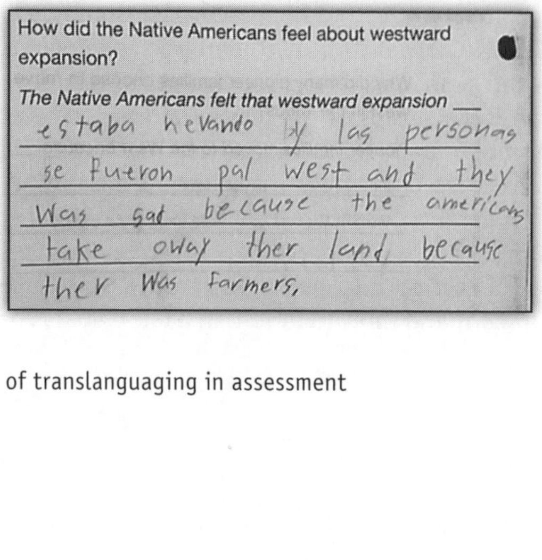

Figure 1.3 Example 2 of translanguaging in assessment

Home Language Assessment

There are typically very few or no formal assessments available in schools for home language, which in this age of accountability leads to a de-emphasis of it (if it's not tested, it's not taught). Another aspect of this issue is accountability. The increase in accountability to measure and show gains in English that came with No Child Left Behind (NCLB) has caused schools – and some bilingual schools – to abandon instructional time for developing the home language because they are no longer held accountable for showing growth in it. And in some cases, schools may even abandon bilingual programs altogether. Kate Menken and Cristian Solorza (2014) studied the decline of bilingual education in New York City schools. Through qualitative research, they studied 10 city schools that have eliminated their bilingual programs in recent years and replaced them with English only programs. The authors found that testing and accountability (high accountability of English, little to none of Spanish) were used as justification and created a disincentive to serve EBs through bilingual education.

Also, many teachers refrain from additional tests beyond those mandated; they feel that their students are already burdened with too many tests. This concern is warranted because many times EBs are tested up to double the amount of non-EBs. If you take each test for EBs and add together the amount of instructional time lost to account for testing and teacher-absence due to scoring and training for testing, the 'cost of testing' for EBs becomes evident. Unfortunately, not to assess the home language is to leave out important information that could be used to inform instruction and build on students' strengths.

Common in schools today is the overwhelming dominance of relatively inflexible assessment practices with EBs. Most assessment and accountability systems focus exclusively on English, reflecting the assumption that English is the only relevant language when instructing and assessing. Common assessment practice with EBs tends to measure each language separately, or not assess the home language at all. For example, in the US, EBs are regularly tested in English using a mandated standardized test, and on a separate day with a separate instrument, perhaps (many times assessing the home language is missing or optional) they are also tested using a Spanish language proficiency test. Typically, the two results are combined to represent the child's bilingualism. In reality, this is considered to be a very narrow view that critically underestimates what the child can actually do as a bilingual person.

Snapshot: Which Lens?

Assessment Practices may lead to Promise: Efrain's teacher invites him to create a writing portfolio to demonstrate how his writing ability in English has improved over the first two marking periods. The primary theme of the portfolio is 'change', and the teacher and Efrain conference together to decide that the four writing samples in English that he will showcase in his portfolio will each describe a recent change in his family (for example, a new dog, his grandfather and cousin from Mexico are living in their house for four months, his brother moves out and gets an apartment two blocks away) with attention to how these changes influence his life. Reflecting the teacher's understanding that reading and writing are interconnected, as are all of the languages in Efrain's linguistic repertoire, included in Efrain's portfolio is evidence of reading comprehension in Spanish. Efrain reads several award-winning children's stories about being Mexican in the US Southwest, focusing on the changes that children go through in the US. Efrain reads the books in Spanish and records a summary of the books in Spanish. The recordings and reflections are included in a section of the portfolio about home language. Also included in Efrain's portfolio is a page on which Efrain reflects on the quality of his work over time, as well as a page on which the teacher evaluates Efrain's writing in stages (using a rubric aligned with state ELP – English language proficiency – standards) and provides feedback. Efrain uses the portfolio to demonstrate his writing ability to his teacher and parents. This exemplifies promising assessment practices because the portfolio is designed to show Efrain's writing ability, and he is expected to be an agent of the assessment process by including a self-assessment of his own work. This is also an example of how promising assessment is culturally relevant. Culturally relevant instruction/assessment is when teachers respond to the differences in students while focusing on the strengths of students. It often mediates the mismatch between home and school that many schools experience. Results from the portfolio are compared to Efrain's interactive journal writing samples and the standardized English (writing portion) test score to chart his progress and determine programmatic changes (if any).

Assessment Practices may lead to Deficit: Efrain's teacher announces that according to state policy, April 10 will be the day he takes the Content and Language Instruction Performance (CLIP) – a state-mandated ELP test. Efrain is reminded on a daily basis starting in January how important this test is and his teacher provides 10 minutes of CLIP practice every day to prepare for the big test in April. The test contains multiple-choice items and prompts in English to generate writing samples upon which Efrain will be evaluated. The prompts change from section to section and are unrelated. For example, first Efrain is asked to write about a day at the beach (he lives in the desert); next, he is asked to write about nature versus nurture; lastly, he is asked to write about the types of things he can learn from peers while playing a sport. Efrain and his teacher are the objects of the assessment – it is being performed *upon* them – and the items are designed by outside evaluators (a psychometric company) unfamiliar with Efrain's language and culture. Creation of the actual test items and most of the scoring are done outside the state, and the test scores are analyzed to show what parts of Efrain's writing needs improvement. The focus is on what Efrain cannot do in writing (searching for deficits). The results arrive at the school in June and Efrain's new teacher reads the results in August. An academic intervention plan to remediate these deficits is

(Continued)

designed for the next school year; and Efrain is tested the following April to see if the deficiencies have been remediated. Based on the test score generated on the ELP test, Efrain will either remain officially designated as an English language learner (ELL) and continue to receive English as a New Language (ENL) services, or be mainstreamed (not receive ENL services).

Discussion questions

- What assessment practices lead to promise or deficit for EBs?
- How can you negotiate both views (promise, deficit) to create a 'compromise' plan that benefits students?
- How can you advocate for better assessment practices for EBs?

Four Guiding Assessment Principles in this Book

The following four guiding principles – both theoretical and practical – guide the work throughout this book:

- **Guiding Principle 1: Assessment practice for EBs is viewed through a lens of promise.** This book assumes that bilingualism is an asset and that assessment methods should highlight this asset (not point to perceived deficits). Assessment is an interactive process that should be integrated into daily routines that occur in a culturally relevant environment (Celic & Seltzer, 2011: 13; Ladson-Billings, 1994). Instruction and assessment should be student centered, involving students and peers in the act of assessment (administering and scoring) and organizing what they know. Assessment should also be multifaceted, involve multiple culturally relevant perspectives and provide authentic and meaningful feedback to improve student learning, teachers' instructional practice and educational options in the classroom. This guiding principle largely draws from the assessment ideas of Evangeline Stefanakis (1999, 2003, 2011) and the author's own practical experience.
- **Guiding Principle 2: Only high-quality assessments are acceptable**. High-quality assessment adheres to the following five standards: (1) clear objectives, (2) focused purpose, (3) proper method, (4) sound sampling and (5) accurate assessment free of bias and distortion. To violate any of these standards places students' academic well-being in jeopardy. This guiding principle draws from the work of Rick Stiggins and Jan Chappuis (2011).
- **Guiding Principle 3: Validity is a unified concept.** Proof that assessment results are valid for EBs should be presented *before* assessments are used to make important decisions. The idea of validity should include the adequacy and appropriateness of inferences and actions, including social consequences, based on test scores or other modes of assessment. This guiding principle draws from the work of Samuel Messick (1989).

- **Guiding Principle 4: Translanguaging during assessment is important for EB students.** For students who speak English and additional languages, translanguaging as a pedagogical practice can serve to validate their home language and cultural practices; plus, they can use their bilingualism in a bilingual context more openly. In assessment, if the purpose of the assessment is to assess content (math or science for example), then translanguaging in assessment will more validly show what students know. Ofelia García (2009) uses the term 'translanguaging' to describe the language *practices* of bilingual people (active) as opposed to the *language* of bilingual people (static). This new focus on dynamic language practices (languaging – translanguaging) represents a major shift in thinking for many researchers and practitioners in the field. This guiding principle draws from the work of Ofelia García (2009) and the practical work of the City University of New York-New York State Initiative for Emergent Bilinguals (CUNY NYSIEB) team.[1]

Figures 1.2 and 1.3 show the use of translanguaging during social studies assessment. The purpose of these assessments was to measure social studies content. This helps students show more fully what they really know because they can use their full linguistic repertoire, which creates more opportunity for access to content and for assessment of a holistic picture of what they know as opposed to a fractional picture if students are limited to one language (Celic & Seltzer, 2013; García, 2009). Using translanguaging in assessment is good pedagogical practice for ENL, bilingual and mainstream teachers – everyone.

Together, these four guiding principles create a foundation for an appropriate model of assessment for EBs. Teachers and administrators can draw on these guiding principles as they make decisions about assessment. The remainder of this chapter introduces a practical and easy-to-remember decision-making process called PUMI that will help teachers adhere to the four guiding principles reviewed above.

PUMI (Purpose, Use, Method, Instrument): A Framework for Decision-Making

This section introduces the 'PUMI' framework, which teachers and administrators can use to make decisions about assessment for EBs. PUMI is an acronym for purpose, use, method and instrument. The PUMI framework is essentially a series of critical questions that educators need to ask in order to select the most appropriate method of assessment and improve the condition of assessment for EBs. Figure 1.4 represents the four major steps in the PUMI framework used throughout this book.

First, educators need to ask themselves and each other, 'What is the **P: purpose** of this assessment?' or, more pointedly, 'Why are we doing this?' For EBs, we often assess for the following purposes: to measure oral language, to measure achievement

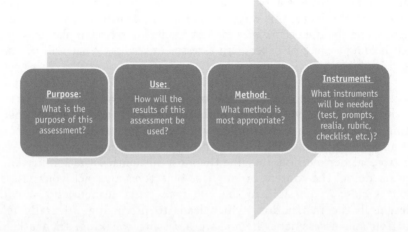

Figure 1.4 A decision making process called PUMI (Purpose, Use, Method, Instrument)

or to measure ELP development in content-based instruction. When answering the first question in PUMI, the answer usually begins with 'to measure…' or 'to assess…'. Every assessment is designed to have a purpose and to measure something, regardless of whether it is developed as a large-scale assessment, mandated by a state as part of its accountability system or is a classroom assessment designed by a single teacher or a team of teachers.

To determine the purpose, articulate exactly what you are trying to measure. If you are using a commercial or state-mandated test, the purpose of the test has already been determined by the test authors. For a commercial test, the purpose is always revealed at the beginning of the technical manual (sometimes called the 'blueprint'), but most teachers would be surprised to read what the test authors say the purpose is – always check. Further, it's important to identify the conceptual or theoretical framework upon which the test was built. If possible, read in the technical manual how the test constructors define language (if it is a measure of language) and on what conceptual or theoretical framework the test is built. Beware of language tests that are vague about articulating a language theory or tests built on the judgment of a committee of experts. If you still don't know the purpose of an assessment, ask your administrator to clarify. Be cautious about moving forward with the assessment without understanding the purpose.

Next, teachers and administrators need to ask critical questions about **U: use.** Use of data is *the most important question to address*. How exactly will the results of the assessment (data) be used after the assessment is completed? The stakes are high for many assessments in schools. Results of assessments are commonly used to determine what program an EB will go into or exit from, whether a child will be labeled as an EB, classification into special education or whether a teacher is effective or not, to name a few. Results of assessments are also used for daily classroom-level decisions, such as how much scaffolding is needed, how to group students, mastery of content, pace of the lesson or unit and so on. Many people confuse purpose and use, so you can think of it this way: The purpose is identified *before* the assessment is designed, and the use occurs *after* the test results are collected. Basically, imagine yourself holding a piece of paper with assessment results. What will you *do* with them? This is use.

It is important to ask PUMI questions in the P*U*M*I order. Following the order, after careful consideration of P: Purpose and U: Use, it is time to select the appropriate **M: method** and instrument. It should make sense that selecting the method and instrument without understanding the purpose and use of an assessment can lead to inappropriate assessment practices. When it is time to consider method, imagine the most authentic situation in which the student is 'doing' the content or language objectives and pick your assessment method as close as possible to the real task. This authenticity should also be present in the instruction, which leads to promising culturally relevant instruction and assessment. If you are assessing speaking, then ask EBs to speak in a natural setting, about something they are comfortable speaking about; if you are assessing problem-solving, then watch them solve a problem and ask them questions about how they solved it; if you are assessing writing, then obtain a sample of writing during a social studies or science lesson; integrated assessment is a guiding principle to select appropriate assessment methods. This author categorizes *all* assessment methods into the following four categories: selected response, written response, performance and one-to-one communication. Chapter 4 provides a deeper discussion and more ideas for methods of assessment.

I: instrument. Outside of education, you can think of a bathroom scale as an instrument to measure weight, a measuring tape is an instrument to measure length, etc.; instrumentation can be thought of as the tools needed to carry out the assessment. Interpreted broadly, instrument consists of the things necessary to carry out the assessment, such as a rubric,[2] a checklist, a standardized test score sheet, props, realia and so on. After you choose the method, it is easy to select the instrument and these are usually easy to find. Instrumentation depends on purpose, use and method and is the final step in the PUMI decision process.

Snapshot: A Teacher's Judgment Counts

Mrs Ortiz is a 6th-grade teacher who assesses EBs in a variety of ways throughout the first two weeks of school to find out important factors she knows affect schooling and language acquisition. She assesses important areas such as schooling history (school intake forms or interview family member), attitudes about English and home language (questionnaire), ELP during a content area lesson (observation of student speaking in content lesson), translanguaging patterns (All About Me poster with emphasis on language use at home) and ELP (state-mandated assessments). However, it has always bothered her that nobody assesses the reading and writing skills of her students in the home language. She understands that the child's home language makes up the whole child (and that viewing the student

Table 1.2 Mrs Ortiz uses PUMI to make decisions

P Purpose	U Use	M Method	I Instrument
To assess reading ability in the home language	To design appropriate instruction using reading in home and new language To design intense alternate program (such as SIFE or Newcomer program) if home reading skills are absent.	Category: One-to-one communication	The General Home Language Reading Assessment Rubric

through English-only assessments may represent only a fraction of the child); she knows that understanding literacy levels in the home language is also a valuable instructional tool to leverage content, learn more English and learn more home language. In addition, her state is now mandating that schools identify students with interrupted/inconsistent (SIFE) schooling. With all this in mind, Mrs Ortiz was introduced to the General Home Language Reading Assessment Rubric[3] at a workshop and decided to use PUMI to make decisions about whether this assessment will meet the needs in her classroom. Mrs Ortiz made a quick PUMI table like the one in Table 1.2 and based on the PUMI analysis, she decided to proceed with using the General Home Language Reading Assessment Rubric.

Discussion questions

- How does this snapshot relate to 2/4 guiding principles presented earlier in this chapter?
- How does Mrs Ortiz use PUMI to help guide her assessment decisions about?

End-of-Chapter Activities (Instructors: see advice at the end of the book)

By completing Activity 1 and 2, the reader will be able to:

(1) Discuss assessment practices that lead to promise and those that lead to deficit for EBs.
(2) Order the steps to PUMI and briefly explain each step. Use PUMI to better understand a mandated English proficiency test in your area.

Activity 1
Discuss assessment practices that lead to promise and those that lead to deficit for EBs.

Either as a whole group or a small group, students will place the instructor-made sticky notes in a blank T-table (formatted like the one on the next page), read the clue to the class and briefly discuss why it fits there.

(Continued)

Leads to Deficit	Leads to Promise

Activity 2
Order the steps to PUMI and briefly explain each step. Use PUMI to guide the decision-making process about assessment for EBs.

Find another student to be your partner. The instructor will pass out four index cards per pair. Each card will display the letter P, U, M or I. With each student taking a turn, explain what each letter means (not just the word – but a definition in your own words). Many people confuse *Purpose* with *Use*. Hint: When talking about purpose, start with 'to measure...' or 'to assess...'; with *Use*, once you have the results in your hand, now what will you *do* with them (what decisions will be made, for example)? Explore a different order of PUMI and explain why you like it. Be prepared to share your definitions of PUMI and one example to the whole class. If you live in the US and you are 1 of the 33 states that uses the World-Class Instructional Design and Assessment (WIDA)[4] test called ACCESS for ELLs, complete a PUMI table for the ELP test called ACCESS (currently used by over half of the US). Otherwise, use a mandated ELP test in your area. For example, New York is not a WIDA state, so with your partner, create a PUMI table for the New York State Identification Test for English Language Learners (NYSITELL) or the New York State English as a Second Language Achievement Test (NYSESLAT).

Notes

(1) CUNY-New York State Initiative on Emergent Bilinguals (NYSIEB) is a collaborative project of the Research Institute for the Study of Language in Urban Society (RISLUS) and the PhD program in Urban Education funded by the New York State Education Department.

(2) Remember: A rubric is not an assessment method; it is a scoring device (or tool) to help make assessment results more reliable and therefore more valid.

(3) This General Home Language Reading Assessment Rubric can be found in a book called A CUNY-NYSIEB FRAMEWORK for the Education of Emergent Bilinguals with low home literacy: 4–12 grades García,O., Herrera, L., Hesson, S., and Kleyn, T. (http://www.nysieb.ws.gc.cuny.edu/files/2013/05/CUNY-NYSIEB-Framework-for-EB-with-Low-Home-Literacy-Spring-2013-Final-Version-05-08-13.pdf). The rubric can be found in Appendix A.

(4) WIDA is no longer using this acronym definition because it no longer represents their mission. Just WIDA now.

References

AERA, APA, NCME (2014) *Standards for Educational and Psychological Testing*. Washington, DC: AERA.

Celic, C. and Seltzer, K. (2013) *Translanguaging: A CUNY-NYSIEB Guide for Educators*. New York: CUNY-NYSIEB, The Graduate Center.

García, O. (2009) *Bilingual Education in the 21st Century: A Global Perspective*. New York: John Wiley.

Ladson-Billings, G. (1994) *Dreamkeepers: Successful Teachers of African American Children*. San Francisco, CA: Jossey-Bass.

Menken, K. and Solorza, C. (2014) No Child Left Bilingual: Accountability and the elimination of bilingual education programs in New York City schools. *Educational Policy* 28 (1), 96–125.

Messick, S. (1989) Meaning and values in test validation: The science and ethics of assessment. *Educational Researcher* 18 (2), 5–11.

Stefanakis, E. (1999) *Whose Judgment Counts? Assessing Bilingual Children, K-3*. Portsmouth, NH: Heinemann.

Stefanakis, E. (2003) *Multiple Intelligences and Portfolios: A Window into the Learners Mind*. Portsmouth, NH: Heinemann.

Stefanakis, E. (2011) *Differentiated Assessment: Finding Every Learners Potential*. Wiley-Jossey Bass Series. San Francisco, CA: Jossey-Bass.

Stiggins, R. and Chappuis, J. (2011) *An Introduction to Student-Involved Assessment for Learning* (6th edn). New York: Pearson.

2 History: How Did We Get Here?

Themes from Chapter 2

(1) The history of testing EB students includes many examples of inappropriate testing and misuse of results.
(2) Despite more than a decade of warning from the measurement community, test scores from tests given in English, to students who don't know English, are still being used for important education decisions.
(3) The current political climate favors accountability over validity.

Key Vocabulary

- Class analysis argument
- Cultural argument
- Eugenics
- Genetic argument
- NCLB
- Test fairness
- Test misuse

PUMI Connection: Use

This chapter focuses primarily on the U (Use) of test scores for emergent bilinguals (EBs). By providing a history and presenting the damaging mistakes that have been made in the past, it is hoped we can prevent the misuse of test scores in the future, and better understand where we are today.

This chapter may seem rather gloomy but its aim is to help explain the present. The author wanted to include a variety of historical perspectives regarding testing, which may be of particular interest to readers who wish to know how present practices took root. First, is a review of the history of test misuse among non-English-speaking and other groups of people, followed by some theoretical frameworks that contradict the old but strong genetic argument of school success/failure. These frameworks may also help EB educators understand and explain the reasons why today, some students succeed and others don't. The second section of the chapter provides a major-event history table documenting important and influential policies in the history of EB assessment over time. The final section emphasizes the changes in assessment policy since No Child Left Behind (NCLB) was introduced in the US.

A History of Misuse

A history of discrimination exists in US education whereby non-English-speaking children have been denied equal educational opportunity based on the use of standardized tests. Standardized tests in English, when presented to non-English-speaking students, raise several obvious validity concerns (a detailed discussion of validity is forthcoming in Chapter 3). The issue of fairness in testing has attracted scrutiny since the 1960s, yet federal and state mandates requiring the testing of students in a language they do not know are increasing.

Understanding test fairness was less of a concern before the 1960s. Many examples exist, pre-1960, of the misuse of intelligence tests to gatekeep or advance some racial groups over others. During this era, for example, some educators, psychologists and others used intelligence test scores to describe American Indian and Mexican children as having many negative qualities such as 'dullness'. For example, Lewis Terman,[1] who was most famous for his Stanford-Binet Intelligence test first used in schools in 1916 (and a version of it is still used today, 100 years later), was also a well-known eugenicist.[2] At the same time as he became a champion for 'gifted' children, he also promoted a very dark social agenda for 'other' groups of children. Terman and other eugenicists claimed that the smartest or more fit people, such as the wealthy with European ancestry, were reproducing too slowly and in danger of being overwhelmed by more 'feeble-minded' races (non-wealthy and non-European). Terman also promoted the idea that America was being jeopardized from within, by the rapid proliferation of people lacking intelligence and moral fiber, and warned that the unchecked arrival of immigrants from southern and eastern Europe would drag down the national stock (Leslie, 2000).

As Leslie (2000) reports, early eugenicists such as Terman managed to advocate and pass several laws aligned with their social agenda. Thirty-three states, including

California, passed laws that required sterilization of about 60,000 men and women at mental institutions. Early eugenicists also affected immigration policy; in 1924, Congress set quotas that drastically cut immigration from eastern and southern Europe (Leslie, 2000).

In 1916, while Terman promoted his Stanford-Binet Intelligence test in schools, he also published a book called *The Measurement of Intelligence*. In this book, Terman discussed his findings after administering the Stanford-Binet test to Spanish speakers and unschooled African Americans. This only supported his preference for white European racial groups over others. In his words:

> [a] high-grade or border-line deficiency...is very common among Spanish Indian and Mexican families of the Southwest and also among negroes. Their dullness seems to be racial or at least inherent in the family stocks from which they come...children of this group should be separated into separate classes...They cannot master abstractions but they can often be made into efficient workers... from a eugenic point of view, they constitute a grave problem because of their unusually prolific breeding.

Although this quote is extreme and old (it dates back to 1916), many still question the roots of intelligence tests used today – especially as entrance criteria for gifted programs and other similar programs. It is a well-known fact that such programs exhibit an under-representation of minorities, with almost no EB representation. Because EBs come from non-dominant cultural and linguistic groups, they are most vulnerable to test misuse based on race or language. Figure 2.1 is a cartoon, dated 1922, showing the powerful assessor and the child as an object of the assessment. As depicted in the cartoon, the assessment is based on intelligence testing and psychological theories. This is new and an improvement on the 'old method' where students were sorted based on race and class. What is better the 'old' or the 'new' method?

Measurement misuse in order to advance one racial group over another can be traced back even further to the use of craniometry in the 19th century. This now-laughable practice measured cranial features in order to classify intelligence and race superiority as well as temperament and morality. Those who practiced craniometry believed that measurements of skull size and shape could determine traits such as intelligence and capacity for moral behavior. The British used such measurements to justify racist policies against Africans, Indians and the Irish. The Nazis and Belgians used similar craniometry methods to claim their superiority. In *The Mismeasure of Man*, Stephen J. Gould (1981) implies that craniometry in the 19th century gave way to intelligence testing in the 20th century.

In 1969, researchers Chandler and Plakos designed a research study to investigate how intelligence (IQ) tests were being used with Spanish-dominant Mexican-American children. They selected 47 Spanish-dominant students to be a part of the study, all of whom were enrolled in educable mentally retarded (EMR) classes after being assessed on the English-only IQ test. Chandler and Plakos retested all 47 students with the Spanish-language version. In most cases, the Spanish-dominant

Figure 2.1 School as sorters

Source: Paul Davis Chapman from Stefanakis, E. (1999) *Whose Judgment Counts? Assessing Bilingual Children, K-3*. Portsmouth, NH: Heinemann

children were found not to be EMR; the decision to classify them as EMR was therefore based on an invalid use of the English IQ test scores. The study concluded that many children of Mexican descent were inappropriately placed in EMR classes.

During the 1960s and 1970s, test fairness became a concern for many. Changes to the testing standards (*Standards for Educational and Psychological Testing*) illustrate the growing concern by the measurement community over testing fairness for non-English-speaking children. The 1966 version of the *Standards* focused on what is required for test-accompaniment manuals. The 1974 version, however, for the first time included standards for the *use* of tests. A decade later, the 1985 *Standards* included a section on standards for 'particular' applications, with a section specifically designated for the testing of linguistic minorities. The 1999 version dedicates one-third of the book to fairness in testing, with a focus on testing individuals of diverse linguistic backgrounds, and the most recent version (2014) includes a more articulated chapter on fairness with more examples than before of EBs (American Educational Research Association [AERA], American Psychological Association [APA], National Council on Measurement in Education [NCME], 1966, 1974, 1985, 1999, 2014). Despite these articulate and supportive standards, test misuse runs rampant.

The issue of fairness in EB assessment has gained more nationwide attention as legislation such as NCLB looks toward the inclusion of all children in large-scale assessments as a way to provide equal learning opportunity. August and Hakuta (1998) warned of the great need to develop guidelines for determining when EBs are ready to take the same assessments as their English-proficient peers, and when versions of an assessment other than the standard English version should be administered. They also emphasized the need to develop psychometrically sound and practical assessments and assessment procedures that incorporate EBs into district- and state-assessment systems.

Standards from the measurement community have warned researchers and practitioners about the potential validity threats for EBs taking tests in English. For non-English speakers and those who speak some dialects of English, every test given in English becomes, in part, a language or literacy test (AERA, APA, NCME, 1985: 73). The 1999 version of the same standards warn that test norms based on native speakers of English either should not be used with individuals whose first language is not English, or such individuals' test results should be interpreted as reflecting, in part, the current level of English proficiency rather than ability, potential, aptitude or personality characteristics or symptomatology (AERA, APA, NCME, 1999: 91). Also in 1999, the National Research Council (NRC, 1999), which formed a Committee on Appropriate Test Use, echoes the same message: The test score for an EB is likely to be affected by construct irrelevant variance (CIV) and, therefore, is likely to underestimate his or her knowledge of the subject being tested.

Many EB educators are aware of the history of test misuse for EBs and have tried to move away from the deficit perspectives of non-English-speaking children in schools, but the practices dominating schools and policies today perpetuate these old ideas. Since the 1960s, several frameworks for interpreting success and failure in schools have been explored to counter the dominant genetic argument so popular in the 1800s and 1900s. Two frameworks from Guadalupe Valdés and John Ogbu are explored below to help EB educators interpret and explain the factors and different perspectives on success/failure of EBs in schools.

Theories that Explain Success and Failure

Throughout history, myriad and complex theories have attempted to explain why some children succeed in school and others do not. The question generally is approached through two broad theoretical frameworks – the deficit argument and the difference argument. The *deficit argument* holds that the impoverished child is failing in school because he or she is not ready for school. The communities, homes and cultures from which the child comes are lacking, and this leads to a disadvantage at school. The *difference argument* targets the school as being unready, rather than the child, and claims that the deficit argument is based on ethnocentric research plus Anglo middle-class norms and values.

Guadalupe Valdés (1996) suggests that explanations of school failure can be categorized in terms of the genetic argument, the cultural argument and the class analysis argument. The *genetic argument* (discussed earlier in this chapter) has been out of favor for a number of years; it views some groups as genetically more able than others, and because of these inherent differences, children of different racial and ethnic groups perform differently in schools.

The *cultural argument* proposes that children who perform poorly in schools are either culturally deprived (devalues the child's culture) or culturally different (values the child's culture) and therefore mismatched with schools and school personnel. In general, this school of thought takes the position that non-mainstream parents do not have the 'right' attitude toward the value of education, do not prepare their children well for school or are not sufficiently involved in their children's education. Valdés (1996) states that there is a fine line between the culturally deprived and culturally different explanations. The cultural difference argument supports the idea that the experiences of all children are rich, even if they are not the values respected by the educational institution.

The *class analysis argument* ascribes school failure to the role of education in maintaining class differences (that is, maintaining the power of some over others). For this argument, it is no accident that children of the middle classes are primarily sorted into the 'right' streams or tracks in school and given access to particular kinds of knowledge. The role of the schools, using testing as a tool, is to legitimize inequality under the pretense of serving all students and encouraging them to reach their full potential. The system succeeds because, although the cards are clearly stacked against some students, these students come to believe that they are in fact given an opportunity to succeed. They leave school firmly convinced they could have done better – perhaps achieved as much as their middle-class peers – if only they had tried harder or worked more. They are then ready to accept low-paying, working-class jobs, and the working class is thus reproduced (Valdés, 1996).

In a classic study that documented the class analysis argument, Jean Anyon (1980) studied a sample of schools from the working class, the middle class and the affluent professional class. In the working-class schools, schoolwork consisted of following the steps of a procedure. The procedure was usually mechanical, involving rote behavior and very little choice or decision-making. In the middle-class schools, work consisted of getting the right answer. If one accumulated enough right answers, one received a good grade. Directions often called for some figuring, some choice and some decision-making. In the affluent professional schools, work was creative activity, carried out independently. The students were continually asked to express and apply ideas and concepts (Anyon, 1980). This differentiated schooling, as highlighted in Anyon's research, inevitably leads to a replication of social class structure and helps to explain the class analysis argument for school success or failure.

Another theoretical framework through which to view student success and failure, is John Ogbu's (1998) cultural-ecological theory. Ogbu is well known for his explanation of how minority students are classified based not upon numbers but upon their different histories. Differences in student performances, explained through a two-part theory, are the result of the treatment of minority groups within both school and society at large, as well as minorities' perceptions of that treatment and their responses in school.

The first part of Ogbu's theory, which concerns what he terms 'the system', explains the way minorities are treated or mistreated in education in terms of educational policies, pedagogy, returns for their investments or school credentials. The second part of the theory concerns 'community forces' – the way minorities respond to schooling as a consequence of their treatment. These minority responses are also affected by how and why a group became a minority.

Autonomous minorities are people who belong to groups that are small in number. They may be different from the dominant group in race, ethnicity, religion or language. Examples of autonomous minority groups in the US are Amish, Jews and Mormons. Although these groups may suffer discrimination, they are not totally dominated and oppressed; thus, their school achievement is no different from the dominant group (Ogbu, 1978). Voluntary (immigrant) minorities are those who have more or less willingly moved to the US because they expect better opportunities (better jobs, more political or religious freedoms) than they had in their homelands or places of origin. Involuntary (non-immigrant) minorities have been conquered, colonized or enslaved. Unlike immigrant minorities, non-immigrants have been permanently incorporated into US society against their will. Involuntary minorities in the US are original owners or residents of the land who were conquered – American Indians, Alaskan Natives and early Mexican-Americans in the southwest. This also includes Native Hawaiians and Puerto Ricans who were colonized, and Black Americans who were brought to the US as slaves.

Clearly, the 'achievement gap' problem is a complex one, connected to history, society and power. The next section discusses the history of policy regarding assessment for EBs.

Accountability With(out) Validity? No Child Left Behind

Educators and families need *more accountability and more validity* for EBs. The following section will take the reader through arguments of accountability and validity. Do we have to sacrifice one for the other?

What is NCLB? The No Child Left Behind Act started in 2002 and ended in 2015; however, its impact will remain for many years to come. Educational reform efforts in the United States in the early 21st century can be largely defined by two characteristics: (1) schools labeled as excellent are those that have good test scores in math and reading, and (2) the use of standards and test-based accountability is the way to achieve such excellence. The intent of NCLB was to provide every child in the US with a good education so that 'no child is left behind'. However, the law's definition of a good education – a high score on standardized tests in English and mathematics – is one most educators would disagree with. To support this definition, NCLB requires that all children in 3rd through 8th grades, even EBs, be given state assessments each year in reading and mathematics.

If a child fails the test, he or she is judged to have not received a good education. If a school or district doesn't make adequate yearly progress (AYP), it is labeled 'in need of improvement' and subject to some kind of major change, such as allowing students to move to another school, moving the principal and half the staff out of the school, closing the school and/or other consequences. Students who perform poorly on math and reading are considered at risk of school failure, regardless of how they perform in other subjects. The logic of NCLB makes sense, unfortunately the test and punish methods don't.

The passage of NCLB completely changed the accountability landscape for EBs. The era before NCLB (pre-2002) can be classified in general as *less accountability/ more validity* because teachers had more flexibility to choose valid measures of what, exactly, EBs knew. Advocates for EBs supported state-level policies that delayed the requirement that EBs take content-area standardized tests in English until they obtained sufficient levels of language proficiency; like many polices regarding EBs, the definition of 'sufficient language proficiency' varied from state to state. These state-level policies were put into place largely in response to years of research showing that as language proficiency increases, so does academic achievement. In other words, we have the best chance to show what content an EB knows if we wait to assess until his or her English proficiency is higher. Schools were seldom asked to be accountable for EBs before those EBs could comprehend the language of the tests. In fact, it was common for EBs to have at least three years (or more) of exemption before they were required to take the standardized tests in English for any purpose (accountability or otherwise). This backfired, though, because delayed accountability for EBs often led to inferior programs and instruction during these formative language-learning years. Advocates for EBs were unhappy with the lack of accountability, arguing that schools and policies continued to ignore the needs of EBs.

The pendulum swung fast and far after NCLB was passed. EB accountability went from nearly non-existent to attaching ultra-high stakes to the performance of EBs on standardized tests in English. Despite the language of the NCLB that called for 'valid and reliable' assessments, the law also required that EBs be tested in English before they know English – a highly contradictory stance.

The era after NCLB (post-2002) can therefore be described, in general, as a *more accountability/less validity* era during which the struggles continue. In August 2006, under the Bush administration, the federal government created a new (ELL/LEP) partnership in Washington, DC, to discuss assessment requirements for EBs. One of the main goals of this meeting was to provide states with the technical assistance they needed to develop valid and reliable assessments for EBs. Three years later, a public forum was commissioned by Barack Obama's administration and was held by the US Department of Education on December 2, 2009, in Denver, Colorado. Three prominent EB researchers were invited (Jamal Abedi, Charlene Rivera and Robert Linquanti), who called for a number of dramatic changes in the way EBs were tested. In the same year (2009), a working group advisory board for EBs was formed through the Center for Applied Linguistics (CAL) to prepare a set of recommendations for the federal reauthorization of the Elementary and Secondary Education Act (ESEA). The board's recommendations focused on improving education outcomes for EBs. Meetings focusing on Race to the Top competitive grants and a new set of tests for the Common Core Learning Standards (CCLS) followed in January 2010.

The sequence of events described above led to heated debates in the field of education, as EB educators were split about whether to support, through advocacy, much-needed accountability at what many say was at the expense of validity. Most EB educators would rather choose neither (less accountability/more validity nor more accountability/less validity) because they strive for a better balance between accountability and validity. Some say that the former ignored the needs of EBs and the latter delivered more harm than benefits to them. One negative result of NCLB was the creation of a two-tiered educational system, in which those who can't pass the test revert to a repetitive, test-preparation curriculum, while those who pass the test receive a high-level, higher-order thinking curriculum aligned with college preparation and professional careers. One side of the debate argues that NCLB actually caused the same inequities that most people believe the law was designed to eradicate, with a huge dollar sign attached to it.

Scholars in the field documented the harmful effects of NCLB as (1) dismantling bilingual education programs as a result of low English language arts (ELA) and English language proficiency (ELP) test scores (for example, see Menken & Solorza, 2014); (2) narrowing the curriculum to focus on content areas (English and math) that count for AYP; (3) declining graduation rates (as school ratings rose, graduation rates went down); (4) increasing the number of EBs classified as having special education needs; and (5) creating more situations where bilingualism is a 'problem' and schools and teachers are discouraged from working with students who may have difficulty passing the test. Wayne Wright (2002) interviewed teachers to explore the effects of high-stakes testing from their perspective and also reported effects such as narrowing of curriculum, linguistic bias, sociocultural and class bias and feelings of inadequacy in many teachers and students. Feelings of inadequacy can be seen in Figure 2.2 in a student drawing to describe how he feels about being tested in English.

Often, student effects are observed, but rarely are students asked how they feel about standardized testing. The illustration in Figure 2.2 was created by an EB in Arizona when his teacher asked him to draw a picture to show how he feels about taking the state's high-stakes test.[3] His response as seen in the picture was 'I felt like not knowing nothing'. The drawing also depicts the student slumped at his desk. Clearly, in addition to a low score, taking the test led him to feelings of inadequacy.

Doubts about NCLB

The logic of NCLB targeted two 'gaps' in achievement. One gap is the differences in test scores and quality of schooling among subgroups within the US (e.g. white vs. African-American or EBs vs. native English speakers). The other gap is the difference in test scores between the US and other countries. Comparing the US to China, Yong Zhao (2009) authored a book titled *Catching Up or Leading the Way* in which he questions whether test-driven accountability will empower the US to 'lead the way' in quality schooling and innovation or whether it will put the US in a position where it is must try to 'catch up' with other nations that

Figure 2.2 Drawing by EB elementary student in response to a high-stakes test: 'I felt like not knowing nothing'

have tried test-based accountability for years but have begun to abandon it. As an example, Zhao demonstrates how China is beginning to abandon its use of test-based accountability and test-based curriculum because of negative consequences such as a lack of innovation and the narrowing of skill sets and curriculum. He argues that since NCLB, US schools are not emphasizing the skills students truly need – such as the new globalization and technology goals – and that such neglect undermines traditional US thought and strength. He also notes that countries such as China are changing their education systems to emulate the pre-NCLB US educational system.

Many researchers, including David Berliner and Stephen Krashen, point to the long history of research on achievement gaps and how gaps in test scores reveal primarily one thing: the most influential factor in achievement – poverty. When compared to other countries with similar degrees of poverty, the US actually fares quite well on a global level. Berliner (2009), a well-respected researcher, argues that six out-of-school factors (OSFs) cannot be ignored in any discussion or policy aimed at closing the achievement gap. The six OSFs include: '(1) low birthweight and non-genetic prenatal influences on children; (2) inadequate medical, dental and vision care, often a result of inadequate or no medical insurance; (3) food insecurity; (4) environmental pollutants; (5) family relations and family stress; and (6) neighborhood characteristics' (Berliner, 2009: 1). Berliner argues that these six OSFs are related to a host of poverty-induced physical, sociological and psychological problems that children often bring to school, ranging from neurological damage and attention disorders to excessive absenteeism and oppositional behavior. Schools in high poverty neighborhoods face significantly greater challenges than those serving wealthier families, and efforts to improve educational outcomes in these schools – such as driving change through test-based accountability – are unlikely to succeed unless they are accompanied by policies that address OSFs. According to Berliner (2009), if the writers of NCLB had taken into account the complexities of poverty and passed co-requisite policies to target them and how they affect schooling, a reduction in achievement gaps might have become a reality. But this did not happen.

The way that Diane Ravitch (2010), an educational historian, sees it, during NCLB years, the Standards Movement was 'hijacked' by the Testing Movement. She notes that the law bypassed curriculum and standards altogether; it demanded that schools generate higher test scores in basic skills, but it required no curriculum at all nor did it raise standards. Moreover, NCLB ignored important topics such as history, civics, literature, science, the arts and geography. Ravitch realized that the new reforms had nothing to do with the substance of learning, and that accountability makes little sense if it undermines the larger goals of education. Parents are not happy.

Parents in the US are rallying across the country and a movement called the National Opt-Out Movement is gradually growing each year. Parents are opting out of state-mandated testing by keeping their children at home or requesting a separate location in school so that children can 'refuse' to take the test. Pennsylvania experienced a five-fold increase in parents 'opting out' between 2012-15. Some school districts in New York experienced over 50% of students opting out of the state-mandated math test. This movement caught the attention of Arne Duncan, former US Secretary of Education, who pledged to urge Congress to set state testing limits. News like this has been broadcast across social media and is popular on public radio stations (see for example, 'More Parents Say No To Testing' Here and Now, Boston NPR news station, February 27, 2015).

Support for NCLB

NCLB has delivered one large and significant positive effect for EBs: a new focus on accountability. If EBs don't perform well, it's everyone's problem. More and more principals, superintendents and state departments of education are talking about the quality of education for EBs, as well as possible solutions. Learning how to appropriately educate EBs is now seen as the responsibility of the whole school, including English as a new language (ENL) and non-ENL teachers. In New York, for example, as of 2014 all teacher candidates have to pass a test called Educating All Students (EAS) to receive any state certification – any. The EAS test has nine indicators on it that directly target an understanding of how EBs learn best. Before NCLB, these conversations rarely happened in the mainstream education environment, and mainstream teachers could become certified without knowing anything about the needs of EBs. NCLB has also ushered in higher-quality, large-scale assessments for

EBs. According to Jamal Abedi (2008), the guidelines set forth by NCLB in 2002 improved the overall quality of large-scale ELP tests compared to those used before NCLB.

A History of Assessment Events

Table 2.1 presents a range of historic events that impacted assessment in the US. This chapter ends with Table 2.2, which shows another perspective on how NCLB, a particularly influential policy, has changed the face of education, in particular, for EBs. In December 2015 the NCLB Act was replaced by the Every Student Succeeds Act (ESSA). President Obama signed ESSA into law in December 2015. The new law ends heavy federal involvement in public schools and sends much of that authority back to states and local districts.

Table 2.1 Important historical events affecting assessment and accountability in the United States

Year	Event	Importance
1954	*Brown v. Board of Education*	The outcome of this landmark case was, that 'no state shall deny any person within its jurisdiction the equal protection of the laws.' This ruling opened the door to future litigation limiting discriminatory practices against students based on, for example language, race, ethnicity, disability, culture, etc.
1964	Elementary and Secondary Education Act (ESEA)	Government funds are granted to meet the needs of 'educationally deprived children'.
1968	Title VII Bilingual Education Act, an amendment to ESEA	For the first time, federal funding provides support to programs specifically designed for EBs, including bilingual education
1970	*Diana v. State Board of Education*	Diana, a Spanish-speaking student, was diagnosed with mental retardation (MR) due to her low score on an IQ test given to her in English. When given the test again from a bilingual psychologist, Diana no longer qualified for special education. This resulted in a consent decree that mandated that IQ tests could not be the sole criteria or primary basis for diagnosis.
1972	*Guadalupe Organization v. Tempe Elementary School District*	The plaintiffs request was to require bilingual/bicultural services to non-English-speaking Mexican American and Yaqui Indian students. Similar to Diana, this consent decree specified that IQ tests could not be the sole criteria or primary basis for diagnosis.

(Continued)

Year	Event	Importance
1974	*Lau v. Nichols*	Supreme Court case; establishes that language programs are necessary to provide equal educational opportunities.
1981	*Castañeda v. Pickard*	An appeals court establishes a three-part test to determine whether schools are taking appropriate action under the 1974 Equal Educational Opportunity Act: (1) programs must be based on sound theory, (2) programs must be supported by adequate funding, and (3) programs must show effectiveness after a certain amount of time.
1984	A Nation at Risk	Fear-driven report that blames the poor education system for the country's ills. This report leads the United States down the path toward greater federal control.
1991	First National Standards	In 1991, the mathematics education community spearheaded the first standards of its kind. National Standards were written by the National Council of Teaching Mathematics (NCTM).
1994	George W. Bush becomes governor of Texas	The 'Texas Miracle' begins. Bush holds office as governor from 1994 to1999. The Texas Miracle impresses Congress and convinces legislators that such a model of accountability can work. Researchers McNeil and Valenzuela (2000) report that the Texas Miracle harms the education of poor and minority students.
1997	First national ELP Standards	*ESL Standards for Pre-K-12 Students* is the first set of national ELP standards.
1997	Individuals with Disabilities Education Act (IDEA) Revisions of 1997	This particular version of the law, among other things, mandated that parent consent procedures must be in the native language, and evaluation materials be free from bias of race and culture and must be provided in child's native language.
1998	Proposition 227 passes in California	This proposition severely limits the use of home languages in California public schools. The US 'English Only' movement is official.
1999	National Research Council forms committee on appropriate test use	Committee Statement: The test score for an EB is likely to be affected by Construct Irrelevant Variance (CIV) and therefore is likely to underestimate his or her knowledge of the subject being tested.
2000	George W. Bush becomes President of the United States	The Texas Miracle concept is adopted as a draft of NCLB.
2000	Proposition 203 passes in Arizona	Like California, Arizona voters severely restrict the use of home languages in public schools. The 'English Only' movement grows stronger.
2001	NCLB becomes law	NCLB is signed into law.

Year	Event	Importance
2002	Question 2 passes in Massachusetts	Like California and Arizona, voters in Massachusetts restrict the use of home languages in public schools.
2002	Title III of NCLB	Requires states to (1) develop and implement ELP standards; (2) implement a single, reliable and valid ELP assessment aligned with ELP standards that annually measures listening, speaking, reading, writing and comprehension; and (3) establish annual measureable achievement objectives (AMAOs) and report progress annually. See Table 2.2 for a more detailed examination of the changes NCLB brought to assessment of EBs.
2002	NCLB Enhanced Assessment Grant	Provides state support to develop an ELP instrument. Four different consortia of states develop ELP tests in an attempt to address the new requirements of NCLB. All new tests focus on the concept of academic language or using language for academic purposes.
2002	World Class Instructional Design and Assessment (WIDA) is born	WIDA Enhanced Assessment Grant is awarded to Wisconsin Department of Public Instruction, WIDA's first home. Eventually, more than 30 states join the WIDA consortium.
2002	Title VII eliminated	The Title VII (Bilingual Education Act) created in 1968 is eliminated and replaced by Title III. (Language Instruction for Limited English Proficient and Immigrant Students)
2004	Rod Paige announces changes to NCLB	Secretary of Education Rod Paige announces two significant changes to NCLB pertaining to EBs: (1) LEP students may be exempt from English Language Arts exams for 1 year; and (2) for AYP purposes, Fluent English Proficient FEPs can stay in the LEP subgroup for two years. The fact that this was announced two years later, demonstrates that EBs were not a priority (more of an afterthought) when NCLB was written.
2004	Pennsylvania challenges EB test validity in state court	*Reading School District v. PA Department of Education*: Challenge denied. It was determined by state court that it was not practical for the Department of Education to administer tests in the child's primary language.
2005	State standards required	NCLB requires that all states develop standards in Science by 2005 (English and math in 2002).
2007	National experts gather	Federal government calls a meeting of national experts (five years after NCLB passes into law) to define what is valid and reliable assessment for EBs. The question remains unanswered.

(Continued)

Year	Event	Importance
2008	California challenges EB test validity in state court	*Coachella Valley v. California*: Nine school districts asked the state to provide tests in Spanish or simplified English. The request was denied and upheld by the state.
2009	National experts gather (again)	Federal government calls a meeting of national experts (seven years after NCLB passes into law) to define what is valid and reliable assessment for EBs. The question remains unanswered.
2009	Obama administration's American Recovery and Reinvestment Act (ARRA) of 2009	Economic stimulus package signed into law by Barack Obama –$831 billion from 2009 to 2019. The US Department of Education calls upon schools to use assessment data to respond to students' academic strengths and needs.
2010	Common Core State Standards (CCSS) released in ELA and math	Design of standards is coordinated by National Governors Association (NGA) and the Council of Chief State School Officers (CCSSO). Forty-five states join in an unprecedented level of national participation in a single set of standards.
March, 2010	US Department of Education announces grant to develop CCSS assessments	Grant reflects concerns about CCSS, including the incorporation of fair and reasonable accommodations for EBs and students with disabilities (SWD). Nearly 10 years after NCLB law required 'valid and reliable' assessments for EBs, the Department of Education still cannot define what that means.
2010	Two assessment consortiums launched (Smarter Balance and Partnership for Assessment of Readiness for College and Careers [PARCC] launched)	Smarter Balance (Assessment Consortium, awarded $175 million) and PARCC (awarded $185 million) are launched with funding from the US Department of Education to create assessments aligned with the CCSS and to be fully operational by the 2014/2015 school year.
2014/ 2015	Forty-two states commit to use common test	Consortia member-states commit to and implement the common assessments as their NCLB assessments. Race to the Top (RTTT) funds pay for the design, development and piloting of the assessment system, plus other costs.
2015	NCLB replaced by ESSA	NCLB Act was replaced by ESSA. At the time that this book was going into production, the intent of the law was to lighten up the federal involvement in public schools and send much of that authority back to states and local districts.
2016	Proposition 58 passes in California	Proposition 227, restricting Bilingual Education in California is repealed.

Table 2.2 Results of NCLB: Major changes that affect EBs

Before NCLB	After NCLB	Implications of the change (positive and negative)
EBs have a three-year waiver.	EBs must take content-area tests; no exemptions. EBs must take English language proficiency tests after one year.	+ Increased accountability for EBs. Schools are worried about the appearance of low test scores and are thus motivated to improve schooling for EBs.
		− Decrease in validity. EBs are taking tests when they are (by definition) not proficient in English. There is no valid use for these scores. Negative effects of using these scores outweigh the benefits.
ELP standards are not required.	States are required to develop and implement English-language proficiency standards (called ELP standards).	+ Consistency: When students move from district to district, they receive a similar curriculum.
		− Districts lose autonomy. Standards may not be written well, but districts are stuck with them.
Districts may choose a language proficiency test from a list of tests.	States are required to implement a single, 'reliable and valid' English-language proficiency assessment aligned to ELP standards that annually measures listening, speaking, reading, writing and comprehension.	+ Consistency across districts. Before this change, a child may be classified EB in one district and not EB in another because he or she took a different language proficiency test. + Psychometric qualities of ELP assessments improved (Abedi, 2008).
		− Districts can no longer choose. The one test chosen by the state department might be too easy or too hard.
AMAOs do not exist. States are not required to report annual EB progress.	States are required to establish annual measureable achievement objectives (AMAOs) and report progress annually.	+ Increased accountability for EBs. Schools with low-quality ENL and bilingual programs need to show evidence of progress.
		− Beginner EBs grow more quickly, and more advanced EBs grow more slowly. AMAOs are not aligned with second language acquisition (SLA). Demanding that students 'move along' with language acquisition is not enough.

End-of-Chapter Activities (Instructors: see advice at the end of the book)

By completing Activities 1–4, the reader will be able to:

(1) Order 10 important historical events that influenced the history of assessment for EBs.
(2) Categorize popular reasons for school success/failure through different arguments and relate them to personal experiences and assessment.
(3) Compare and contrast the benefits and risks of validity and accountability scenarios for assessing EBs.
(4) Make two comments in an academic discussion about school practices today and how they relate to the history of assessment for EBs.

Activity 1
Order 10 important historical events that influenced the history of assessment for EBs.

Pairs of students will practice the order of historical events and the implications of these events. The instructor will bring paper and sticky notes to class for each pair of students to create a timeline. The instructor will post a list of historical events (from Table 2.1) out of order and ask students to order them with a partner on their 'timeline' and explain why the event was important. The sticky notes are used so that students can reorder events and change the order of events while discussing/learning. An alternative way to introduce this activity using more movement is to create a 'human timeline'. Pass out 10 index cards with the name of an important historical event and have the whole class input on how to order the students holding the cards. This allows for a group discussion of the historical events.

Activity 2
Categorize popular reasons for school success/failure through different arguments and relate it to assessment.

In a group activity, be prepared to state two reasons why some students succeed in school and others don't. After the group activity, give assessment examples in each part of a word web and share with a partner.

(Continued)

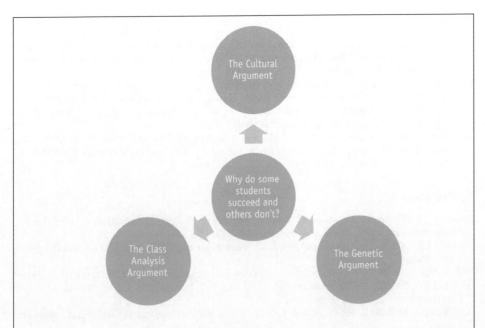

Activity 3

Compare and contrast the benefits and risks of validity and accountability scenarios for assessing EBs.

In groups of three or four students for small-group discussion, answer the following questions and be prepared to share with the whole class: (1) name and describe the two validity accountability scenarios discussed in this chapter; (2) list two specific examples per scenario.

Activity 4

Make two comments in an academic discussion about school practices today and how they relate to the history of assessment for EBs.

After reading this chapter, come to class prepared for an academic discussion worth points on the syllabus (this also models authentic assessment). Each student should be prepared to comment twice in the academic discussion and will be scored on the following rubric. This assessment method is called discussion with a rubric.

Quality of Comments. Student contributes at least two timely and appropriate comments, thoughtful and reflective, responds respectfully to other students' remarks and provokes questions and comments from the group (suggested *four points*).

Resource/Document Reference. Clear reference to chapter being discussed/has done the reading with some thoroughness, comment contains detail or critical insight (suggested *four points*).

Active Listening. Posture, demeanor and behavior clearly demonstrate respect and attentiveness to others (suggested *two points*).

Notes

(1) Lewis Terman is also noted as a pioneer in educational psychology for his research with 'gifted' children by Stanford University. In addition, he served as president of the American Psychological Association.
(2) A eugenicist is a person specializing in eugenics. Eugenics is a social philosophy advocating the improvement of human genetic traits through positive genetics – the promotion of reproduction among people with desirable traits, and negative eugenics – reducing the reproduction of people with undesirable traits.
(3) The drawing is part of an unpublished study to explore the feelings of EBs taking achievement tests in English in a restricted language policy state (Arizona). Mahoney, K., Mahoney, A., Rossi, R. (unpublished).

References

Abedi, J. (2008) Measuring students' level of English proficiency: Educational significance and assessment requirements. *Educational Assessment* 13, 193–214.
AERA, APA, NCME (1966) *Standards for Educational and Psychological Tests and Manuals.* Washington, DC: Author.
AERA, APA, NCME (1974) *Standards for Educational and Psychological Tests.* Washington, DC: Author.
AERA, APA, NCME (1985) *Standards for Educational and Psychological Testing.* Washington, DC: Author.
AERA, APA, NCME (1999) *Standards for Educational and Psychological Testing.* Washington, DC: Author.
AERA, APA, NCME (2014) *Standards for Educational and Psychological Testing.* Washington, DC: AERA.
Anyon, J. (1980) Social class and the hidden curriculum of work. *Journal of Education* 162, 67–92.
August, D. and Hakuta, K. (eds) (1998) *Educating Language Minority Children.* Washington, DC: National Academy Press.
Berliner, D.C. (2009) *Poverty and Potential: Out-of-School Factors and School Success.* Boulder, CO/ Tempe, AZ: Education and the Public Interest Center & Education Policy Research Unit. See http://nepc.colorado.edu/publication/poverty-and-potential.
Gould, S. (1996) *The Mismeasure of Man* (revised edition). New York: W.W. Norton & Company.
Leslie, M. (2000) The vexing legacy of Lewis Terman. *Stanford Alumni Magazine* July/August.
Menken, K. and Solorza, C. (2014) No Child Left Bilingual: Accountability and the elimination of bilingual education programs in New York City schools. *Educational Policy* 28 (1), 96–125.
McNeil, L. and Valenzuela, A. (2001) The harmful impact of the TAAS system of testing in Texas: Beneath the accountability rhetoric. In M. Kornhaber and G. Orfield (eds) *Raising Standards or Raising Barriers? Inequality and High Stakes Testing in Public Education* (pp. 127–150). New York: Century Foundation.
National Research Council (NRC) (1999) *High Stakes: Testing for Tracking, Promotion, and Graduation.* Washington, DC: National Academy Press.
Ogbu, J. (1978) *Minority Education and Caste: The American System in Cross-Cultural Perspective.* New York: Academic Press.
Ogbu, J. (1998) Voluntary and involuntary minorities: A cultural-ecological theory of school performance with some implications for education. *Anthropology & Education Quarterly* 29 (2), 155–188.
Ravitch, D. (2010) *The Death and Life of the Great American School System: How Testing and Choice are Undermining Education.* New York: Basic Books.
Valdés, G. (1996) *Con respeto.* New York: Teachers College, Columbia University.
Wright, W. (2002) The effects of high stakes testing in an inner-city elementary school: The curriculum, the teachers, and the English Language Learners. *Current Issues in Education.* See http://cie.ed.asu.edu/volume5/number5/
Zhao, Y. (2009) *Catching Up or Leading the Way: American Education in the Age of Globalization.* Alexandria, VA: ASCD.

Recommended reading

Baserra, M., Trumbull, E. and Solano-Flores, G. (eds) (2010) *Cultural Validity in Assessment: Addressing Linguistic and Cultural Diversity* (Language, Culture and Teaching Series). New York: Routledge.

The authors address the disproportionately negative impact on students who do not come from mainstream middle-class backgrounds. The book is unique in that it accounts for cultural validity by articulating through validity terms the cultural and linguistic variations that jeopardize assessment results. Criteria for culturally valid assessment are included.

Glass, G. (2008) *Fertilizers, Pills, and Magnetic Strips*. Charlotte, NC: Information Age Publishing (IAP).

Glass argues and shows with data that the central education policy debates at the start of the 21st century (vouchers, charter schools, tax credits, high-stakes testing and bilingual education) are really about two underlying issues: (1) how can the costs of public education be cut and (2) how can the education of the white middle class be privatized at public expense? He uses demographic data across 30 years to support these points.

McNeil, L., Coppola, E., Radigan, J. and Heilig, J. (2008) Avoidable losses: High-stakes accountability and the dropout crisis. *Education Policy Analysis Archives* 16 (3). See http://epaa.asu.edu/ojs/article/view/28.

These researchers used large-scale data to show that the current high-stakes, test-based accountability system puts our most vulnerable youth – the poor, EBs, African American and Latino children –at risk of being pushed out of their schools so the schools can reach acceptable status according to NCLB.

Ravitch, D. (2013) *Reign of Error: The Hoax of the Privatization Movement and the Danger to America's Public Schools*. New York: Alfred A. Knopf.

In this book, Diane Ravitch argues that graduation rates are the highest and dropout rates the lowest they have ever been. She argues that NCLB and RTTT set unreasonable goals and punish schools and teachers in an unfair way. She also documents how Wall Street, individual billionaires and major foundations are eyeing public education as an emerging market for investors, which will lead to its downfall.

3 Validity

Themes from Chapter 3

(1) Tests aren't bad; it's how we are using them that's bad.
(2) Viewing emergent bilingual (EB) test scores through the Unified View of Validity puts overdue importance on how we use EB test scores. This includes paying more attention to social consequences of test-use.
(3) Construct Irrelevant Variance (CIV) is a major validity threat for test scores of EB students.
(4) Social consequences of using test scores or 'side effects' are having a wide-range impact on the field of ENL and bilingual education.

Key Vocabulary

- Unified view of validity
- Construct
- CIV (Construct Irrelevant Variance) otherwise known as bias
- Test interpretation
- Test score use

PUMI Connection: Use

This chapter primarily focuses on the U (Use) by explaining a theory of validity called the 'Unified View of Validity'. The Unified View of Validity shifts the thinking on validity from validating tests (outdated thinking) to validating how we *use* test scores (current thinking). This is an important shift because it places more emphasis on test-score-use, which will lead to more appropriate and fair decisions about testing for EBs.

This chapter is the most theoretical of all the chapters in this book. After this chapter, the remainder of the book focuses on the practical issues of assessing EBs. The author uses the concerns over assessing EBs (achievement and language) in the US as the context to better understand the important topic of validity. This chapter raises concrete concerns about the validity, ethics and ideologies of using test scores. It is important for the reader to process some of this theory/framework to draw more meaning from the practice-oriented chapters immediately following this chapter.

In the past, we asked: Is this *test* valid or not? Now we ask: Is a particular *test score use* valid for EBs? This change represents a fundamental shift in thinking about validity, from validating the instrument (presumably for all students) to validating how we use test scores for a particular purpose. Although different types of validity still exist, it is now considered inappropriate not to consider this unified view. Most people refer to the *Unified View of Validity* as *Validity* now.

Construct-related Validity Threats

Construct Irrelevant Variance (CIV) is a major threat to the validity of using EB test scores. CIV is a systematic measurement error that reduces the ability to accurately interpret scores or ratings (Haladyna & Downing, 2004). Simply put, tests in English are likely measuring something other than what it seems for EBs, at least partly, and in a systematic way that may go undetected.

To break CIV down – *Construct*[1] is the concept we are attempting to measure. With EBs we often measure the construct of language proficiency and/or academic achievement, with high stakes attached to test use. The term 'construct' reminds us that these ideas are constructed by experts in the field and are informed by a theoretical or conceptual framework chosen to guide the test construction. *Irrelevant* means not relevant to the construct. *Variance* is a way of explaining what accounts for the test score in a statistical way. No psychological construct is perfectly definable or perfectly measureable; language proficiency and achievement are no exceptions to this rule.

CIV is a major validity threat for EBs because irrelevant constructs often contaminate test scores. In other words, if the CIV is high, then the test may be measuring something different than it was designed to measure. Measurement scientists mostly call these construct-irrelevant variables, but some call them nuisance variables, extraneous variables or contaminants. For example, if an EB takes a math test in English that is full of word problems, the assessment becomes more of a measure of language than of math. The CIV in this case is language because the assessment was designed to measure math. The term CIV can also be replaced with the term bias.

Another validity threat related to the construct is when the test does not cover the entire ability (the term for this in the measurement field is 'construct underrepresentation'), like language for example. For instance, many tests narrowly measure speaking, listening, reading and writing and many times not very well, but they claim the test measures 'language proficiency'. This is an example of the test claiming to measure language, but in reality only a very small fraction of language is measured.

Most experts that study language become frustrated with the way schools define and assess language in such narrow and calculated ways, and with so many high stakes attached (advancement of grade, graduation from high school, entry to special education or gifted programming, etc.). Elana Shohamy points out that our conceptions of language should include multimodal representation such as visuals, graphics, images, dance and even silence. These forms of 'languaging' are far more representative of real language use for EB children. She also says that when language is treated as discrete categories with fixed boundaries, political entities use such boundaries to maintain an 'us versus them' attitude and give preference to some language varieties over others in order to harness political power (Shohamy, 2006). Those having political power give preference, and privilege, to certain forms of language, like Standard English over non-Standard English. This privilege is justified through test results. These types of validity threats lead to one group claiming superiority over another (see Chapter 2 for historical documentation of this).

Language-Related Validity Threats

Although they function closely together, language proficiency and academic achievement are two distinct constructs and should be measured separately. Language proficiency signifies knowing a language, whereas academic achievement signifies knowing a particular domain of content made available through formal schooling. On the one hand, the emphasis of academic achievement is on content, which consists of the concepts and generalizations within a subject matter. Language proficiency, on the other hand, is the medium through which students access these domains of content. Academic achievement is the result of cognitive learning, whereas language proficiency is a result of language acquisition or language learning. Because language proficiency is a medium for academic achievement, the task of measuring each construct and separating how one influences the other has proved to be an important scientific challenge.

There is no denying a strong relationship between language and achievement. The relationship between language factors and student performance in content-based areas has been well established in the literature (see, for example, Abedi, 2003).

When two constructs, such as achievement and proficiency, function so closely together, how much of the test score is due to true achievement.[2] and how much is due to CIV? EB educators understand that language factors threaten the validity of achievement test scores because they are trained in how to instruct and assess EBs, taking language factors into consideration, through concepts like scaffolding and comprehensible input. However, non-educators may not see the harm in testing EBs in English on academic achievement tests. When those who advocate for testing EBs in English are asked why they think this is a good idea, two responses are typical. First, for many, its the law. State and federal laws in general leave no option but for schools to comply with mandatory testing. State policymakers rationalize that scores need to be collected right away, sometimes even before an EB can speak English, to provide solid 'baseline data'. Second, it is argued that even though the test may not be a good measure of content, at least it can measure language. In fact, some state policies use content-area test scores to inform the identification process for EBs. School districts rationalize this because children must know English reasonably well to understand the questions of a test, lower scores reflect limited knowledge of English and higher scores reflect greater knowledge of English. Many researchers point out that an achievement test, not specified by second language acquisition theories to measure language, is inappropriate and that children may score low on a standardized achievement test for reasons wholly separate from language.

Because true achievement is an abstract idea, and since no test is perfectly reliable, providing empirical evidence that can quantify exactly how much of the test score is due to true achievement, is a question that can never really be answered with 100% accuracy. Every (achievement) test score is made up of the true construct (achievement) plus some amount of error. Too much error results in an unreliable test score and an invalid representation of what a child really knows. The problem worsens when we use unreliable data to make decisions.

Use and Interpretation is the Most Important Concept in Validity

Good validity takes into account how a test will be used, the consequences of using it in those ways and for whom the test was intended. It also includes empirical evidence, with external checks, that the intended use of the test does work as it should for EBs. According to standards from the measurement community, this should be done on a case-by-case basis, meaning each and every test use for EBs should be 'tested'. It takes longer to 'test the test' but it's worth it, because when you increase validity you strengthen accountability in a meaningful way. We are currently in an historic era that favors accountability over validity. That means we are holding schools and teachers accountable, but often with the use of invalid data.

As mentioned above, each *use* of the test must be considered for validity on a case-by-case basis. Common ways we interpret/use test scores for EBs are as follows: give grades, decide program, decide promotion, EB classification or Special Education (SPED) classification, to name some important uses. Particularly controversial is the question of whether achievement tests should be used to evaluate teachers. During NCLD, New York state, 20% of a teacher's annual performance reviews was derived from state-mandated standardized test results. When considering validity, the consequences of test use are critical. Consider the consequences of labeling a teacher as needing improvement because the EBs in his or her class were mostly new to the English language and generated low test scores (some did not finish the test). Consequences of inappropriate test-use could include: (1) the teacher may move to a school with fewer EBs or quit, (2) the parents begin to doubt the teacher's ability and request to place their student in another class, or (3) the teacher is put on a Teacher Improvement Plan and becomes discouraged.

The measurement community – American Educational Research Association (AERA), American Psychological Association (APA) and the National Council on Measurement in Education (NCME) (2014: 23) – makes very clear the importance of *test designers* to establish intended uses and interpretations as shown by the following standards (for a full review, read Chapter 1 in the standards document called 'standards for validity'):

1.1 The test developer should set forth clearly how test scores are intended to be interpreted and consequently used. The population(s) for which a test is intended should be delimited clearly, and the construct or constructs that the test is intended to assess should be described clearly.

1.2 A rationale should be presented for each intended interpretation of test scores for a given use, together with a summary of the evidence and theory bearing on the intended interpretation.

1.3 If validity for some common or likely interpretation for a given use has not been evaluated, or if such an interpretation is inconsistent with available evidence, that fact should be made clear and potential users should be strongly cautioned about making unsupported interpretations.

1.4 If a test score is interpreted for a given use in a way that has not been validated, it is incumbent on the user to justify the new interpretation for that use, providing a rationale and collecting new evidence, if necessary.

Snapshot: The Validity of Using Stanford English Language Proficiency (SELP) Results for Reclassification?

This is a true story. A requirement of No Child Left Behind (NCLB) was that all states select one English language proficiency (ELP) test and use it across the entire state. In response, the State Department of Education in Arizona purchased a commercial test off the shelf called the Stanford English Language Proficiency Test – the SELP. At the time, Arizona state code regulated that the test publisher's recommendation for when a child is 'ready for a mainstream' class be used as the cut-off score to reclassify EBs. In other words, in this case, the publisher (Harcourt Brace) determined when EBs were ready to be mainstreamed (based solely on their SELP test score), and by law all Arizona schools needed to comply. In 2006, after using the SELP for reclassification purposes, many teachers felt that the SELP was 'too easy' as many students were placed in mainstream classes before they were ready. Unfortunately, the teachers who spoke up were accused by the state superintendent, as quoted in a newspaper article, of wanting to keep students classified as EBs to raise more money for their school (Ryman, 2006). This accusation was founded on the fact that a school is awarded a certain amount of money per student when they are classified as EBs and the superintendent implied teachers wanted to keep students classified for the money.

Teachers began to call me and my colleagues at Arizona State University. Tom Haladyna, Jeff MacSwan and I began a study of the validity of using the publisher-recommended cut-off for reclassification using achievement (as measured by the Arizona's Instrument to Measure Standards (AIMS)) as an external proxy for success – a study that should have been conducted before the state adopted the test (if we concern ourselves with validity before accountability, that is), before the publisher suggested a cut-off score and definitely before this became state code. We asked: How does a testing company from another state know when EBs in Arizona are ready for mainstream classrooms? This is a critical question that EB teachers with many years of experience struggle with, yet a test maker from another region was able to determine this with precision (via a cut-off score). What evidence is presented by the publisher with this score to ensure that we're making good educational decisions? How are EBs in Arizona doing after being reclassified by the SELP? These are all case-by-case validity questions mentioned as a heading earlier in this chapter. When the study was complete, it showed that teachers were correct; using the SELP for reclassification exited students too early. This conclusion was verified when a large percentage of students did not meet state academic standards after reclassification. We knew this because we looked at the evidence of success after classification.

Had a validity study been conducted *before* the test was adopted, thousands of students would not have been misclassified that year. This study was conducted using Samuel Messick's (1990) *Unified View of Validity* as a framework to highlight the need to examine validity on a case-by-case basis. (See Mahoney *et al.*, 2009 for the full validity study.)

We must *slow down* accountability regulations until we're able to study valid ways of using results from tests for EBs. We need better assessments, not more assessments.

Discussion Questions

- What part of validity was ignored by policymakers in this example?
- What can teachers do when they judge a test use to be invalid?

What is a Unified View of Validity?

In 1985, major measurement organizations recognized validity as a unified concept (APA, AERA, NCME, 1985) The unified view of validity is an integrated evaluative judgment of the degree to which empirical evidence and theoretical rationales support the adequacy and appropriateness of inferences and actions based on test scores (Messick, 1989), which is a mouthful but here is how to break it down.

A unified view of validity matters for EBs because the actions we take based on test scores and test interpretation are critical in making the appropriate educational decisions. If you find yourself asking questions focusing on meaningfulness and appropriateness of using test scores for EBs, these are validity questions. The following is a list of validity questions you may have considered:

• How do we know what test scores for EBs really mean?
• What does it mean if an EB scores a level two on state mathematics exam?
• What does it mean if an EB scores at the advanced level on the state's English proficiency test? How should we use these scores?
• How was it determined that students are ready for reclassification?
• Do we have evidence to show that students scoring below proficiency are *not* ready to participate meaningfully in the classroom outside of English as a new language (ENL)?
• What evidence has been presented to show that these cut-off scores work accurately to inform these critical educational decisions?
• How does the test publisher know how to make recommendations for student placement?
• Have the recommendations been investigated empirically (with data)?
• Have test publishers considered the social and educational consequences of using the test scores based on their recommendations?

These are examples of important validity questions that we need to ask (and find answers to!) to increase validity for EBs. For example, two researchers decided to investigate the validity of language proficiency test results by comparing them to other tests designed to measure and use results in the same way. Jeff MacSwan and Kellie Rolstad (2006) conducted a study in which 150 elementary school EBs took three language assessments to see if they led to similar results. They used two common language proficiency assessments, the Language Assessment Scales-Oral (LAS-O) and the Idea Proficiency Test I-Oral (IPT-Spanish), along with one natural language measure. The results of the LAS-O identified 74% of the students as not proficient in their primary language and the IPT-Spanish identified 90%, whereas the natural language sample found only 2% of the sample to have high morphological error rates (remember – this was the same group of students given different instrumentation). The authors of this study argued that using test results such as these to make important educational decisions, partly leads to disproportionate representation of EBs in special education and other serious consequences.

Part science, part ethics

The most important question for EBs, however, is how test scores *should be used* – the *should* question. Examples of should-questions surrounding EBs under the current testing accountability climate include:

• Should EB results of achievement tests in English be used to judge teacher performance?
• Should scores be used to evaluate programs?

- Should one score on a language proficiency test determine whether an EB receives language services?
- Should scores be used to judge whether a school or neighborhood is good?
- Should these scores decide whether a principal is effective?

Some of these questions highlight the social consequences of using (or not using) the test score as part of the validation process. A true understanding of validity involves giving science and ethics equal consideration. Figure 3.1 depicts the delicate balance between science and ethics.

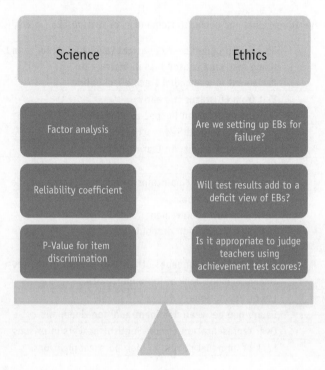

Figure 3.1 Balancing science and ethics in validity

Let's use a pharmacy analogy to better understand the consequences of testing. Federal policies and procedures ensure that a new drug is not used with the general public until it and its side effects have been studied over a period of time. To use a test score without a thorough (and empirically driven) understanding of its meaning is as dangerous as trusting a drug to work without knowing what it intends to treat and its potential side effects. The social consequences of test score use are viewed as the 'side effects' of testing and are very important in the consideration of testing EBs in English; in reality though, the actual appraisal of social consequences is a difficult task. One side effect of testing EBs that is often heard through personal communication with EB teachers, is the amount of crying, fear and disappointment that occurs at test time. Many teachers describe the sense of helplessness they and their students feel when given a high-stakes test that they can't read well. These types of side effects contribute to a negative schooling experience that often spirals downward over time. Table 3.1 presents a list of some of the potential negative educational and social consequences, or potential 'side effects' in the appraisal of the appropriateness, meaningfulness and usefulness of test scores. There could be a parallel table showing the positive consequences and casting each of these ideas in a promising light (for example placement in a gifted program or feelings of achievement or increase number of bilingual schools); however, these happen much less frequently.

Table 3.1 Negative educational and social consequences of testing EBs (in English)

	Bilingual program de-emphasizes languages other than English
	Home language is used less in instruction
	Placement in a remedial track of schooling
	Exit from EB status too early
	Over-representation in special education
	Access to less-qualified teachers
	Unequal opportunity to learn (OTL)
	Grade retention
	School/community maintains deficit perspective of EBs
	Disinterest in school
	Feeling of low achievement
	Low graduation/high dropout rate
Social/political	
	Devaluation of languages other than English in society
	Unemployment, lack of job opportunities
	Lower-paying jobs
	Salary gap between dominant and non-dominant
	Over-representation of non-English speakers in prisons
	Lack of bilingual people in high political positions

The role of ideology (language and culture)

Ideology and (cultural) values also play a role in validity. Because of national and state policy, schools are mostly concerned with measuring achievement and language proficiency (in English) for accountability purposes. Because accountability tests are administered mostly in English only in the US, this gives a great advantage to English-speaking students and teachers of English-speaking students. At the same time, testing what students can do in home languages or additional languages goes undetected, feeding a deficit perspective of EBs and ignoring the great value that bilingual children offer. Many important constructs, in addition to achievement and language, such as acculturation and motivation, go unnoticed for EBs. Acculturation is when a student is confronted with new norms and a new culture; this is known to directly impact learning. Because of the connection between acculturation and learning, it is important to assess acculturation with EBs new to school culture (Adelman Reyes & Kleyn, 2010). Assessing acculturation is usually done through interview with a checklist. The checklist may focus on the amount of time in a country, district and school. It also may focus on proficiency in the home language, new language and whether there are people in the school who share the home language or culture.

Constructs such as achievement and language, which are broad and difficult to define/measure, leave room for other factors such as ideology and cultural values to become part of the unintended or irrelevant construct. In the context of schooling in the US, the values of the dominant culture (white, English-speaking middle class) have become intimately intertwined with the concept of evidence, interpretation and meaning of test scores. The very nature of norm-referenced testing (comparing students to one another to see who is better) is embedded in the competitive values of the middle class in a way that gives advantage to those already dominant in the US. A classic study conducted by Rhodes (1988) offers an example of how culture and values can significantly affect test score. In studying the very low achievement test scores of Hopi and Navajo students, Rhodes points out that tests require quick answers, guessing, risk taking and the elimination of options in the selection of only one response. This contradicts what is taught in some Native American cultures in which decisions are made slowly and surely. Therefore, Hopi and Navajo children may be at a disadvantage in demonstrating achievement not because they are so-called low achievers, but because the construct of achievement, as measured through a standardized and timed test, may require cultural values not aligned with Hopis and Navajos.

Further, the construct of achievement and language proficiency are largely influenced by language ideology. Language ideologies are the assumptions, interpretations and judgments about vocabulary, grammar, accent and so on, that are based upon political, religious, class or other views. In the US, a strong language ideology is expressed by the 'English-only movement' – that is, a view that supports the idea that language homogeneity is beneficial to US society and is evidenced by the requirement to take and pass standardized achievement tests in English. We know these ideologies exist in assessment, but as Sammual Messick (1980) pointed out 30 years ago, exposing the value assumptions of a test construct and its more subtle links to ideology – possibly to multiple cross-cutting ideologies – is a daunting challenge. For EBs, potential cross-cutting ideologies embedded in the constructs of achievement and language proficiency include, for example, political ideologies (English is the language of power), sociocultural and sociolinguistic ideologies (middle-class language and culture is normal), and race ideologies (white privilege).

In summary, one cultural group may use tests to control other cultural groups. This idea can be used to explain the history of misuse that was presented in Chapter 2. Using very broad constructs for testing may also support a system of cultural hegemony, whereby one cultural group (English speaking and white) can manipulate the system of values in order to create a world view favoring its authority over other cultural groups (non-white and non-English speaking). Cultural hegemony is the domination of a diverse society by one world view, instead of multiple world views. Holding EBs and teachers of EBs accountable to standardized tests in English and not holding them accountable for home language development, promotes this sort of cultural hegemony.

Achievement Test Results Used the Wrong Way

Test score results should not be used to evaluate teachers and principals. We have better ways, which researchers have studied for years, to measure teacher and principal effectiveness. One is the National Board certification, which includes explanations, data and reflections about its extensive methods for measuring teacher effectiveness. Some of these include observation, videotaping and integrating a culturally responsive pedagogy that matches the local community.

Academic achievement tests measure the academic achievement of a group of students for whom the test was designed. Along the same lines, language-proficiency tests are designed to measure language proficiency among a certain group of students. Each instrument is intended to be used in a certain way, as outlined in the technical manual. Academic achievement test results are meant to measure student academic achievement against a set of standards, not to evaluate teachers. This is an example of not using test scores the way they were intended to be used. Because of policies promoting teacher evaluation using student test scores, teachers are reluctant to work in schools with many EBs and alternately seek employment at schools with lower numbers of EBs in order to improve their teacher rating. Students who are known to score low on tests are not wanted in classrooms where teachers are threatened about their APR. In a high school that the author visited recently, one teacher who felt stuck deterred an EB student with lower English proficiency from enrolling in her English language arts (ELA) class, but allowed the student to audit the class, thus avoiding having the low test score attached to her annual professional performance review (APPR). The student in such a case receives no credit for taking the class. This is an example of a negative unintended consequence of high-stakes testing.

Snapshot: Missed Opportunity

Recently, I visited a bilingual school that has had problems recruiting and maintaining bilingual teachers. In the hallway, I was surprised to run into a new fourth-grade teacher – Ms Rodriguez, the daughter of a well-known bilingual teacher who has been a very effective teacher of EBs over the years. When I mentioned that I hadn't seen her name on the teacher list for the bilingual program and wondered if she had changed her name, she replied, 'I am not certified in ESL or bilingual'. She then explained to me that her mother and other teachers had warned her how difficult teacher evaluations are for teachers with large numbers of EBs and advised her to approach teaching through a mainstream teaching certificate, and she heeded their warning. Owing to an evaluation system that puts teachers with large numbers of EBs at an unfair disadvantage, we are losing our best. This is a case of a missed opportunity.

Discussion questions

- Why was Ms Rodriguez reluctant to join the field of bilingual education?
- What positive incentives do districts offer for teachers to become bilingual educators?
- Why is it more difficult for teachers with high numbers of EBs to receive positive evaluations?

Two major validity concerns are shown through the previous and following snapshots, both of which are based on true stories. The previous snapshot is an example of a serious negative consequence (good teachers deterred from the profession) of using tests scores for teacher evaluation. The following snapshot is an example of two things. A negative effect (narrowing of curriculum) and the misuse of academic achievement results to evaluate quality of teaching.

Snapshot: The Higher the Test Score the Better the Teacher?

Teacher A: Cathy spent all of her time preparing students for the ELA test. She reduced the time spent teaching Spanish language arts, science and social studies, and she cancelled the field trip to the city's art museum so she could have more time to prepare for the test. Every day, she talked about the importance of the test, practice items were reviewed again and again and test-taking strategies became a very important topic. Students memorized a song about doing well on the test, and a letter was sent home to parents indicating the importance of their children being ready for the test. Cathy spearheaded a school initiative to invite students to come early to school to jog and exercise during the weeks of testing (this initiative ended as soon as state tests ended) to help stimulate their brains during test week.

Teacher B: Despite pressure to drop traditional subjects and focus only on math and English, Roberto decided to continue teaching all subjects in school with a heavy emphasis on biliteracy. He spent time at the beginning of each school year assessing each student and increasing his cultural competency so that the instruction was culturally relevant – a method coined by Gloria Ladson-Billings to denote a pedagogy where teachers focus on cultural competence, high expectations and raising social consciousness. To teach social studies, mathematics and an ELA project, Roberto launched a community project in which his students mapped all the abandoned buildings within two square miles of the school and wrote a report to the City Development Department citing the negative impact these buildings have on youth in their community and proposing solutions to the excessive number of such buildings. The report included the community consequences of multiple abandoned buildings and how they affect children and their learning; it also suggested productive ways to renew these buildings. At state testing time, Roberto spent the two weeks before the test preparing the students for the test. However, he made it a point not to overwhelm students with anxieties about the test because they should be as comfortable as possible on test day, and outside factors were already making them nervous.

(Continued)

Result: The students in Cathy's classroom scored much higher on the test than in Roberto's. Roberto is being considered for a Teacher Improvement Plan; if he doesn't raise test scores within a certain time frame, he might not receive tenure. Cathy was evaluated as a highly effective teacher and was recognized at the district level as a good mentor for new teachers. Unfortunately, in this example, it might be the case that the weaker teacher was labeled as effective and the stronger teacher was labeled as ineffective.

Although NCLB and policies like it are intended to reward highly qualified teachers while weeding out the ineffective ones, in some instances it may achieve the exact opposite. Thus, we must always ask the most pressing question: What does a high test score really mean? Does a test score represent true achievement? A high score may mean in part that the teacher narrowed the curriculum to focus on test preparation; thus, in some cases it may be that a higher score might actually indicate a less effective teacher.

Discussion questions

- Whose students benefitted more?
- Who has an advantage under this accountability system? Who is benefitting from a system of accountability like this?
- Do higher test scores mean better teachers?

End-of-Chapter Activities (Instructors: see advice at the end of the book)

By completing Activities 1 to 4, the reader will be able to:

(1) Write your own definition of validity as a unified concept.
(2) Identify key 'unified validity' vocabulary terms and use them in a sentence related to EBs.
(3) Shift thinking about test validity from whether *tests* are valid to whether *how we use test scores* is valid.
(4) Agree or disagree with the following statement and provide evidence: *Testing EBs in the US using broad constructs may support a system of cultural hegemony.*

Activity 1

Write and say your own definition of validity as a unified concept. In small groups, students brainstorm a list of qualities that help define the unified view of validity. After 20 minutes, be prepared to share the group's definition of a unified view of validity. Afterward, students write their own definition of validity on an index card and submit to the instructor for evaluation.

Activity 2

Identify key 'unified validity' vocabulary terms and use them in a sentence related to EBs.

Play 'vo-back-ulary' with the whole class. The instructor projects a list of key vocabulary words related to the unified view of validity (use the list at the beginning of the chapter) and provides a brief review of each term. One student stands in front with his or her back facing the class, and

the instructor places a large sticky note on the student's back with one of the key words. The standing student must guess what word it is and use it in a sentence related to EBs. The next person at the table gives clues, being careful not to give too many clues or any that lead directly to the key vocabulary word. Even if the list of words is smaller than the number of students, reuse the words until all students have a chance as many of the concepts are difficult and review may be necessary. Since the concepts in this chapter are difficult, perhaps play vo-back-ulary with a team of two guessing the term.

Activity 3

Shift thinking about test validity away from whether tests are *valid* to whether *how we use test scores* is valid.

(Continued)

Review the law in your state about teacher evaluation and, in particular, how test scores are used to evaluate teachers. Ask one small group to review teacher accountability (teacher's perspective), another group to review principal accountability (principal's perspective) and a third group to review state policy regarding the consequences of low test scores for schools and districts (school/district's perspective). Review the policies as a whole group. Give each group 45 minutes to prepare an advocacy statement to a board of education about how test scores are used for schools with large numbers of EBs and whether or not the state-mandated use of test scores is fair. Are these test scores valid for all students? Is the state department of education using test scores in a valid way?

Activity 4

Agree or disagree with the following statement and provide evidence: *Testing EBs in the US using broad constructs may also support a system of cultural hegemony.* Be prepared to use a value line, where 1 is strongly disagree and 10 is strongly agree.

In the US, a strong language ideology is expressed by the English-only movement – that is, language homogeneity is beneficial to US society. Exposing the value assumptions of a test construct and its more subtle links to ideology – possibly to multiple cross-cutting ideologies – is a daunting challenge (Messick, 1980). For EBs, potential cross-cutting ideologies embedded in the constructs of achievement and language proficiency include, for example, political ideologies (English is the language of power), sociocultural and sociolinguistic ideologies (middle-class language and culture is normal) and race ideologies (white privilege).

Notes

(1) A construct is a hypothetical (or constructed) idea not easy to observe. Constructs can be supported by theories, frameworks or expert judgment. Important constructs for EBs are achievement, language proficiency (home and new language), motivation and acculturation, to name a few.
(2) Classical test theory supports the idea that each person has a 'true score' or in this example 'true achievement' that would be obtained if there were no errors in measurement. However, through assessments, we only have access to an 'observed score'.

References

Abedi, J. (2003, April) Impact of linguistic factors in content-based assessment for EB students: An overview of research. In M. Alkin (Chair) Linguistic modification in the assessment of English language learners. Paper presented at the American Educational Research Association, Chicago.

Adelman Reyes, S. and Kleyn, T. (2010) *Teaching in 2 Languages: A Guide for K-12 Bilingual Educators.* Thousand Oaks, CA: Corwin Press.

AERA, AERA, NCME (1985, 2014) *Standards for Educational and Psychological Testing.* Washington, DC: American Psychological Association.

Haladyna, T. and Downing, S. (2004) Construct-irrelevant variance in high-stakes testing. *Educational Measurement: Issues and Practice* 23 (1), 17–27.

MacSwan, J. and Rolstad, K. (2006) How language tests mislead us about children's abilities: Implications for special education placements. *Teachers College Record* 108 (11), 2304–2328.

Mahoney, K., Haladyna, T. and MacSwan, J. (2009) The need for multiple measures in reclassification decisions: A validity study of the Stanford English Language Proficiency Test (SELP). In J.S. Lee, T.G. Wiley and R.W. Rumberger (eds) *The Education of Language Minority Immigrants in the United States* (pp. 263–294). Bristol: Multilingual Matters.

Messick, S. (1980) Test validity and the ethics of assessment. *American Psychologist* 35 (11), 1012–1027.

Messick, S. (1989) Meaning and values in test validation: The science and ethics of assessment. *Educational Researcher* 18 (2), 5–11.

Messick, S. (1990) *Unified View of Validity*. Research Report RR-90-11. Princeton, NJ: Educational Testing Service.

Rhodes, R.W. (1988) Standardized testing of minority students: Navajo and Hopi. Paper presented at the annual meeting of the National Council of Teachers of English, St. Louis, MO.

Ryman, A. (2006, March 2) Teachers, state at odds over whether test should pass or fail. *The Arizona Republic*.

Shohamy, E. (2006) *Language Policy: Hidden Agendas and New Approaches*. New York: Routledge.

4 Methods

Source: L.L. Kopf. In Teaching about testing in K. Swope and B. Miner (eds) *Failing Our Kids: Why the Testing Craze Won't Fix Our Schools* (p. 53). A Special Publication of Rethinking Schools, Ltd. Milwaukee, Wisconsin.

Themes from Chapter 4

(1) Selecting an appropriate method of assessment is directly related to aligning with the purpose of the assessment.
(2) Rubrics and checklists can be made easily from standards and criteria (purpose).
(3) Main categories of methods are: One-to-one communication, written response, selected response and performance.
(4) Interviews, portfolios, storytelling and teacher observation are all very popular methods of assessment with emergent bilinguals (EBs). Which one you should use depends on your purpose.

Key Vocabulary

- *Four categories of methods*: Selected response, written response, performance, and one-to-one communication

- *Four categories of modalities*: One-to-group, one-to-one, group-to-group, or self (examples: teacher-to-student, student-to-student, or peer assessment, student-to-group, student-to-family or teacher-to-family)
- Content or language target
- Oral interview
- Portfolio
- Role play
- Rubric
- Story retelling
- Teacher observation

PUMI Connection: Purpose, Method and Instrument

This chapter focuses on the M (Method) and I (Instrument) in PUMI. And, of course, you wouldn't know what method or instrument to use if you haven't articulated the P (Purpose). Identifying your target (purpose), picking the best method and creating or finding an instrument to support the assessment are integral ideas to good assessment. Readers are invited to explore a variety of methods and create checklists and rubrics to support the method chosen.

This chapter is designed to introduce the reader to the basics of selecting appropriate methods of assessment for EBs. Later in the chapter, popular methods of assessment are introduced and examples are given showing specific language or content targets. Table 4.1 outlines the judgments that EB educators can make about selecting an appropriate method of assessment. Table 4.1 also suggests methods, and the remainder of the chapter outlines the thinking behind the judgments and suggestions. When possible, share and discuss a rubric with students before the assessment takes place. The teacher decides what modality (one-to-group, one-to-one, group-to-group, or to-self) is best for each of the methods, depending on the individual needs of the students and class.

How are methods categorized?

There is no crystal-clear way to categorize assessment methods broadly. For the purposes of this book, all methods will be placed loosely into four categories. It is less important to know what category of assessment method you are using than to pick the appropriate individual method. Each example from Table 4.1 is listed so that you can see how these categories work:

Selected response – any method where a student has to choose from predetermined responses (no examples in Table 4.1, but true/false and multiple choice are popular methods).

Written response – any method where student has to write the response (example method: essay with rubric, written short responses).

Performance assessment – any method where a student is doing, completing or performing something, action oriented (example methods: oral presentation, observation with checklist, anecdotal records, think aloud with rubric).

Table 4.1 Sample lesson plan considerations: Pick an appropriate method

	Select key practices from core standards	*Methods of assessments to consider and why*
ELA	Analyze complex texts	**Discussion with rubric** because this allows the students to think aloud and the teacher to document analysis of text.
	Produce clear and coherent writing	**Essay with rubric** because this generates a writing sample and the rubric can articulate clarity and coherence.
	Construct arguments	**Graphic organizer with checklist** because students can practice building arguments visually and the checklist will guide students and teachers into building a solid argument.
Math	Solve problems	**Observation with checklist** because it is most authentic to watch students solve a problem. Questioning and think-aloud methods also work very well for assessing problem-solving.
	Reason abstractly	**Think aloud with rubric** because students can think aloud to express reasoning. Written responses (if writing proficiency is high) with rubric also work well.
	Use appropriate tools	**Observation with checklist** because it is most authentic to watch students use appropriate tools.
Science	Ask questions	**Anecdotal records because scientific** questions will emerge naturally throughout the learning process. Self-assessment using a rubric can guide students to ask better questions and more frequently.
	Define problems	**Written response with rubric** because students will define problems based on real-world factors. Questioning or oral presentation of problems provides nice scaffolding for key principle.
	Analyze and interpret data	**Graphic organizers (table, figure, etc.) with checklist** because the graphics will assist the teacher to focus student work on analysis and interpretation. Short oral or written responses can help assess interpretation of data.

One-to-one communication – any method where the student and teacher, for example, are working together one-to-one (example methods: discussion with rubric, interview, questioning).

What's your purpose?

If you want to hit the bull's eye, you need to know exactly what the target is. The single most important concept in assessing EBs is to have a clear purpose for the assessment. For example, if a teacher is using a story retell as an assessment method, the purpose could vary greatly. The purpose could be a variety of things such as

(1) to assess reading – focus on reading cues; (2) to assess oral language – focus on speech output; or (3) to assess a certain skill such as using the present tense – focus on oral language form, or other measurable factors. Good assessment practice requires knowing your purpose and sharing it with students before the assessment begins. Purpose can also be called targets, achievement targets, language targets, standards, anchors or objectives, among other terms.

For most states, the Common Core State Standards (CCSS) and the Next Generation Science Standards (NGSS) dictate what *content targets* teachers are required to use; these come in the form of knowledge and associated processes such as analyzing, producing, constructing, reasoning, defining, developing, using, etc. To develop *language targets* for instruction and assessment, EB educators use the required English language proficiency (ELP) standards chosen by your area. In your ELP standards, language targets should represent communicative activities such as language use (student and teacher) and language tasks, as well as different modalities and registers of the classroom (Valdés & Lee, 2013). The ELP standards in your area should articulate an academic discourse quite different from everyday discourse to allow teachers to focus on content and language targets toward school success. With core standards, it is recognized that EBs must have access to core standards from the first day of school. An assumption that most EB educators know (but that perhaps is not known to others) is that EBs can master content *before* they acquire native-like performance in English. There is no need to wait for students to develop English fully before teaching rigorous content.

To view standards more conceptually, career- and college-ready standards cover a small fraction of the total universe of content and language. Having said that, the language and content targets used in this book represent the content and language EB educators are accountable for – the required content and language in schools today. The language targets of your area ELP standards should reflect the language expectations and underlying language practices embedded within the CCSS and NGSS. Keep in mind that content and language targets found in standards documents are not representative of all; hidden discourses, socio-emotional, family interests, translanguaging and other important targets are rarely included in these documents but are still critically important.

Home languages are not included in the CCSS or the NGSS, but EB educators should not underestimate the importance of knowing where (assessing) a child is in his or her home language. The New York State Education Department (NYSED) supported the development of the Bilingual Common Core Initiative (BCCI) to better articulate the content and language demands of the Common Core Standards, in order to help all teachers develop purpose and targets aligned with the new standards. This initiative addressed (home and new) Language Arts. Authors of the BCCI articulated the main academic demand (content) of every Language Arts anchor standard as well as the main linguistic demand (language). These are organized by grade level to help teachers develop language targets and give examples of how to address core-related linguistic demands in English and the home language (NYSBCC, 2013).

Snapshot: How Much Home Language Literacy?

Mrs Caruso is a fifth grade teacher who has new students from the Dominican Republic, Puerto Rico, Burma and Bangladesh. Her district has conducted many English assessments but no home language assessments, and Mrs Caruso wants to know where students are with their home language writing ability because she wants to design some instruction to transfer writing ability from the home language to the new language. Assessing the home language will also allow her to use a variety of translanguaging strategies. She also wants to know if any of her students are not able to write in their home language because she will refer to a specialized framework[1] for students with low home language literacy. Mrs Caruso knows Spanish but has to find people who know Karen and Bengali. A writing assessment can be very authentic, is not very time-consuming and can help guide teachers in explaining how students are responding to the curriculum and instruction in their class. The General Home Language Writing Assessment Rubric can be used as a stand-alone general measure of home language literacy, or combined with another test of home language to see if results match (and confirm valid results). A quick PUMI study shows this (Table 4.2).

Table 4.2 General home language writing assessment rubric

| P | U | M | I |
Purpose	Use	Methods	Instrument
To measure writing ability in home language	To assist instruction (can the teacher use home language to help teach English and content?) To help decide if a special framework or program may be necessary to provide appropriate programming, early	Written response	Prompts, rubric

Teacher prompts: Ask students to write either (1) a memory they have of a special person in their lives (encourage students to write the steps of the story first using a timeline or other graphic organizer) or (2) an informative text about their life in their home country (give students ideas about what they might include, such as information on food, clothing, holiday traditions, school, free time and activities, friends and family, home, etc.).

Student name:	Grade:		Date:
Criteria	4	3	2	1
Response to prompt	Student fully responds to writing prompt given.	Student mostly responds to writing prompt given.	Student vaguely responds to writing prompt given.	No response given.
Details in writing	There are details to support and enhance the response.	There are some details to support and enhance the response.	There are few details to support and enhance the response.	There are no details to support and enhance the response.

Organization	Response is well organized.	Response is somewhat organized.	Response is poorly organized.	Response is not organized.
Mechanics of writing	There are less than four errors in spelling and grammar that distract the reader from the content.	There are less than six errors in spelling and grammar that distract the reader from content.	There are less than eight errors in spelling and grammar that distract the reader from the content.	There are eight or more errors in spelling and grammar that distract the reader from the content.
Use of transition words	Student uses transition words to create a cohesive writing piece.	Student uses one or two transition words to create a cohesive writing piece.	Student does not use transition words, but sentences follow a somewhat logical sequence.	Response is disjointed. Sentences do not follow a logical sequence. No transition words used.

Total score (out of 20)	Comments:
Writing fluency	
16 to 20	Average LOTE home literacy
13 to 16	Low home literacy. Needs this framework
8 to 12	Low home literacy. Certainly needs this framework
5 to 7	Very low home literacy. Needs an intensive program

* See Note 1 on p. 78 for source details

Discussion questions

- How does Mrs Caruso use PUMI to decide if this assessment is appropriate for her students?
- How will Mrs Caruso use the results of the assessment to improve instruction for EBs?

Some Assessment Methods Highlighted

The following sections highlight assessment methods that have been very popular over the years. The purpose of this section is to introduce the reader to EB-friendly assessment methods; however, specific targets are not given. And really, a method such as interview could possibly have 100 different purposes. The first five methods (interview, retelling, portfolio, teacher observation, role play) are typically used as assessment practices leading to promise, which is to say they embrace student-centered participation in authentic contexts. In addition to selecting method, the role of the EB educator is to use his or her expertise to select modality, content and language objectives, appropriate differentiation, classroom methods, non-academic targets, and to make instruction and assessment culturally relevant to the particular class.

Interview (One-to-One Communication)

This method is considered by many to be authentic because interviewing someone is an authentic experience (it will really happen throughout one's life in a variety of contexts). Within this method of assessment, EB educators can ask questions (input) and evaluate answers from EBs (output). Such interviews can be time-consuming because they are administered one-on-one. Questions to ask might depend on the level of English or home language and could include: What is your family like? What is your favorite activity with friends? Do you like English? Do you like school? Tell me about your experience on the first day of school. What is the easiest part of school for you? What is difficult about school? These questions can lead to further questions, yielding a high-quality, authentic language sample to assess (depending on your purpose), not to mention a deeper understanding of factors that affect second language acquisition such as motivation and experience with English. The purpose of an interview could be to measure motivation, to measure attitude, to measure speaking complexity (among others). The EB educator can assess while the child is speaking, immediately following

Table 4.3 Example of using an interview to measure speaking complexity

P	U	M	I
To measure speaking (complexity)	To design appropriate instruction for content areas	Interview (one-to-one communication)	Interview prompts, rubric

Interview questions			
	Who is in your family?		
	What do you do with friends?		
	Tell me about your experience on the first day of school. How did you feel?		
	What is the easiest part of school for you? Do you like English?		
	What is difficult about school?		

Rubric below: After reviewing student responses to the questions above, put an X through the box

Level 1	Level 2	Level 3	Level 4	Level 5
Single words, short phrases, chunks of memorized speech.	Speaks with short sentences or phrases.	Speaks with expanded sentences or phrases. Responses show some detail.	Speaks with a variety of sentence lengths with varying complexity. Speech is emerging as clear and cohesive.	Extended discourse – organized and supported with details.

the interview, or the interview can be recorded and assessed later. Interviews can be conducted in the new or home language and in the following modalities: teacher-to-student, student-to-student (peer assessment), student-to-family, or teacher-to-family. There are excellent suggestions for interview questions to ask families for Dual Language Learners (DLL) in early childhood. Many of these questions can be modified to use across the grade levels. This publication by Head Start offers great questions, plus gives an explanation about why this is important. Visit http://eclkc.ohs.acf.hhs.gov/hslc/tta-system/cultural-linguistic/fcp/docs/dll_background_info.pdf.

Tables 4.3 and 4.4 show two examples of how EB educators might use the method of interviewing to measure two distinct purposes. Table 4.3 is an example of using interview to measure speaking complexity and Table 4.4 is an example of using interview to measure language use in content area.

Table 4.4 Example of a math interview to measure language used for academic purposes in math

P	U	M	I
To measure communication during math	To design appropriate language objectives for instruction	Interview (one-to-one communication)	Interview prompts, checklist

Interview questions: These questions are designed to measure language used for academic purposes in math during a unit on triple digit subtraction using exchanges. The student has a set of base 10 blocks and has been asked to solve two problems. This interview takes place after the student has had time to solve the problem. (Note: Some may call this assessment method questioning.)
Tell me about how you solved your problem. What steps did you take?
Is this a good solution?
Why is this a good solution?
Now explain to me in words why this is a good solution.
How are these two problems similar and how are they different?
Can you show me on paper how to solve these two problems?

Checklist for language used for academic purposes (*answer yes or no*)
Summarizes steps taken to find a solution
Uses sequential language to describe steps in solution in a logical order
Uses formal math terms (exchange, subtract, trade, tens, ones, etc.) and symbolic notation to defend her solution
Describes similarities and differences between two problems
Gives evidence to support/defend solution

Table 4.5 shows an actual interview between a teacher and an EB student from Puerto Rico who was currently enrolled in an 'English-only' program. The results of this interview may provide evidence for the teacher to introduce translanguaging pedagogy to provide a more holistic view of Roberto.

Table 4.5 Informal interview with Roberto

Teacher question	Student response
What is your favorite subject?	I like science, it is my favorite.
Do you like math class?	It is okay, sometimes it is really hard for me. I like when we go to the computer lab.
What is difficult for you in math class?	There are a lot of numbers and sometimes I don't know what to do. It is hard when the questions are long and you have to do a lot of things. Sometimes I forget what the questions want me to do.
What could I do to help you in math?	Um I don't know. Sometime it helps me when I can talk to Yolanda or Maeva in Spanish, but we aren't supposed to use Spanish. I like English better, but sometimes I don't know what the question wants me to do. It helps me when I can ask questions.
Did you like math class in Puerto Rico? Can you teach me how to say some of these words in Spanish?	No, I don't like math class in Puerto Rico. I liked science and playing soccer. I know how to say these in Spanish, but I'm not supposed to talk in Spanish.

Story Retelling (Performance)

This method is considered authentic because storytelling is familiar to many students in some form from a young age. EBs read or listen to text and then retell the main ideas and some details. This type of assessment usually has two purposes – to assess something in English Language Arts (ELA) and to assess something in ELP. Through story retelling, EB educators can assess a variety of targets, like how the student describes the events in a story (ELA), or assess signifiers such as fluency, grammar or tense usage (ELP). For ELP, the language functions used to retell a story usually include summarizing, describing details and giving information. Story retelling, along with other performance and one-to-one communication, provides ample opportunity for translanguaging, even if the teacher does not know the home language. For example, students can retell a story and create a short audio recording in the home language retelling the story. Students can retell the story in Spanish, for example, then retell in English. Alternatively, students can retell the story to one another in their home language and then retell in English. To make the assessment more culturally relevant, have the child retell a personal story or one that is popular in his or her family or community. If your purpose is to assess oral language proficiency, the actual story choice does not matter, but will yield more valid results if it is culturally relevant.

The general directions for a story retell are to read the story to the child or play a recorded reading of the story. Ask the child to retell the story, but avoid having it feel like an interview – one of the true strengths of a story retell is the opportunity that the student is given to talk. The EB educator documents the assessment by using a rubric or checklist. This method of assessment can be easily aligned with the CCSS like the one in Table 4.6.

Table 4.6 Common core speaking and listening standards K-5

Presentation of Knowledge and Ideas: Grade 3

(1) Report on a topic or text, tell a story or recount an experience with appropriate facts and relevant, descriptive details, speaking clearly at an understandable pace.

Example checklist used with story retelling

P	*U*	*M*	*I*
To measure ability to tell a story	To guide instruction	Story retell (performance)	Story, checklist
Checklist			
	Student initiates	*Responds to teacher prompt*	*Comments or details*
Important factors in story retelling			
Uses chronological order to recall events			
Identifies major events			
Uses appropriate and relevant facts from the story			
Uses details to describe main character			
Uses details to describe setting			

Portfolio Assessment (May Include All – or a Mix of – Assessment Methods)

Portfolio assessment may include a *profile* of assessment methods and therefore does not fall into only one category of methods. It may contain a mix of selected response, written response, performance assessment and one-to-one communication. Traditionally, portfolios are associated with the arts; the word evokes the image of artists carrying their best work in a portfolio to demonstrate their talents. However, a portfolio can be created and maintained for any student to showcase growth through time and a whole body of work. Usually, it contains samples of student work, selected by the student and the teacher systematically and purposefully to show evidence that the student is learning core standards. Unlike a single test score that documents one point in time, the portfolio is multidimensional and charts student growth across multiple points throughout the school year; it can therefore reveal much more about what an EB can actually do. The teacher uses the portfolio to integrate the results of individual assessments and make instructional decisions based on this evidence. The key is to make portfolio building an important part of instructional time and to make students the agents of their own assessments.

In the digital age, portfolios can be much more compact; they might be digital with audio and video components, or they can be presented in a simple three-ring binder with plastic sleeves to organize and hold the content. For an example of digital portfolios built around the theme of Howard Gardner's multiple intelligences, see the work of Evangeline Stefanakis (2002) in the Recommended Readings list at the end of this chapter.

Getting started with a portfolio entails the following steps, similar to PUMI: (1) articulate the purpose of the portfolio; (2) articulate how the results of the portfolio will be used; (3) set criteria (usually CCSS and ELP standards selected by state) and pick or make tools in the form of checklists or rubrics to help document the criteria; and (4) review the contents to make sure they match Purpose and Use. It is very common to have a portfolio that addresses both language and content goals, as well as other goals.

One strength of the portfolio is that it supports a holistic classroom in which instruction is student centered, meaningful and authentic. Teachers may choose to allow students to select the contents of the portfolio and also take part in evaluating their own work. The act of self-assessment is critical; many educators believe that it is important to allow students to be active learners who construct their own knowledge, set their own goals and check their own progress. Most teachers who practice portfolio as an assessment method report that students become more responsible about their learning. One way in which EBs can reflect on their own work is to ask them to review their work and set some goals to improve it. The feedback can be combined with peer and teacher assessment to show three points of view of the student's work. See Table 4.7 for suggestions for self-assessment.

Table 4.7 Suggested questions for portfolio self-assessment

Look at your writing sample that describes important characters from the story called 'Father Hawk' and answer the following questions:
(1)   What did you do well in this writing sample?
(2)   What do you need to do better?
(3)   Write one thing you will do better when writing the next draft.

Another powerful aspect of the portfolio as assessment is its direct alignment with instruction and the CCSS. Usually the portfolio assessment process includes a conference between the teacher and the child and perhaps a presentation to parents. EBs can prepare for the conference by completing some reflective questions, as shown in Table 4.8.

Margo Gottlieb and Diep Nguyen (2007) describe a pivotal portfolio that has worked well in dual and transitional bilingual education programs. The pivotal portfolio is a hybrid of both a working portfolio (contains work-in-progress) and the showcase portfolio (contains display of best work), with three main distinctions: in the pivotal portfolio, each teacher gathers what the teachers collectively consider evidence of essential student learning and achievement; all of the teachers use common assessments of that essential student work; and it follows the student for the length of his or her career in the language education program. In fact, in Schaumburg School District 54, this portfolio follows each student from year to year and becomes the student's graduation present at the end

Table 4.8 Suggested questions to prepare for the portfolio conference

Please review your entire portfolio.

(1)	What does this portfolio tell about you as a student in English and math?
(2)	What are you good at? Where is evidence of this in the portfolio?
(3)	What goals will you continue to work on?

of eighth grade. For more detail on this particular model and on portfolios, see Gottlieb and Nguyen (2007).

Figure 4.1 shows a rubric for a Poetry Portfolio from Adelman Reyes and Kleyn's (2010) book *Teaching in 2 Languages: A Guide for K-12 Bilingual Educators*. The authors warn that although portfolios are relatively common, the danger is that they turn into nothing more than a folder of mandated assignments, rather than a collection of work that students select which showcases their progress and learning over time. Figure 4.1 is an example of a rubric used to assess a poetry anthology that connected the genre of poetry with the topic of identity (Adelman Reyes & Kleyn, 2010).

Language Portfolio

The Language Portfolio has been developed in Europe over the past 10 years, with each country creating its own versions, accredited by the Council of Europe (Celic & Seltzer, 2011[2]). Celic and Seltzer review the Language Portfolio and offer links and directions on how to create a Language Portfolio in your class, or even school- or district-wide. The Language Portfolio is an example of how to encourage an environment that celebrates languages and cultures and also raises multicultural competence for all students. Students keep the Language Portfolio with them as they proceed through grade levels. The Language Portfolio has three sections: Language Biography – to record experiences emphasizing intercultural understandings; Language Passport – includes rubrics and checklists to document what students know and can do in different languages; and Language Dossier – where multilingual academic work is showcased and includes setting future goals.

Teacher Observation (Performance Assessment)

Teacher observation is an assessment method used by all teachers, but not all teachers consider it a 'serious' method. Whether teaching young children or college students, all good teachers will change their instruction – perhaps even mid-lesson – based on what they observe the students to be doing. For example, if a teacher sees that most of the students are off-task and unsure about how to start an activity, he or she will adjust the instruction by modeling the directions better, or by having a student paraphrase the instructions for a second time. The teacher continues to observe and make instructional decisions based on what he or she sees. The following Spanish as a second language (SSL) rubric was created by faculty in a dual language program to create an assessment using teacher observation to document performance in SSL from K-6 (Gottlieb & Nguyen, 2007). Table 4.9 shows the rubric

	4—Exceptional	3—Proficient	2—Developing	1—Beginning
Content	Student has written more than 5 poems. They may include • 1 identity poem • 1 family poem • 1 culture experience poem • 1 object poem • 2 or more poems of his or her choice	Student has written 5 poems. They may include • 1 identity poem • 1 family poem • 1 culture experience poem • 1 object poem • 1 poem of his or her choice	Student has written 3 or 4 poems. They may include • 1 identity poem • 1 family poem • 1 culture experience poem • 1 object poem • 2 poems of his or her choice	Student has written 1 or 2 poems. They may include • 1 identity poem • 1 family poem • 1 culture experience poem • 1 object poem • 1 poem of his or her choice
	Poems have many poetic elements, including metaphors and similes	Poems have some poetic elements, including metaphors and similes	Student attempts to use poetic elements, including metaphors and similes	Poems do not have any poetic elements, including metaphors and similes
	Poems include many concrete and sensory images	Poems include some concrete and sensory images	Student attempts to include concrete and sensory images	Poems do not include any concrete and sensory images
	Student's identity is clearly reflected throughout all poems	Student's identity is clearly reflected in most poems	Student attempts to reflect identity through poems	Student's identity is not reflected through poems
Word Choice	Many interesting vocabulary words used	Some interesting vocabulary words used	A few interesting vocabulary words used	No interesting vocabulary words used

	4–Exceptional	3–Proficient	2–Developing	1–Beginning
Process	All steps of the writing process are turned in: draft, revisions, and final copy	Most steps of the writing process are turned in: draft, revisions, and final copy	Some steps of the writing process are missing	Few steps of the writing process were followed
	Student edited paper independently and with partner	Student edited paper with help from teacher	Student relied on teacher to edit work	Student did little or no editing

Figure 4.1 A rubric for a Poetry Portfolio (topic identity)

Source: Created by Elizabeth Silva, Surky Mateo, Jaqueline Rodríguez, and Wenn Siak. From Adelman Reyes, S. and Kleyn, T. (eds) *Teaching in 2 Languages: A Guide for K-12 Bilingual Educators*. Thousand Oaks, CA: Corwin Press. Reproduced with permission.

for first grade only as an example of observation as an assessment method. However, the full K-6 checklist can be found in Gottlieb and Nguyen (2007: 202).

Role Play (Performance Assessment)

Role play is often overlooked but can be quite valuable as an assessment method with EBs due to its reliance on physical movement and comprehension. (Other versions of role play are sometimes referred to as improvisations or simulations.) Role play invites students to speak or act through the identity of others. This type of dramatic activity can make the classroom an exciting place. At the same time, it can provide an authentic context for students to learn language and content, and for teachers to assess it. When preparing a lesson, survey the whole lesson to see if there are opportunities to role play (ORP[3]). Almost every lesson offers ORPs, yet ORPs in instruction and assessment are underutilized. For example, students can act out a dinner party as characters from a story such as Pig 1, Pig 2, Pig 3 and their mother. If you are teaching social studies, each student could be a different president. The students then study their role and dramatize an event. Role play offers an authentic setting for EBs to practice natural language use, such as facial expressions, hesitations, repetitions and so on. In addition, many important language functions can be practiced during role play, such as agreeing/disagreeing, giving or evaluating an opinion, persuading and so on. It also offers an authentic situation to use translanguaging.

To get started with role play, as with all assessments, identify the purpose. Allow students time to practice their roles. Make sure any reading or cue cards are at the students' level. Differentiate the activity by language level – for example, more

Table 4.9 Example of first-grade Spanish as a second language (SSL) checklist

P	U	M	I
To measure SSL development over time	To evaluate and show effects of dual language program to parents and administrators	Observation (performance assessment)	Checklist
Checklist			

Oral performance indicators	Beginning	Developing	Secure
Initiates, responds to greetings appropriately for time of day.			
Uses familiar phrases and simple sentences in appropriate context.			
Lists vocabulary words according to specific categories.			
Actively participates in routine oral language activities (songs, shared reading, calendar, daily routine).			
Reading performance indicators			
Recognizes the letters and sounds of the Spanish alphabet.			
Demonstrates interest in Spanish books.			
Reads aloud controlled vocabulary with understanding (colors, numbers, etc.).			
Reads aloud simple picture books and matches text to picture with teacher guidance in order to demonstrate comprehension.			
Actively participates in shared reading and demonstrates comprehension by retelling in English.			
Uses cognates to guess meaning of words.			
Demonstrates comprehension of key vocabulary from a story with prompting.			
Writing performance indicators			
Writes short familiar phrases and sentences using sentence starters.			
Spells familiar words correctly in writing activities (journal, dictation).			
Grammar usage performance indicators			
Uses the present tense in the following verbs in first person singular (estar, ser, tener, ir, gustar).			
Vocabulary knowledge performance indicators	0–20 words	20–35 words	35–50 words
Demonstrates comprehension and usage of new core, targeted vocabulary words.			

advanced students will agree/disagree and evaluate, while beginner students will be cued to ask simple questions or supply one- to two-word utterances to the other players. Before using role play as an assessment, be sure the students have sufficient time to practice in school. If the purpose is to assess oral language skills, a rubric or checklist can be used to systematically document the assessment. Share the rubric to help students prepare for the assessment. Videotaping the role play is another way to allow for self-assessment or peer assessment. This method of assessment can align with CCSS standards; Table 4.10 shows a popular rubric used for some role-play assessments in history. Don't forget to use the same supports (scaffolds) for EBs in assessments that are used in instruction. Table 4.10 shows a rubric with the purpose of measuring history content and presentation skills; however, the purpose may also be to measure speaking skills in history class by simply changing the purpose (and content) of the rubric.

Standardized Test (Selected Response)

Most textbooks do not talk much about standardized tests as a method of assessment for EBs, but the stark reality is that they are very *high stakes* and used often. Many important decisions are made on the basis of standardized test results. Unfortunately, and unlike the other popular methods (interview, observation, role play), teachers typically do not design these; in fact, they usually cannot see the high-stakes tests until moments before they begin.

There are many downfalls to selected response when used as a high-stakes assessment, but when selected response assessment is not used as high-stakes assessment (low-stakes), this assessment can yield quick and accurate data to inform instruction (Table 4.11).

Incorporating Two Languages in Assessment Products

Using two languages in instruction and assessment is not just for bilingual programs. ENL teachers, bilingual teachers and monolingual teachers can encourage more than one language in a variety of settings to better match the student. Table 4.12 suggests ideas for translanguaging for a final product. Many teachers don't discourage use of the home language; however, they don't often encourage it either. Some view the integration of home language as a waste of time. To represent the child more holistically, try to find more creative ways to use and value home languages in your classroom in your final assessment products.

Rubrics and Checklists

Broadly speaking, rubrics and checklists count as Instruments (I) in PUMI; they can be thought of as 'instruments of documentation'. In good assessment, there is a fine line between instruction and assessment, but what distinguishes the two is the way student-progress data are recorded or documented. Checklists and rubrics are the most popular instruments to collect data in a reliable manner. They can be used in

Table 4.10 Common core key design considerations

Students adapt their communication in relation to audience, task, purpose and discipline; they set and adjust purpose for reading, writing, speaking, listening and language use as warranted by the task. They appreciate nuances, such as how the composition of an audience should affect tone when speaking and how the connotations of words affect meaning (CCSS, Key Design Consideration [2011]).

Example of a role play rubric

P	U	M	I	
To measure history content and presentation skills	To contribute to 30% of history marking period grade	Role play (performance assessment)	Rubric, props	
	Excellent (4)	Good (3)	Adequate (2)	Needs improvement (1)
Works cooperatively with group	Always willing and focused during assigned talk	Usually willing and focused during assigned talk	Sometimes willing and focused during assigned talk	Rarely willing and focused during assigned talk
Presentation of perspective	Convincing communication of character's role, feelings and motives	Competent communication of character's role, feelings and motives	Adequate communication of character's role, feelings and motives	Limited communication of character's role, feelings and motives
Use of non-verbal cues (voice, gestures, eye contact, props, costumes)	An impressive variety of non-verbal cues in an exemplary way	Good variety (three or more) of non-verbal cues were used in a competent way	An acceptable variety of non-verbal cues were used in a competent way	Limited variety of non-verbal cues were used in a competent way
Historical accuracy	Historical information appears to be always accurate	Historical information appears to be usually accurate	Historical information appears to be sometimes accurate	Historical information appears to be rarely accurate

Table 4.11 Examples of selected response assessment

Multiple choice

What causes night and day?

(a) The earth spins on its axis.
(b) The earth moves around the sun.
(c) Clouds block out the sun's light
(d) The earth moves into and out of the sun's shadow.
(e) The sun goes around the earth.

Matching

Match the word to the definition

(1) ___ tradition
(2) ___ enable
(3) ___ maneuver
(4) ___ request
(5) ___ exclaim

(a) To ask for something politely or formally.
(b) To allow someone to do something.
(c) To say something excitedly.
(d) Something special done for a long time.
(e) To move or turn skillfully.

True/false

(1) Many food chains make a good web.
(2) An empty lot is a habitat.
(3) All food chains start with the sun.
(4) Plants can survive without light.
(5) A habitat can recover from flood.

Table 4.12 Examples of translanguaging with a final assessment product

Final product	Add translanguaging
Write persuasive reviews about local restaurants	Write one in English and one in home language to target more audiences.
Write about cause/effects of WW2	Create a short audio recording summarizing causes/effects of WW2 in home language.
Research a country of their choice	Take notes in home language and English. Read research on internet from home language websites and English websites.
Write a document-based question (DBQ). A DBQ is a type of essay that provides the writer with documents to serve as sources of information for the writing.	Write a DBQ in home language. Include one sentence in English and English key vocabulary words.
Write a story	Use home language and English to write a story.
Create campaign advertisement	Create one advertisement in home language and one in English.
Critique a poem	Choose a poem in the home language and create a PowerPoint in English to explain the poem to peers. Include comparison of English to home language. Give oral presentation in English.

different modalities, perhaps by the teacher, the student or even a parent, to make the assessment process less teacher centered and to generate multiple points of data. The rubric is not the assessment method – it is a tool to keep the data collection systematic and focused on the same purpose or target (usually the Common Core or ELP standards, for example). Rubrics are an important part of good assessment because they increase predictable (or reliable) results.

If the teacher judges a curriculum appropriate for EBs, he or she should use existing rubrics and checklists from the curriculum already used at his or her schools. However, curriculum-based checklists and rubrics may align with the curriculum, and they *may not be* aligned with core content and language standards documents. In addition, curriculum-based rubrics and checklists (and all assessments) are usually designed for native English speakers and therefore need to be differentiated the same way that instruction is differentiated. Table 4.13 shows one of the Common Core math standards.

From Table 4.13, the EB educator designs content and language objectives such as those shown in Table 4.14 using ELP standards and expertise as guidance. Many EB educators now use the Sheltered Instruction Observation Protocol (SIOP) model (Echevarria *et al.*, 2012) to create language and content objectives aligned with the content standards to support a sheltered learning environment for EBs, which further promotes language learning in a meaningful academic context. Remember: Standards tell teachers *what* to teach, not *how* to teach (or assess). Moving from the standard in Table 4.13 to the content and language objectives in Table 4.14 is the first step toward appropriate standards-based assessment.

Table 4.13 Common Core math standard example

Number and operation, fractions, 4.NF

Build fractions from unit fractions by applying and extending previous understandings of operations on whole numbers.

Decompose a fraction into a sum of fractions with the same denominator in more than one way, recording each decomposition by an equation. Justify decompositions, e.g. by using a visual fraction model.

Examples: 3/8=1/8+1/8+1/8

3/8=1/8+2/8

2 1/8=1+1+1/8

Checklists collect dichotomous data; this means that there are only two choices in responding, such as yes/no, complete/incomplete, present/not present and so on. Because checklists generate dichotomous data, their usefulness to illustrate growth is limited. However, they are quick and easy to carry around on a clipboard. Usually, the data are in the form of checkmarks (√). Checklists are easy to make – simply use Microsoft Word to create a table with the objectives in the first column and the names of students in the remaining columns (Table 4.14).

Table 4.14 Teacher-designed checklist for EBs aligned with CCSS (math)

	Student #1	Student #2	Student #3	Student #4	Student #5
Place a check next to student's name when he or she completes the task. Check √ means complete. Blank means the student did not complete.					
Student will be able to (SWBAT) match the equation 5/8=1/8+4/8 to the appropriate visual model (using Cuisenaire rods).					
SWBAT produce short phrases to explain why the matched Cuisenaire rods model 5/8=1/8+4/8.					
SWBAT sort pattern blocks by denominator 1/2, 1/3, 1/6 and show two different ways to make an equation with the same denominator (e.g. 1/3+1/3=2/3 or 1/6+3/6=4/6).					
SWBAT write two equations with the same denominator in more than one way with visual models (Cuisenaire rods or pattern blocks), writing it in symbols and saying the equations aloud to peers.					

Making a checklist for the whole class, a small group or one student (the teacher decides the modality of assessment) from the content and language objectives is relatively easy using the Microsoft Word table feature (see Table 4.14). The checklist can be carried by the teacher and used while sitting next to students and watching them learn, or it can be used in a different modality, such as one-to-group, one-to-one, group-to-group, or to-self, with slight or no modifications.

Using a checklist like this is convenient for observing large or small groups of students and documenting at the same time on the same sheet of paper. The checklist can be easily turned into a rubric (see Table 4.15 for example) for one student showing whether he or she is developing, meeting or exceeding this target. In addition to a check mark, there is room for anecdotal information to help provide evidence for this level or note what the student can improve upon. Table 4.15 shows this type of rubric.

Table 4.15 Teacher-designed rubric for EBs aligned with CCSS (math)

	Developing (1)	Meeting (2)	Exceeding (3)
Place a check next to student's name when he or she completes the task. Check means complete. Blank means the student did not complete.			
Student will be able to (SWBAT) match the equation 5/8=1/8+4/8 to the appropriate visual model (using Cuisenaire rods).			
SWBAT produce short phrases to explain why the matched Cuisenaire rods model 5/8=1/8+4/8.			
SWBAT sort Cuisenaire rods by denominator 1/4, 1/3, 1/2, 1/8 and show two different ways to make an equation with the same denominator 6/8.			
SWBAT write two equations with the same denominator in more than one way with visual models (Cuisenaire rods), writing it in symbols and saying the equations aloud to peers.			

Creating a good rubric is more time-consuming than creating a checklist, because the teacher has to unpack the levels of performance and the categories of the construct being measured. RubiStar, a free website funded by the US Department of Education, can help generate rubrics if they are unavailable to you or if you are not satisfied with the rubrics presented in your curriculum. You must register to use RubiStar services; go to http://rubistar.4teachers.org. (An alternative is to use the Microsoft Word table tool to create your own rubric from scratch.) The rubric shown in Table 4.16 was created in just a few minutes using RubiStar. Try one!

This rubric focuses on mathematical concept, explanation, diagrams and sketches, working with others, as well as mathematical terminology and notation. Selection of categories is *very* important because this is your target (directly related to purpose – remember PUMI) unpacked into levels (usually three to five levels). Also,

Table 4.16 Teacher-designed rubric (using RubiStar) aligned with CCS (math)
Math – Problem-solving: fractions 4.NF

Teacher name: Ms. Mahoney

Student name: _____

Category	4	3	2	1
Mathematical concepts	Explanation shows complete understanding of the mathematical concepts used to solve the problem(s).	Explanation shows substantial understanding of the mathematical concepts used to solve the problem(s).	Explanation shows some understanding of the mathematical concepts needed to solve the problem(s).	Explanation shows very limited understanding of the underlying concepts needed to solve the problem(s) or is not written.
Explanation	Explanation is detailed and clear.	Explanation is clear.	Explanation is a little difficult to understand, but includes critical components.	Explanation is difficult to understand and is missing several components or was not included.
Diagrams and sketches	Diagrams and/or sketches are clear and greatly add to the reader's understanding of the procedure(s).	Diagrams and/or sketches are clear and easy to understand.	Diagrams and/or sketches are somewhat difficult to understand.	Diagrams and/or sketches are difficult to understand or are not used.
Working with others	Student was an engaged partner, listening to suggestions of others and working cooperatively throughout lesson.	Student was an engaged partner but had trouble listening to others and/or working cooperatively.	Student cooperated with others, but needed prompting to stay on-task.	Student did not work effectively with others.
Mathematical terminology and notation	Correct terminology and notation are always used, making it easy to understand what was done.	Correct terminology and notation are usually used, making it fairly easy to understand what was done.	Correct terminology and notation are used, but it is sometimes not easy to understand what was done.	There is little use, or a lot of inappropriate use, of terminology and notation.

EB educators need to keep in mind that the categories on RubiStar are designed for native English speakers and may need to be modified to meet the needs of beginner and intermediate EBs for the language objectives only. When comparing the rubric to the checklist, you can see that the rubric has four categories and four levels of performance. This gives your data four levels of performance per category, allowing you to document much more detail than a checklist. (Again, choosing an assessment depends on the purpose, and often checklists are sufficient.) It is very convenient to save the customized rubric in your RubiStar space; you can also download it as an Excel file, then modify and save it without having to log on to RubiStar for access.

End-of-Chapter Activities (Instructors: see advice at the end of the book)

By completing Activities 1 and 2, the reader will be able to:

(1) Make a list of products that EBs can create using translanguaging strategies.
(2) Create one checklist and two rubrics aligned with the CCSS and give examples of how to use with home and new languages.

Activity 1

Make a list of products that EBs can create using translanguaging strategies. Throughout this chapter, hints are given about how to use more than one language to create final products. Final products can act as formative or summative assessments but usually summative. In small groups, make a list of 10 ways that students in your class can use translanguaging methods to create final products.

Activity 2

Create one checklist and two rubrics aligned with the CCSS and give examples of how to use with home and new languages.

In small groups, examine the Common Core standard in Table 4.17. Follow these steps to practice making checklists and rubrics. *Step One:* Read the standard and brainstorm content and language objectives. Write one content and one language objective on chart paper, starting with 'Student will be able to (SWBAT)...' *Step Two:* Make one checklist, one rubric, and another rubric using RubiStar – similar to the ones presented earlier in this chapter – from the content and language objectives your group wrote.

Table 4.17 Common Core speaking and listening standards K-5

Vocabulary acquisition and use: Grade 3

(6) Acquire and use accurately grade-appropriate conversational, general academic and domain-specific words and phrases, including those that signal spatial and temporal relationships (e.g. 'After dinner that night we went looking for them').

Notes

(1) A framework (for students with low home literacy) and the General Home Language Writing Assessment Rubric used in this snapshot can be found in *A CUNY-NYSIEB Framework for the Education of Emergent Bilinguals with Low Home Literacy: 4–12 grades* by Garcia *et al.* (Spring 2013) and can be found at the following URL: http://www.nysieb.ws.gc.cuny.edu/files/2013/05/CUNY-NYSIEB-Framework-for-EB-with-Low-Home-Literacy-Spring-2013-Final-Version-05-08-13.pdf. The rubric is in Appendix B.
(2) This translanguaging handbook is available free as a PDF at the following link: http://www.nysieb.ws.gc.cuny.edu/files/2013/03/Translanguaging-Guide-March-2013.pdf.   Rubrics, checklists and a step-by-step process is included starting on page 23.
(3) This in an acronym the author invented to use with teacher candidates to review lesson plans and search for opportunities to role play – or ORPs.

References

Adelman Reyes, S. and Kleyn, T. (2010) *Teaching in 2 Languages: A Guide for K-12 Bilingual Educators.* Thousand Oaks, CA: Corwin Press.
Celic, C. and Seltzer, K. (2011) *Translanguaging: A CUNY-NYSIEB Guide for Educators.* New York: CUNY-NYSIEB, The Graduate Center.
Echevarria, J., Vogt, M. and Short, D. (2012) *Making Content Comprehensible for English Learners: The SIOP Model* (4th edn). New York: Pearson.
Gottlieb, M. and Nguyen, D. (2007) *Assessment and Accountability in Language Education Programs: A Guide for Administrators and Teachers.* Philadelphia, PA: Caslon.
New York State Bilingual Common Core Initiative (NYSBCC) (2013) See http://www.engageny.org/resource/new-york-state-bilingual-common-core-initiative (accessed 11 October 2016).
Stefanakis, E. (1999) *Whose Judgment Counts? Assessing Bilingual Children, K-3.* Portsmouth, NH: Heinemann.
Valdés, G. and Lee, O. (2013) English language learners and the next generation science standards: Using the English language proficiency development (ELPD) framework (PowerPoint). A webinar hosted by the Council of Chief State School Officers.

Recommended reading

Gottlieb, M. (2006) *Assessing English Language Learners: Bridges From Language Proficiency to Academic Achievement.* Thousand Oaks, CA: Corwin Press.
The main topic of this book is how to appropriately assess language proficiency and content learning. It includes many tools to help educators organize, interpret and report data for educational decision-making. In addition to including evaluation instruments, the author guides readers in understanding the pros and cons of different types of assessments.
Stefanakis, E. (2002) *Multiple Intelligences and Portfolios: Window into the Learner's Mind.* Portsmouth, NH: Heinemann.
In this book, Stefanakis provides practical tips, guidelines, teacher anecdotes and examples of digital portfolios that can guide teachers from kindergarten through high school toward documenting a child's progress in school through multiple intelligences.
Stefanakis, E. and Meier, D. (2010) *Differentiated Assessment: How to Assess the Learning Potential of Every Student.* San Francisco, CA: Jossey-Bass.
In this book, Stefanakis and Meier provide detailed and practical tools to implement a classroom portfolio program. It includes real-world examples of model assessment programs from five school environments containing multilingual students and large numbers of underperforming students. The authors emphasize student portfolio assessments and personalized learning profiles.
Stiggins, R. and Chappuis, J. (2011) *An Introduction to Student-Involved Assessment for Learning* (6th edn). New York: Pearson.
This introductory text on assessment is written for teacher candidates who have little or no classroom experience. It provides an initial and thorough orientation to classroom assessment.

5 Content and Language

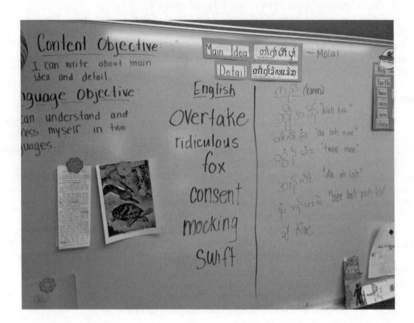

Themes from Chapter 5

(1) When assessing <u>content</u>, minimize or simplify the language so you can focus on content (you can never completely eliminate language, but there are ways to reduce it, without reducing content).

(2) <u>Language</u> is best assessed in context and over time. Language is not assessed well out of context (decontextualized) and at one point in time.

(3) The <u>environment</u> of language assessment should be integrated, natural and authentic but the <u>purpose</u> should be articulated, isolated and clear.

Key Vocabulary

- Content categories
- *Knowledge*
- *Reasoning*
- *Key practices*
- *Dispositional*
- Formative assessment
- Summative assessment

PUMI Connection: Purpose and Use

This chapter focuses on the Purpose (P) and Use (U) of assessing school-related content and language, broadly defined. A variety of purposes and assessment methods are explored in relation to content and language. Whether or not an assessment is formative or summative depends on how the assessment is used. Is it used to <u>form</u> or <u>summarize</u> what students can do?

Introduction to this Chapter

The photograph[1] at the opening of this chapter is typical in classrooms with emergent bilingual (EB) students where the teacher articulates how language and content are separated and also practices translanguaging by connecting content and language to the home language (in this case, Karen – a popular language in Burma). This chapter emphasizes the importance of separating language and content in assessment, and knowing whether the purpose of the assessment is to do with language or assessment.

The first half of this chapter covers content and the second half language, that is content and language typically found in schools.[2] Most of this chapter focuses on logically thinking about your purpose in order to pick the right method of assessment for content and language. Because content and language are never completely separate constructs, there is a discussion of the relationship between content and language in the middle of the chapter, which transitions the reader into the second half on language. Both formative and summative assessment examples are provided for language and content.

How to think about writing a lesson plan with PUMI

Regardless of what lesson plan format you use, somewhere in the plan is a place to articulate the assessment method. When planning for assessment, you should create a PUMI table for each objective to guide you into selecting the appropriate assessment. Usually teachers are expected to measure each objective; therefore each objective requires a PUMI table. After considering the purpose and use of an objective, then select an appropriate method and instrument. When assessing students in a language they are not proficient in, be very careful with the level of language required to successfully complete the assessment. If the language demands of an assessment are too high, then the assessment and results become less meaningful and therefore less valid. Does the assessment require a rubric and if yes, how is that related to the purpose? Before introducing assessment external to the lesson, look inside your instruction for authentic pieces of student work that can be assessed; this leads to more authentic assessment practice. And finally, the assessments of a lesson plan should happen in natural places; assessing every procedure is too much. Strive for one meaningful assessment for each objective that won't disrupt instruction. Best assessment practice looks almost exactly like instruction!

Formative and Summative

Formative and summative assessment has to do with how we *use* the results of the assessment. It's easy to remember the difference between formative and summative assessment if you focus on the base words 'form' and 'sum'. Teachers use formative assessments to gather information in order to 'form' or shape student learning; another way to think about it is teachers are still 'forming' their professional judgement of what students can do. Formative assessment is ongoing and happens most often in classrooms. Benchmarks, which are mini goals set to scaffold a student to reach an end goal, guide formative assessments. Most assessments used in classrooms are meant to show how students are progressing toward language and content goals throughout the year. The results of formative assessments also help shape and form the teacher's instruction. Good formative assessments should lead to better summative outcomes. Summative assessments are intended to 'summarize' the progress of a program or a child after a long period of time such as a marking period or an academic year. Summative assessments often look like grades, final exam scores, regents tests, a research project or a language-proficiency test score.

Types of Content

There are different types of content used in schools that are oftentimes highlighted in content standard documents. Drawing from content standards, this author will organize and explain content in the following ways: *knowledge, reasoning, key practices* and *dispositions*. As discussed in Chapter 4, knowing what kind of content you are targeting is required to pick the appropriate assessment method. Please note that these categories are not mutually exclusive; they are used to help organize the different types of content. For example, it takes *knowledge* and *reasoning* to perform the *key practices*.

Knowledge

Knowledge can be defined in many ways, but within a school setting it is usually defined as subject matter content that teachers want EBs to master. Every discipline or content area has a set body of *knowledge* that defines it. For example, mathematics *knowledge* may consist of measurement, geometry, number sense and algebra. In science, *knowledge* may consist of life, earth, space and physical sciences. *Knowledge* of content typically means that teachers ask students to learn important content as defined by the standards. Teachers design instruction and give notes and study guides to help them master *knowledge* in their content areas. Students then study the content and attempt to memorize it by test time. Examples of *knowledge* include labeling the parts of a cell or an eye, using multiplication and listing the dates of the Revolutionary War. *Knowledge* can easily be assessed by using selected response type assessments (multiple choice, true/false or matching). A base of *knowledge* is a prerequisite to move into other types of content targets such as *reasoning* and *key practices*.

Table 5.1 Appropriate assessment methods for *knowledge*

Category	Method	Comment
Selected response	True/false, matching or multiple choice test	If items are written simply (linguistic simplification – see Chapter 7: Accommodations and snapshot example later in current chapter), this can be a quick and efficient way to assess *knowledge*. Selected response can be translated or read to student in home language.
One-to-one communication	Questioning, survey, conference, interactive journal	Can assess *knowledge* but may be too time-consuming. Home language can be used if student prefers.
Written responses	Essays, written reports, short or extended responses, etc.	*Construct-irrelevant variance (CIV)*[1] *warning*: Written responses sample *knowledge* but depend on student writing ability. Other two methods preferred.

[1]CIV was discussed in depth in Chapter 3: Validity. For example, if you are trying to measure *reasoning* (construct), you don't want writing ability (irrelevant construct) to interfere. CIV is a validity threat to many assessment results for EBs and is also known as 'bias'.

Table 5.1 presents suggestions for assessing *knowledge*. In order of preference, selected response, one-to-one communication and written responses are recommended. Performance assessment is not recommended for assessing *knowledge*. Keep in mind, since the main purpose is to measure content, then any of these assessments can be administered (input) or responded to (output) in the home language or using a translanguaging pedagogy (both home language and new language).

Reasoning

Most people think *knowledge* gives rise to *reasoning*, and some think *knowledge* and *reasoning* grow together. *Reasoning* means that students will think, understand and form judgments using logic. Students should be able to use their *knowledge* to figure things out, relate *knowledge* to other *knowledge*, critique information based on *knowledge* and more. *Reasoning* usually includes skills such as classifying (e.g. sort from smallest to largest), comparing (e.g. compare the US to Mexico) and synthesizing (e.g. what do two stories have in common?), to name a few. Just as all content areas are defined by a certain base of *knowledge*, they are also defined by the ways that students reason within the discipline. For example, *reasoning* could include comparing and contrasting presidents, debating opposing political views or explaining why an amount becomes smaller as the denominator becomes larger.

Note that while *reasoning* is tied to higher levels of thinking, it also entails a type of language use often referred to as academic language, or language used for academic purposes, which is a separate construct[3] needed to *express reasoning*. English language proficiency (ELP) standards in the US have shifted to focus more sharply on language used to access core standards, which was a requirement of No Child Left Behind (NCLB). Just like other aspects of language, language proficiency used in academic areas develops across a continuum of the second language acquisition (SLA) process. For EB educators, developing students' language skills used to express *reasoning* in content areas is now a major priority. There is a major emphasis on the edTPA[4] (a common assessment for teacher candidates in the US used to determine who receives teacher certification) for teacher candidates to document growth in ELP in the content areas, which is primarily a language assessment, not content. The edTPA also encourages teacher candidates to use the home language in creative ways to help determine more accurately what students know and can do.

Table 5.2 presents suggestions for assessing *reasoning*. In order of preference, performance, one-to-one communication and written response are recommended. Selected response is not recommended for assessing *reasoning*.

Table 5.2 Appropriate assessment methods for *reasoning*

Category	Method	Comment
Performance assessment	Teacher observes *key practices* (analyzing, producing, constructing, building, asking, etc.)	Natural context; students can show what they know in content without high levels of literacy (nice for language beginners). Students can use new language or home language.
One-to-one communication	Questioning, survey, conference, interactive journal, observation (of students while they think aloud). Questioning: Teacher asks questions to probe *reasoning*.	These methods provide a window into *reasoning* without relying on literacy (nice for language beginners). Teacher can ask student to respond in new language or home language.
Written response	Essays, written reports, short or extended written responses, etc.	*CIV warning*: Students can explain their *reasoning* through writing; however, beware of CIV – make sure the writing doesn't interfere with students' ability to express their *reasoning*. Keep the constructs of writing and *reasoning* as separate as possible. Student can write in new language or home language.

Key practices

Practices or procedures (what we do with content) are sometimes called *key practices*; see Table 5.3 for a sample of popular *key practices* across some content areas (drawn from current core standards documents). The idea of *key practices* within a content area can be thought of as 'things we do with the content' or otherwise thought of as the application of content.

Table 5.4 provides suggestions for assessing *key practices*. In order of preference, performance and one-to-one communication are recommended. Selected response is not recommended as a method of assessing *key practices*. Since the purpose is assessing content, flexible combinations of home and new language are welcome.

Table 5.3 *Key practices* across content standards

English language arts
- Analyze complex texts
- Produce clear and coherent writing
- Construct arguments

Math
- Solve problems
- Reason abstractly
- Use appropriate tools

Science
- Ask questions
- Define problems
- Analyze and interpret data

Table 5.4 Appropriate assessment methods for *key practices*

Category	Method	Comment
Performance assessment	Teacher observes *key practices* (analyzing, producing, constructing, building, asking, etc.) Project.[1]	Performance assessment is best for less literacy-based *key practices*; this method can demonstrate 'practice' or 'performance', 'doing' or 'creating' something. Home or new language can be used.
One-to-one communication	Questioning, survey, conference, interactive journal	Very strong match if key practice involves assessing oral communication (such as asking questions, constructing explanations). Home language encouraged.
Written responses	Essays, written reports, short or extended written responses, etc.	Very strong match if key practice involves assessing written communication (such as producing clear and coherent writing and written explanations of problems). Home language encouraged.

[1] Projects such as posters, inventions, models and so on are categorized as performance assessment in this book. It is suggested that performance assessment should be used as one method to assess proficiency in creating things as well as assessing the attributes of the product itself. Even though 'performance' and 'product' are different, they are both very appropriate for *key practices*.

Dispositional

The final category of content, and an especially important one to EBs, is *dispositional* targets. *Dispositional* targets are important to EBs because they include the measurement of important factors that we know add to or subtract from students' experience with second language acquisition (SLA). *Dispositional* targets help EB educators understand factors affecting SLA such as motivation, attitude, negative and positive experiences with immigration or English or school and so on. *Dispositional* factors contribute to what Stephen Krashen calls the 'affective filter' (a filter that may accelerate or slow down SLA), which focuses on factors such as anxiety, motivation and self-confidence. All EB educators know how important it is to monitor these factors because, on the one hand, if any of these dispositions are 'too high', this may negatively impact SLA. On the other hand, when these factors are kept 'low', SLA is more apt to typically develop. Other examples of *dispositional* targets may include EBs' attitudes about reading, how confident they are in joining a whole class discussion and how their family contributes to their success in school.

Table 5.5 presents suggestions for assessing dispositions. All four categories of assessment approaches are recommended (one-to-one communication, written responses, selected responses and performance assessment). Home or new language is preferred. Choose the method that will lead to more meaningful answers. If the teacher does not have the home language skills to do this, *seek someone who does*. Don't forget to ask peer teachers, teacher aides, parents, other students or interpreters, in addition to using new technologies like Google Translate (with audio) and Jibbigo, an offline translator – both can record phrases in English and translate into other languages. Google Translate and Babelshot can be used to interpret writing as well.

Table 5.5 Appropriate assessment methods for dispositions

Category	Method	Comment
One-to-one communication	Questioning, conference, interactive journal, questionnaires	EB educators can talk with students and families about dispositions toward content, school, home and community.
Written responses	Questionnaire with open and written responses	If appropriate to student's writing level, open-ended responses can show window to dispositions.
Selected response	Questionnaires with selected response	Simple and quick questionnaires can access student feelings. Closed responses good for beginners.
Performance assessment	Teacher observes *key practices* (analyzing, producing, constructing, building, asking, etc.)	Weaker than the other three, but teachers may be able to assess and infer feelings based on observations of behavior at school, home and community.

The remainder of this chapter shifts from assessing school-related content to school-related language. The transition from content to language starts with a discussion of the relationship between content and language, where content and language are narrowly defined as the content and language in school.

Language Plays a Role when Measuring Content

The majority of assessments – no matter what the subject area – depend upon language for their administration and for the ways in which students provide their responses. For example, when an EB educator gives a content-area assessment, the directions typically are administered orally or in writing (most of the time in English only) and therefore depend on language. Even in a mathematics test, students more than likely have to read the item to discern what the answer is, and often must write extended responses to show what they 'know'. With this in mind, one of the most significant challenges is to select and use assessments that are sensitive to the language needs of EBs.

Using translanguaging assessment practices offers teachers ways to access and assess rigorous content with bilingual students. Celic and Seltzter (2011) list the numerous benefits to planning for instruction and assessments using many languages. The two points in the list most relevant to the assessment of content are in bold below, but all should be considered as important.

(1) Scaffold EBs' development of academic content, language and literacy abilities in English.
(2) Help EBs better understand the content by utilizing their home language as a vehicle for learning.
(3) Help EBs develop language and literacy abilities in their home language.
(4) **Provide an opportunity to EBs to best demonstrate what they know and can do.**
(5) **Help teachers more accurately assess EBs' *knowledge* and understanding of both content and language.**

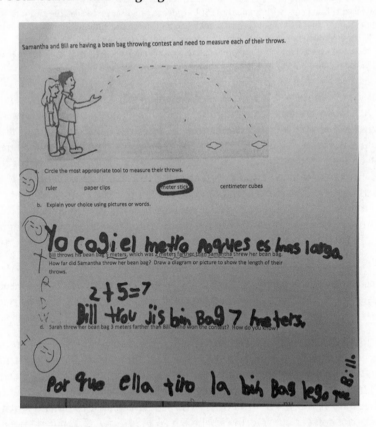

Figure 5.1

(6) Help EBs think critically and at a higher level by asking them to create something in multiple languages and for multiple purposes and/or audiences.
(7) Help EBs engage with the *knowledge* they bring from home.
(8) Help EBs affirm and build their multilingual identities by encouraging them to use their home language practices at school.

Review Figure 5.1 as a content assessment. How much language is necessary to show what she knows in math? To translate the student responses into English, see Table 5.6.

Table 5.6 Interpreting student responses from Figure 5.1

Item	Student response	Interpretation in English
2a	No written response – just a circle.	No interpretation needed.
2b	Yo cogiel metro poques es mas largo.	I chose the meter because it's larger.
2c	2+5=7	2+5=7
	Bill trow jis bin bag 7 meters	He threw his bean bag[1] 7 meters.
2d	Por que ella tiro la bin bag lego que Bill.	Because she threw the bean bag farther than Bill.

[1] When Mahoney used this activity with graduate TESOL students, we discovered that the two international students (India, Saudi Arabia) had never thrown a bean bag and were unfamiliar with any games related to bean bags. But the 14 domestic students had all thrown a bean bag previously. These types of cultural referents may make the assessment more comprehensible to students from mainstream US culture. It's these types of cultural constructs in assessments that many times go unnoticed.

That's a lot of language for a math assessment. Most assessments like Figure 5.1 are filled with both content and language – it's never just a content assessment. The following paragraph reviews the format of responses and the general language demands found in Figure 5.1. The first item (2a) uses selected response, which requires the student to read, comprehend and circle the answer. The second item (2b) uses open-ended response, which requires the student to read, comprehend and explain her answer in writing. The third item (2c) requires her to read, comprehend and draw. And the fourth item (2d) requires her to explain her answer by writing. Table 5.7 shows a summary of language and content required for the assessment in Figure 5.1. A PUMI study further clarifies what this looks like as a content area assessment.

P	U	M	I
To assess understanding of distance using meters.	To provide one grade toward report card (end of unit summary).	Selected response, written response.	Worksheet downloaded from engage.org.

The student answered incorrectly for 2c, but why? Is the reason related to language or content? At first glance, an error analysis of 2c shows that this student was able to use English to answer the questions; but the mathematics was incorrect. The correct answer is 'Samantha threw her bean bag three meters and the correct equation is 5–2=3'. It is likely the student is able to do the math – add and subtract (the correct subtraction is shown in Figure 5.1, 2c), but if the student

Table 5.7 Breaking down the content and language required in Figure 5.1

Content	Language
Knowing how to use measuring tools	Reading for understanding
Knowing what a meter is	Reading academic math language
Thinking abstractly about a bean bag that was thrown even further (pre-algebra)	Comprehend the sentence using superlative 'farther'
Reasoning about who won the contest	Writing using language used to explain *reasoning*

does not understand the English word 'farther[5] than' then English may have led to the error. Probably not having ELP in math[6] was the source of the error, not the math. Even though this is primarily a summative assessment, her teacher will use these responses to design an ELP in math mini lesson on comparative adjectives and how to write comparative adjectives as math equations. If so, this could be listed as an additional use in the PUMI table: to inform instruction.

Because the purpose of the assessment shown in Figure 5.1 was to measure content, the language of the responses can be in English or Spanish or a combination of both. This student used translanguaging in her responses by choosing to answer 2b in Spanish and 2c in English and 2d in Spanish. She also used English (la bin bag) in the Spanish sentence (2d). This is encouraged, because allowing students to use their full linguistic repertoire in content area assessments provides an opportunity for EBs to best show what they know, *when the purpose is assessing content.*[7]

In content assessment, it is also critical to modify the language demands of the content area learning and assessment – *but not the content itself.* In other words, EBs are due the same rigor of content as non-EBs but with reduced language demands. Reducing the language demands of content area assessment increases the chances for EBs to reveal their strengths because they can more directly access content. Opening up assessments to include multiple languages will better support EBs. Conversely, content area assessments with too much language interference or in English only can cover up or disguise content area strengths.

Snapshot: Assessing Content or Language?

Mrs Weiss was frustrated by the district-level math tests because they seemed too wordy and her EB students were guessing or leaving blanks on their tests because it appeared that the language was too difficult for them. Mrs Weiss knew that many of her students were unable to show what they really knew about math because of the way the items were written. Of her own will, she typed into Google search the terms 'simplify language', 'test items', 'ESL' and 'strategies', and she found two documents to help guide her. One was a recent chapter in the *Handbook of Test Development* by Dr Jamal el Abedi (2015) titled Language Issues and Item Development. This researcher studies the language that gets in the way of assessing content

(Continued)

(linguistic features that may hinder student understanding of test items). Mrs Weiss followed his advice and made changes (called 'linguistic simplification') like the ones below the test items:

Original #1: A certain reference file contains approximately six billion facts.

Revision #1: Mack's company sold 6 billion hamburgers (replaced unfamiliar words with familiar ones).

Original #2: The weight of three objects was compared.

Revision #2: Sandra compared the weight of three rabbits (replaced verbs in the passive voice with verbs in the active voice).

Original #3: If X represents the number of newspapers that Lee delivers each day...

Revision #3: Lee delivers X newspapers each day (replaced conditional 'if clause' with sentence).

Mrs Weiss anticipated that the other math teachers in her department might suggest that she was dumbing down the test or changing the math content in some way to make it easier. So, she documented the linguistic modifications she made and cited Abedi (2015). Then, she circulated the items and asked her peer teachers to judge whether the content was changed. Overwhelmingly, they agreed that by deleting the 'language that gets in the way', she had not change the difficulty level of the content (math). She also found an article on translanguaging strategies and decided to implement translanguaging assessment strategies in her math class: (1) students were permitted to answer open ended questions in their home language if they chose and (2) the directions to every section and subsection were read to the students in their home language and their new language. After implementing the linguistic test item modifications and the translanguaging assessment strategies, Mrs Weiss observed an increase in math scores, self-esteem, interest and motivation in math. This was worth the extra time and work. Her peers began to take notice.

Discussion Questions

- Do you think Mrs Weiss made the content easier? Why or why not?
- Can you ever fully separate language from content? Explain.

The remainder of the chapter now turns toward ways of assessing language in school.

Method Suggestions for School-Related Language

When assessing school-related language, special consideration should be given to selecting the appropriate method to match the language target. Table 5.8 suggests methods. With language assessments, obviously you should stay focused on the target language, whether it is the new language (English) or the home language (Spanish) for example. Translanguaging is acceptable within language assessments.

Table 5.8 Matching purpose to method (<u>PUMI</u>): Good and bad choices

Assessment Method[1]

	Bad Choices		Good Choices	
Speaking	*Multiple-choice test:* Method doesn't match language target.	*Written essay:* Method doesn't match language target.	*Teacher observation* (with checklist) of student speaking in social studies debate.	*Interview or questioning:* Provides lots of opportunity for assessing language in context.
Listening	*True or false test:* Not preferred. Other language constructs such as literacy may interfere.	*Short essay:* Doesn't match language target.	*Teacher observation:* Teacher can observe student responding to commands/ requests.	*Interview or questioning:* Teacher can ask questions and evaluate answers.
Writing	*Matching test:* Language target doesn't match method.	*Role play:* Language target doesn't match method.	*Written science lab:* Can provide highly authentic sample of writing.	*Interactive journals:* A written conversation between teachers and student.
Reading	*Multiple-choice test:* Usually decontextualized, therefore, not a good language assessment.	*Extended written response:* Language target doesn't match method.	*Running record[2]:* Provides a natural context thorough documentation.	*Interview or questioning:* Teacher can ask questions and evaluate answers in a natural setting.

[1] To make any language assessment 'standards based', suggested methods should be used with a rubric or checklist designed from standards such as your state ELP standards.
[2] See figures showing examples of running records in current chapter.

This can be done by creating instruction and assessment using the target language; but encouraging students to use both languages to expand meaning-making opportunities.

Assessing Language: To Integrate or Not?

Despite the presentation of language as four distinct areas as presented in Table 5.8, that's not really how language works. Integrated assessment (language, literacy and content) creates a more authentic environment to collect assessment data. The *environment* should be integrated, natural and authentic but the *purpose* of the assessment should be articulated, isolated and clear. Since real language practice is not segmented, the practice of separating language in assessment erodes the authenticity (and validity) of assessment results. Integrated assessment involves finding a meaningful way to develop language, literacy and content learning over an extended period of time. Don't overlook the multiple opportunities for EBs to hear, speak, read and write within meaningful content instruction. Integrated instruction and assessment within a culturally relevant environment that supports translanguaging is ideal for EBs – the type of environment that may be captured using portfolio assessment. This is the main reason portfolio assessment was and continues to be so popular among educators. Portfolios are one of the only assessment methods used in schools today that show change over time and integrate ideas in authentic ways. Plus, the format is flexible and allows for the integration of language, literacy and content.

Language standards and language criteria can be easily turned into rubrics and checklists for use in formative authentic classroom assessment. Check for language standards at international level (for example, teaching English to speakers of other languages [TESOL]: http://www.tesol.org/), regional level (for example, WIDA: https://www.wida.us/) and state level (for example, the Bilingual Common Core [BCC] in New York State: https://www.engageny.org/resource/new-york-state-bilingual-common-core-initiative). For ease of discussion, the following section focuses on four language topics popular in school: speaking, listening, reading and writing.

Speaking

Speaking and listening naturally interact; despite this, they are usually assessed separately. What is clear from research studies on SLA is that speaking, also referred to as oral language development, almost always continues to develop among EBs in two or more languages, even if they do not have exposure to languages other than English for instruction and assessment. Students continue to speak and acquire other languages during school and outside school with family, friends and the community. This can be a huge benefit for EB educators who can use their EBs' multiple language abilities as a classroom asset.

Assessment of speaking should involve interactive and two-way communication in which one person conveys a message and the other person interprets the message. Speaking can be measured more holistically, as a whole conversation, or by its components (grammar, vocabulary, pronunciation, fluency). EB educators listen regularly to oral language samples in their classrooms, but most teachers do not have a systematic way to document and analyze oral language proficiency to record growth over time. Oral language proficiency is an important step in scaffolding EBs into reading and writing, but it is most often overlooked in instruction and assessment.

Table 5.9 is an example of an assessment for the purpose of measuring listening and speaking. Method is observation with a checklist. This checklist was modified from Genesee and Upshur (1996) to include a classroom context and core ideas.

This language assessment can happen in a very natural (authentic) classroom setting, where students are engaging with academic tasks. The EB educator can use this as a checklist by marking a check for yes and leaving a blank for no. Alternatively, a rating scale (1=low, 2=average and 3=high) can be used to generate slightly more descriptive data. A PUMI study is shown below.

P	U	M	I
To assess listening, comprehension and speaking during classroom instruction.	To differentiate instruction based on individual language needs and share with other content teachers.	Teacher observation.	Checklist.

Table 5.9 Example of a listening/speaking assessment: Observation with checklist

Listening during content instruction		Speaking during content instruction	
1	Understands simple directions.	1	Pronounces vowel sounds correctly.
2	Understands simple sentences.	2	Pronounces consonant sounds well.
3	Understands simple yes/no.	3	Pronounces blends correctly.
4	Understands plurals.	4	Uses word stress correctly.
5	Understands content vocabulary appropriate to age.	5	Uses tone correctly.
6	Understands adjectives appropriate to age.	6	Gives one-word responses.
7	Understands several related sentences.	7	Produces simple sentences/questions.
8	Understands contractions and other common shortened forms.	8	Gives simple directions.
9	Distinguishes tones and understands their meaning.	9	Uses tense markers correctly.
10	Understands meaning of difference intonation patterns.	10	Uses prepositions correctly.
11	Understands more complex directions.	11	Forms complex sentences.
12	Understands rapid speech.	12	Gives descriptions.
13	Understands language in content-area activity.	13	Uses vocabulary appropriate to age.
14	Understands language when peers speak to him/her.	14	Uses classroom language easily.

Listening

Whereas classroom instruction usually involves meaningful interaction with teacher and peers, large-scale assessments of listening are generally restricted to a paper and pencil test simultaneously administered to a large group of EBs. Theoretically, test constructors design the listening items on discrete point (taken at one point in time) tests to measure only listening. An example of a discrete point listening assessment, which is very popular in schools, is measuring phonemic discrimination through a task such as recognizing minimal pairs (a minimal pair comprises two words that differ only by a sound, or phoneme). Figure 5.2 shows a listening assessment (selected response) that is considered decontextualized (out of a meaningful context) and likely measured at one point in time. It is decontextualized because it is lacking any meaningful or culturally relevant context. For example, there is no authentic relationship between cot, cat, mat and dot. And there is no

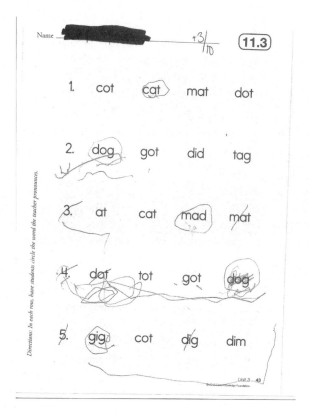

Figure 5.2 Listening assessment

meaningful two-way interaction (for example, the assessment is not administered in a communicative-based manner).

As discussed earlier in this chapter, it is nearly impossible to separate listening from content in a school context. For example, if a student is asked during a listening assessment to sequence events in a story using story pictures, he or she must have listening comprehension, *knowledge* of the story and the ability to sequence events, each of which is a construct outside of listening. Not recognizing the many constructs is called *confounding constructs* (when strong constructs get mixed, like language and content) and are considered a validity threat. The need to keep language constructs such as listening from confounding with other language or content constructs has been a challenge for psychometricians (measurement scientists) and educators. It may seem feasible on paper to separate languages, but the reality is that no one item measures only listening. It is more meaningful and natural to assess listening in a communicative-based manner, such as questioning with a rubric. Teacher observation is also an appropriate method for a communicative-based listening assessment. A teacher can observe an EB performing many classroom-based listening activities. A rubric or checklist can easily be developed (see Chapter 4 for how to construct a rubric or checklist) to document how well an EB listens within academic contexts[8] and what progress he or she makes. For example, teachers can observe and document how EBs respond when they are asked to follow simple directions (put away the book, line up at the door), construct maps or figures from oral directions (identify symbols on a map, places from models) or sequence a series of events or illustrations using hands-on material from oral directions.

Reading

EB educators assess reading for a variety of reasons. They might want to assess prior *knowledge*, decoding skills, reading comprehension strategies, interest and family practices in reading or many other reading measurables. The key, again, is to identify the purpose of the reading assessment and align the instruction and assessment with it. Often, reading assessments are done by encouraging productive language skills (speaking and writing). However, when a teacher asks a student to retell a story (for the purpose of assessing reading comprehension), this is also an assessment of speaking. In the same way, asking a student to write about the story he or she just read can be an assessment of writing and speaking. It

"¡Apúrense! ¡Tenemos que salir!"

	Errors	SCs
Mi mamá me tomó de la mano. "¡Apúrense!		
¡Tenemos que salir!" le gritó a David que estaba		
en su cuarto. "Tenemos que salir de la casa,		
¡AHORA!"		
Íbamos corriendo y tropezándonos por		
el pasillo, que de repente empezó a crujir como		
un barco en una tormenta. Sansón, nuestro perro,		
también corría detrás de nosotros. "Pero no	1	1
traigo puestos los zapatos," gritaba yo.		
"¡No importa! La casa se está cayendo."		
Todo alrededor de nosotros se tambaleaba.		1
Salimos a la calle cubierta de nieve y		
nos caímos, porque el suelo se abrió.		1
Apenas salimos, la casa se cayó. Oímos		
el ruido de los vidrios al romperse y de	1	
las maderas al quebrarse, pero el terrible		
estruendo del temblor seguía y seguía.		1

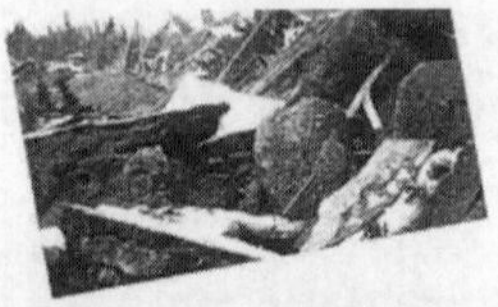

	Errors	SCs
Cuando volteé hacia arriba vi que los árboles		
grandes que había alrededor de la casa se movían		
como látigos. Entre la nieve, aparecía un hoyo negro		
enorme, cada vez que un árbol se caía. Con el	1	
movimiento, se abrían grietas enormes. De repente,		
el lugar en el que estábamos parados empezó a	1	
ladearse, primero un poco y después más y más.		
Se empezó a abrir una grieta que nos separó a mí		
de mi mamá y mi hermano, y yo me empecé a	1	
resbalar, alejándome de ellos. Yo estaba aterrorizada,		
pero mi mamá estiró la mano, me agarró y me jaló		
hasta donde estaba parada.		
Entonces, ¡el temblor se acabó!		
Total errors and self corrections	6	4

Fluency (✓)

Reads smoothly and expressively	✓
Reruns or repeats words or phrases	
Is slow and hesitant	
Ignores punctuation	✓

Strategies used (✓)

Do attempts look similar?	✓
Do attempts sound right?	✓
Do attempts make sense?	✓
Does the reader monitor for accuracy and meaning?	✓

Accuracy Chart

Uncorrected errors	%	Uncorrected errors	%
1–3	99	13–15	94
4–5	(98)	16–17	93
6–8	97	18–20	92
9–10	96	21–22	91
11–12	95	23–24	90

Retelling

After the student has finished reading, ask: *¿Me puedes decir de qué se habla en este texto?* (Retells details)

Record details		
su familia estan en casa, hay un temblor, ellos se apuran y cojen toda la familia y cuando salen afuera se cespeló y su mamá la salvó	Many facts (4 or more)	(3)
	Few facts (1 to 3)	1
	No facts	0

Figure 5.3

is important for EB educators to be aware of this natural confounding of variables and to find ways to isolate skills when necessary – but it's also important to understand that confounding language is a natural and authentic classroom use of language.

Another very natural way to read texts with EBs is to read content area texts in the home language, where available; this allows EBs to build more background *knowledge* and understand the English text more. This type of translanguaging method can be used during assessment and instruction. Also, consider running records when assessing reading; these are an in-depth way to observe a student's reading performance and have been used for many years by reading experts. They allow the teacher to quickly assess strengths and weaknesses and to identify reading strategies used by the student, as well as those not used. The following two figures show how reading records are documented with bilingual children by conducting the assessment in Spanish (Figure 5.3) and in English (Figure 5.4). Many times educators combine the results of English and Spanish assessment to view a fuller linguistic repertoire.

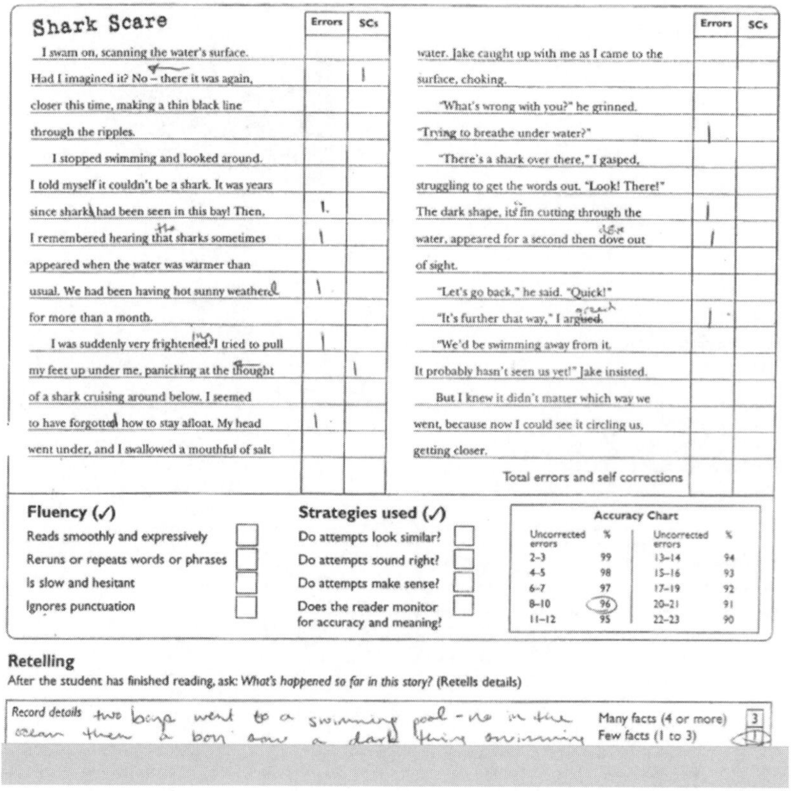

Shark Scare

Errors | SCs

I swam on, scanning the water's surface. Had I imagined it? No – there it was again, closer this time, making a thin black line through the ripples.

I stopped swimming and looked around. I told myself it couldn't be a shark. It was years since sharks had been seen in this bay! Then, I remembered hearing that sharks sometimes appeared when the water was warmer than usual. We had been having hot sunny weather for more than a month.

I was suddenly very frightened. I tried to pull my feet up under me, panicking at the thought of a shark cruising around below. I seemed to have forgotten how to stay afloat. My head went under, and I swallowed a mouthful of salt water. Jake caught up with me as I came to the surface, choking.

"What's wrong with you?" he grinned. "Trying to breathe under water?"

"There's a shark over there," I gasped, struggling to get the words out. "Look! There!" The dark shape, its fin cutting through the water, appeared for a second then dove out of sight.

"Let's go back," he said. "Quick!"

"It's further that way," I argued. "We'd be swimming away from it. It probably hasn't seen us yet!" Jake insisted.

But I knew it didn't matter which way we went, because now I could see it circling us, getting closer.

Total errors and self corrections

Fluency (✓)

- Reads smoothly and expressively ☐
- Reruns or repeats words or phrases ☐
- Is slow and hesitant ☐
- Ignores punctuation ☐

Strategies used (✓)

- Do attempts look similar? ☐
- Do attempts sound right? ☐
- Do attempts make sense? ☐
- Does the reader monitor for accuracy and meaning? ☐

Accuracy Chart

Uncorrected errors	%	Uncorrected errors	%
2–3	99	13–14	94
4–5	98	15–16	93
6–7	97	17–19	92
8–10	96	20–21	91
11–12	95	22–23	90

Retelling

After the student has finished reading, ask: *What's happened so far in this story?* (Retells details)

Record details two boys went to a swimming pool – no in the ocean then a boy saw a dark thing swimming

Many facts (4 or more) 3
Few facts (1 to 3) 1

Figure 5.4

WIDA has developed rubrics designed specifically for language in content areas. The rubric below might be used to measure ELP in the content area (reading in science for example). This rubric was adapted from WIDA (2014).

Table 5.10 Rubric to measure reading in content area (adapted from WIDA, 2014)

	4	3	2	1
Reading in the content area (in English).	Student work demonstrates that the student can read and comprehend specific content area language in English.	Student work demonstrates that the student can read and comprehend some content language in English.	Student work demonstrates that the student can read and comprehend limited content language in English.	Student work demonstrates that the student cannot read and comprehend any content related language in English.
Content area symbols	Student work demonstrates a well-developed understanding of specific and technical content area symbols in math.	Student work demonstrates a general understanding of specific and technical content area symbols in math.	Student work demonstrates a limited understanding of general content symbols in math.	Student work demonstrates no understanding of general content related symbols.

Writing

As with reading, students write for a variety of purposes and utilize a number of different genres. Writing to share *knowledge* and give information and details on a topic is called informative or *expository writing*, whereby EBs rely on existing *knowledge* to integrate new ideas or analyze or synthesize ideas. Autobiographies or creative types of writing are based on observations that students have made in their lives; this is called *expressive* or narrative writing. *Persuasive* writing, which is evaluative in nature, combines some background *knowledge* with the author's view or opinion. Danling Fu (2009) emphasizes the following to develop writing skills and other language skills among EBs:

- Provide plenty of writing opportunities.
- Teach writing across content subject areas.
- Understand and guide students through writing stages.
- Give students the freedom in their language choice for expression.
- Allow students to move back and forth from their native writing to English writing.
- Urge bilingual, ESL and regular classroom teachers to collaborate on their curriculum for ELL literacy and language development.

My granmother ② an'd I ⒠talk
about a lot of ~~th~~things,
line stories about when she
worked with~~a~~ her husband in
the field, and when my
sister was little and she ~~a~~ eat
Hot food, she said, "my sister
said is hot ~~to~~ but is good,"
When I am ~~with~~ with my friend
we talk about the class, the
things that we both lме or
we line to listening mosin and
watch how the boy play
~~football~~
~~————~~ or basnetbull, some
time we play domino, and
we tan pictores togeter.

Figure 5.5 Contextualised writing sample

Figure 5.5 shows a culturally relevant writing sample from a high school girl from Mexico who works four to eight hours a day on a dairy farm in western New York, seven days a week, and also attends high school in a rural area five days a week. The writing sample in Figure 5.5 can be assessed using the rubric immediately following it. The rubric in Figure 5.6 is from WIDA (2014).

This chapter ends with a snapshot of a situation where a summative language assessment was causing students to be labeled as non-nons, or not knowing any language. This demonstrates the danger of assessing language out of context and at one point in time (see assessments leading to deficit in Chapter 1), then using the results to make program and student-level decisions that negatively impacted students and families. At the time, most people didn't question the test; unfortunately, they trusted the test and questioned the children. This is further explained in the snapshot.

WIDA Performance Definitions – Speaking and Writing Grades K-12

Within sociocultural contexts for language use…

	Discourse Dimension	Sentence Dimension	Word/Phrase Dimension
	Linguistic Complexity	Language Forms and Conventions	Vocabulary Usage
Level 6 - Reaching	Language that meets all criteria through Level 5, Bridging		
	At each grade, toward the end of a given level of English language proficiency, and with instructional support, English language learners will produce…		
Level 5 Bridging	• Multiple, complex sentences • Organized, cohesive, and coherent expression of ideas	• A variety of grammatical structures matched to purpose • A broad range of sentence patterns characteristic of particular content areas	• Technical and abstract content-area language, including content-specific collocations • Words and expressions with precise meaning across content areas
Level 4 Expanding	• Short, expanded, and some complex sentences • Organized expression of ideas with emerging cohesion	• A variety of grammatical structures • Sentence patterns characteristic of particular content areas	• Specific and some technical content-area language • Words and expressions with expressive meaning through use of collocations and idioms across content areas
Level 3 Developing	• Short and some expanded sentences with emerging complexity • Expanded expression of one idea or emerging expression of multiple related ideas	• Repetitive grammatical structures with occasional variation • Sentence patterns across content areas	• Specific content language, including cognates and expressions • Words or expressions with multiple meanings used across content areas
Level 2 Emerging	• Phrases or short sentences • Emerging expression of ideas	• Formulaic grammatical structures • Repetitive phrasal and sentence patterns across content areas	• General content words and expressions • Social and instructional words and expressions across content areas
Level 1 Entering	• Words, phrases, or chunks of language • Single words used to represent ideas	• Phrase-level grammatical structures • Phrasal patterns associated with common social and instructional situations	• General content-related words • Everyday social, instructional and some content-related words

Figure 5.6 Example of Rubric used to access ELP in content area (WIDA, 2014)

Snapshot: Most People Questioned the Children Not the Test

The research study described here was launched by Dr Jeff MacSwan of the University of Maryland to investigate reports of large numbers of 'non-nons' (EBs who allegedly have no language) in states throughout the United States. The Idea proficiency test (IPT)-Spanish and other Spanish language instruments were leading districts and state departments to conclude that students – who were known to be dominant Spanish speakers – did not know Spanish and were limited speakers of their primary language. These children were also not proficient in English; hence, they were labeled as semilingual or 'non-non'. The educational consequences of this label were severe. Students were often denied ESL or bilingual services and instead were mainstreamed. Some students were placed in special education programs, contributing to the over-representation of EBs in special education (SPED). Instead of questioning the instruments that measured language, most people questioned the children. MacSwan launched a major convergent validity study to investigate the (construct of many Spanish language proficiency) tests.

MacSwan, as reported in MacSwan and Mahoney (2008), investigated approximately 150 Spanish-dominant students who had been assessed in Spanish using the IPT-Spanish. The purpose of this test, as articulated by the test manual, was to measure Spanish oral language proficiency. Only 17 students were determined by the IPT-Spanish to be fluent in their native language. Upon further inspection, it was discovered that four items that required students to respond in a full sentence skewed the results. As the directions outlined, children who missed all four of the items shown in Table 5.11 were told to stop after that section and were consequently labeled as limited speakers of their native language. Many features of these items go against what we know to be good assessment practice for EBs: The items were decontextualized, the students must respond in a full sentence or their answer was wrong and the content of the items was peculiar and confused many students. It didn't help that at the time of this study, the Disney movie *Dumbo* was re-released and some students answered that yes, elephants can fly (see Item #22).

Even more troubling was a curve reminiscent of a bell shape that was formed by the results (Figure 5.7), which highlighted how strong test design (normal referencing) over (language) theory or conceptual framework can be. Keep in mind that the bell shape does not occur naturally; it is manipulated during test construction, and the pilot study in particular, when the measurement scientists select the items that behave properly (discriminate well) to create a 'normal' curve (on a norm-referenced test). This introduced many problems because first language acquisition does not function like a bell curve – nearly all students learn their first language orally, fluently and without much effort. This is in direct opposition to the assumptions of the bell curve.

The authors argued that requiring speakers to respond in complete sentences reflected a naive view of language proficiency, inconsistent with linguistic research, and characterized the requirement as 'academic bias' – that is, a prejudice that results from confusion between academic content *knowledge* related to language arts and actual linguistic ability. Consequently, the result produced an arbitrary favoritism toward members of the education classes (MacSwan & Mahoney, 2008).

Discussion questions

- Should the IPT-Spanish be used for Spanish language assessment with Spanish-speaking children?
- How can language assessments using decontextualized items lead to invalid test scores?
- What were the consequences of using invalid test scores for EBs?
- What do you notice about the test items commonly missed by students in Table 5.11?

Table 5.11 Four items on the IPT-Spanish that skewed results

Item #17	*Qué está haciendo el niño?* (What is the boy doing?)
	Correct answer is *'El (niño) está leyendo/estudiando'*.
Item #18	*Cuántas manos tengo yo?* (How many hands do I have?)
	Correct answer is *'Usted tiene dos manos'*.
Item #21	*Pueden correr los caballos?* (Are horses able to run?)
	Correct answer is *'Sí, pueden corer'*.
Item #22	*Vuelan los elefantes como los pájaros?* (Do elephants fly like birds?)
	Correct answer is *'No, los elefantes no vuelan'*.

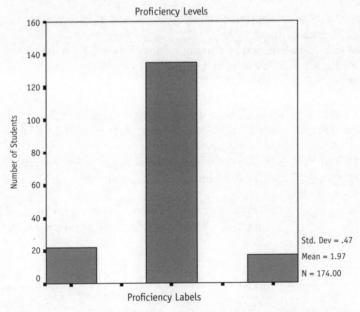

Figure 5.7 An example of how norm-referenced tests, by design, produce the bell curve. NSS: non-Spanish speaker; LSS: limited Spanish speaker; FSS: fluent Spanish speaker (From MacSwan & Mahoney, 2008.)

End-of-Chapter Activities (Instructors: see advice at the end of the book)

By completing Activities 1 to 4, the reader will be able to:

(1) Sort eight clue cards into four content categories (*knowledge, reasoning, key practices* and *dispositional*) and describe one method of assessment that aligns best with this type of content.
(2) Choose the most appropriate assessment method for a given objective and instruction by completing an alignment table.
(3) Use ELP standards and PUMI to design assessment for EBs.
(4) Differentiate a language assessment by five levels.

Activity 1

Sort eight clue cards into four content categories (*knowledge, reasoning, key practices* and *dispositional*) and describe one method of assessment that aligns best with this type of content.

The instructor will give each table 10 clue cards to sort. At your table, sort the clue cards into the five content target categories (*knowledge, reasoning, key practices,* products and *dispositional*) and discuss with your group why you think it belongs in that categories. After 15 to 20 minutes of practice, the instructor will have each group, one by one, bring up one clue card and deposit it into the correct brown bag and tell the class why your group thinks it belongs there. Each group has the exact same clue cards, so there will be opportunity for agreement/disagreement and good discussion as a whole group.

Activity 2

Choose the most appropriate assessment method for objective and instruction by completing an alignment table.

By yourself, complete two alignment tables (Tables 5.12 and 5.13) to practice selecting an appropriate assessment method.

Activity 3

Use ELP standards and PUMI to design an assessment for EBs.

Step 1 is done for you (given below). With a partner, complete Steps 2 and 3 to design a standards-based language assessment.

Step 1: From WIDA ELD (Standard 3, The Language of Mathematics, Grade 1, Level 2 Emerging). Cognitive function: Students at all levels of ELP analyze the relative length of objects.

Step 2:_____ (insert one observable and measurable language objective.)

Step 3:_____ (practice PUMI to select an appropriate assessment method.)

(Continued)

Activity 4

Differentiate a language assessment by five levels.

Using the content from Activity 2 and the six levels of language development introduced by WIDA (entering, emerging, developing, expanding, bridging and reaching), with a partner choose a graphic organizer using MSWord Smart Art to differentiate the language assessment by five levels. How might you differentiate the assessment? Hint: Whenever you differentiate the objective or instruction, you must also differentiate the assessment to maintain good alignment (Figure 5.8).

Table 5.12 Planning for assessment

Objectives	Instruction	Assessment
Content: SW (Student will) be able to compare and contrast the attributes of a square and a rectangle.	Is a square a rectangle? TW (Teacher will) model use of blocks to identify characteristics of square and rectangle. SW use a graphic organizer to collect evidence for or against.	What is a good method to assess content (think PUMI first)?
Language: SW be able to produce a written argument for why a square is a rectangle.	TW model using graphic organizer to write arguments and how to turn those arguments into a short paragraph.	What is a good method to assess language (think PUMI first)?

Table 5.13 Planning for assessment

Objectives	Instruction	Assessment
Content: SW be able to calculate the number of protons, electrons and neutrons in an element, given its atomic number and atomic mass.	TW use clue cards which have a question side and an answer side. SW rotate cards around small circle and practice reading and answering chemistry Q&A.	What is a good method to assess content (think PUMI first)?
Language: SW be able to listen to a question and tell a partner the number of protons/electrons/ neutrons in an element.	In pairs, each student will listen to their partner read a chemistry clue card and practice answering it.	What is a good method to assess language (think PUMI first)?

Reaching

- Little to no language differentiation necessary

Bridging

- Follow multi-step oral instructions to compare the lengths of objects

Expanding

- Follow oral instructions to compare the lengths of objects using a template

Developing

- Follow oral instructions to order objects according to their lengths following a model

Emerging

- Follow oral instructions to categorize objects according to their length following a model

Entering

- Follow oral instructions to identify lengths of objects following a model

Figure 5.8 Differentiated instruction for EBs (From WIDA, 2012: 24.)

Notes

(1)   Photograph courtesy of Ms Nicole Nichter, a dynamic ENL teacher at #45 International School, a Buffalo public school.

(2)   The author recognizes that content and language are huge constructs and that studying language and content in schools in this chapter is just a small fraction of the universal concepts of content and language. For a full book on language assessment, see Bachman and Palmer (2010) referenced in the recommended reading section at the end of this chapter.

(3)   The idea of 'construct' is also discussed in detail in Chapter 3. A construct is a complex concept such as achievement, language proficiency, motivation, readiness, creativity etc. None of these concepts are 'visible', like height and weight are and, therefore, cannot be measured in a simple way like height and weight.

(4)   edTPA is a performance-based assessment that pre-service teachers in approximately 40 out of 50 United States need to pass to obtain teacher certification. edTPA was developed by the Stanford Center for Assessment, Learning and Equity (SCALE) at Stanford University.

(5)   Farther and further are comparative adverbs or adjectives. They are the irregular comparative forms of far. By not comprehending 'farther than' – language used in math class, she is led to create the math equation, $2+5=7$ instead of $5-2+3$.

(6)   For students completing the edTPA, this is the same as ELP in content area, a major section of the edTPA.

(7)   Note: If the purpose was to assess Spanish language used in math (perhaps in a bilingual program), then it would be appropriate to assess in Spanish only. Along the same lines, if the purpose was to assess academic English used in math, then it is appropriate to assess in English only. The language of instruction depends on the purpose. But when the purpose is to assess content, translanguaging is encouraged and allows for more access to content.

(8)   This is another example of assessing *ELP in the content areas* as most teacher candidates now have to provide evidence for/analyze as part of edTPA requirements for teacher certification in the United States. Assessing ELP in content area is a language assessment.

References

Abedi, J. (2015) Language issues in item development. In S.M. Downing and T.M. Haladyna (eds) *The Handbook of Test Development* (pp. 377–398). Mahwah, NJ: Lawrence Erlbaum Associates.

Celic, C. and Seltzer, K. (2011) *Translanguaging: A CUNY-NYSIEB Guide for Educators. CUNY-NYSIEB.* New York: The Graduate Center.

Fu, D. (2009) *Writing between Languages.* Portsmouth, NH: Heinemann.

Genesee, F. and Upshur, J. (1996) *Classroom-Based Evaluation in Second Language Education.* Cambridge: Cambridge Language Education.

MacSwan, J. and Mahoney, K. (2008) Academic bias in language testing: A construct validity critique of the OPT I Oral Grades K-6 Spanish Second Edition (IPT Spanish). *Journal of Educational Research and Policy Studies (JERPS)* 8 (2), 86–101.

WIDA (2014) English language development (ELD) standards. See https://www.wida.us/standards/eld.aspx (accessed 12 October 2016).

Recommended reading

Ascenzi-Moreno (2016) An exploration of elementary teachers' views of informal reading inventories in dual language bilingual programs, literacy research, and instruction. DOI: 10.1080/19388071.2016.1165318.
This article is a study examining how elementary teachers in a dual language program view assessment to support their students' reading growth. This article highlights reading assessment for EBs through the perspective of dynamic bilingualism.

Bachman, L. and Palmer, A. (2010) *Language Assessment in Practice.* New York: Oxford University Press.
This book presents the fundamental theory and application of design, development and use of language assessment.

Valdés, G. (2001) *Learning and Not Learning English: Latino Students in American Schools.* New York: Teachers College Press.
Valdés highlights four Mexican children in an American school and the struggles they face. She highlights the policies/instruction/assessment surrounding their learning of English. Her book offers a comprehensive view of real issues surrounding English language learning in US schools.

Valdés, G., Capitelli, S. and Alvarez, L. (2010) *Latino Children Learning English: Steps in the Journey.* New York: Teachers College Press.
Valdés, Capitelli and Alvarez describe the challenges faced by K-3 students who currently attend segregated schools. They highlight the ways in which English language proficiencies develop in newly arrived immigrants and challenge the myth that young children learn a second language effortlessly and quickly.

6 Psychometrics

Source: Gary Huck and Mike Konopacki Labor Cartoons Collection; WAG 264; Box 26; Folder 63; Tamiment Library/Robert F. Wagner Labor Archives, New York University. Reproduced with permission.

Themes from Chapter 6

(1) Criterion referenced tests (CRT) are more popular than norm referenced tests (NRT); however, both have drawbacks.
(2) There are many types of scores but they are all generated from the same raw score.
(3) Teachers and parents have grown to not trust test scores due to multiple public test items or scoring errors made by testing companies.

Key Vocabulary

- Criterion referenced
- Cut score
- Norm referenced
- Normal curve equivalent (NCE)
- Percentile rank

- Proficiency level
- Psychometrics
- Raw score
- Scale score
- Standard score
- Standardized
- Stanine
- Tests

PUMI Connection: Use

This chapter focuses on the U (Use) and interpretation of test scores by explaining test score results in a way that teachers and parents can understand. When emergent bilingual (EB) educators receive reports back from publishing companies, it can be an overwhelming experience due to the large number of test scores presented. This chapter reminds the reader that all test scores are derived from one raw score and usually from a test given at one point in time. In addition to deconstructing the meaning of test scores, suggestions are also given on how to use test scores in appropriate ways.

As outlined by the American Educational Research Association (AERA), American Psychological Association (APA) and the National Council on Measurement in Education (NCME) (2014) in *The Standards for Educational and Psychological Testing*, the test development process is completed in four phases: (1) development of test specifications, (2) development, tryout and evaluation of items, (3) assembly and evaluation of new test forms and (4) development of procedures and materials for scoring and administration. One of the major differences in tests is whether they are norm referenced or criterion referenced. CRTs are more popular in schools today because the focus is now on evaluating how students perform against standards such as English language proficiency (ELP) or core standards (the standards are the criteria). Table 6.1 shows the differences and similarities between them.

What Exactly Does Standardized Mean?

Everything is standardized (the same) about the assessment: the items, the amount of time, the responses, the directions, etc. Typically, standardized tests consist of some combination of selected response (multiple choice or true/false, for example) and open response (short constructed response or extended constructed response) and usually standardized tests are given to a large group of students at the same time. Everything about the test is standardized, except of course the students. The illustration chosen to open this chapter demonstrates this idea in cartoon form.

Even though we usually discuss standardized assessments as large-scale NRTs or CRTs, the concept of standardization can apply to assessments that are alternatives to testing, such as oral presentations, observation checklists and journals. Most people see the strengths of standardized testing as being (1) they are an efficient way to assess things like achievement or language proficiency, (2) the fact that many students can be tested and scored in rapid time and/or (3) standardized assessments allow for large-scale comparisons.

Table 6.1 Similarities and differences between NRTs and CRTs

	NRT	*CRT*
Differences	Performance is determined based on comparison to peer group	Performance is determined based on comparison to standards
	The norm is a rank at the 50th percentile	Cut score determines the point between proficient and not proficient
	Half score above the 50th percentile and half score below	Theoretically, all students can meet the standard
	Half score above grade level and half score below	Theoretically, all students can meet the standard
Similarities	Standardized	Standardized
	Usually high stakes	Usually high stakes
	Linguistic complexity of items can introduce error for EBs	Linguistic complexity of items can introduce error for EBs
	EBs are expected to perform similarly to students who can read the test	EBs are expected to perform similarly to students who can read the test

What is the Difference between Norm-Referenced and Criterion-Referenced Scores?

An important basic property of assessment is whether it is characterized as norm referenced or criterion referenced. The biggest difference between NRT and CRT achievement testing is who or what the scores are compared to. With NRT scores, students' performances are compared to another group of students' performances to judge how well they learned (did they perform better or worse than other students?). The other group is known as the norming group (sometimes called the peer or cohort group). In CRT testing, students' performances are compared to a set of behaviors, usually standards (did they meet the standard or not?). Normative scores – scores derived from NRTs – are far easier to obtain and as a consequence have been historically the most popular.

Test Fairness

Fairness in testing is closely related to bias. After the 1960s, the topic of test fairness became more and more popular and is still growing. Many test designers are extremely concerned with test fairness, especially with groups of students with unique needs like EBs. When a test favors one group of students over another, there are test fairness concerns. The classic validity concern with NRT and EBs is the underrepresentation of EBs in the norming group. This means that when the test was designed, it was not 'tried out' with EBs to see if the test functioned in a similar way for EBs. This also means that the group of children chosen to compare scores with, 'the norm', includes an underrepresentation of EBs. These practices lead to comparing EBs to native English-speaking children; this will always lead to a low ranking of EBs. It is much more methodologically appropriate to compare EBs to

EBs; ideally, norming groups should consist of EBs. Now, test designers have become sensitive to norming-bias issues and use sophisticated measurement methods to construct fair norming groups and more articulated instruction about who should use their instruments. Unlike in the past, they now select large groups of children to participate in norming studies, including African American, white, Hispanic, Native American and Asian, as well as affluent, middle class, poor, urban, suburban and rural. Thus, test publishers develop various kinds of 'local norms' so that comparisons can be made with similar demographics.

AERA, APA, NCME (2014) views fairness as a fundamental validity issue that requires attention throughout all stages of test development and use. They also review two major concepts that have recently emerged to minimize bias and increase test fairness. The first concept is accessibility – the notion that all test takers should have an unobstructed opportunity to demonstrate their standing on the construct being measured (AERA, APA, NCME, 2014). The second new concept is universal design – an approach to test design that seeks to maximize accessibility for all intended examinees. Universal Design intends to reduce construct irrelevant variance (CIV) for examinees like EBs. A detailed discussion of Universal Design can be found in the 'Fairness in Testing' chapter of the *Standards* (AERA, APA, NCME, 2014: Part 1 Chapter 3).

Michale Zieky (2006) discusses how fairness reviews happen when designing tests. He gives six fairness review guidelines in the *Handbook for Test Development*. A more detailed discussion of fairness can be found in the *Handbook*.

(1) Treat people with respect.
(2) Minimize the effects of construct-irrelevant knowledge or skills.
(3) Avoid material that is unnecessarily controversial, inflammatory, offensive or upsetting.
(4) Use appropriate terminology to refer to people.
(5) Avoid stereotypes.
(6) Represent diversity in depictions of people.

Cut Scores

In test fairness, cut scores have become increasingly controversial because important educational decisions are made about EBs (and non-EBs alike) on this basis. Cut scores are often recommended by the test publisher, but oftentimes final determination is made by state departments of education. CRT is appealing to parents and teachers in general (especially those tired of NRTs) because it moves away from using one group of children as normal or standard; however, CRT design and valid implementation are not as easy as one might expect. Pitfalls include determining cut scores, specifying educational outcomes with enough clarity to measure them, using a limited range of behaviors to represent larger educational goals, the increased stakes associated with cut scores (graduating or not, advancing grade level or not, retaining teachers, closing schools, etc.) and accounting for the measurement error inherent in tests.

The process by which testing companies set proficiency levels (cut scores) for standards is largely based on judgment because test designers call upon teachers, instructional staff, community members and others to make judgments about how well students should perform on standards-based assessments. What exactly is the cut between being proficient at something or not? Imagine making the incredibly difficult judgment about when a student is proficient in a language and when she is not based on a number. Because language is a process, developmental and a continuum of growth, choosing a cut score for language proficiency tests is always questionable (and should be questioned!). These issues for CRTs have never been resolved; in fact, the need to resolve them has intensified as the sanctions for not passing CRTs have increased. Another inherent problem with CRTs is that educators often disagree about the quality of a given set of standards. Some state standards have been criticized for including too little or too much information, for being too difficult, for undermining local curriculum and instruction and for taking sides in political and educational controversies. That said, a CRT can only be as good as the standards it is trying to measure.

How Do I Know If a Test is Norm Referenced or Criterion Referenced?

The quickest way to tell whether a test is an NRT or a CRT is to review how the results are presented. If test scores are presented through grade equivalent (GE), percentile rank (PR) or any rank score, these are associated with norm-referencing – they are all used to compare test takers to one another. If the results are presented through some type of categorical scale (approaching, meeting or exceeding the standard), they are associated with criterion-referencing. However, the most thorough way to investigate a test is to read the test manual (sometimes called a blueprint) that must be made public and must thoroughly explain the test design, standards and theories used to design it, the test-construction principles and much more. The test manual contains detailed information and reading the technical test manual is the best way to understand if a test is based on norms or criteria.

How Should I Interpret Test Scores?

Raw score

A raw score is exactly what it implies – nothing has been done to it yet or it hasn't been 'cooked' yet. For example, if you scored 20/30 on an assessment, this is the raw score; you answered 20 items correctly and 10 items incorrectly. It is not ranked or compared to groups of children. Alone, the raw score has no independent meaning. It is not appropriate to compare across subjects or across grade level. It is an independent score and not very useful. All other scores are derived from the raw score. So, if it looks like a child has five scores, it is likely the child has one score (raw) and it is dressed in five different ways (see all test score types below).

Scale score

The scale score is derived from the raw score, and it links together all test forms (different forms for different grade levels) within one content area. Therefore, it is acceptable to compare across grade levels or other forms of the test with scale scores as long as you remain in the same content area. This score is useful if you want to study change in performance over time. As with a language proficiency test, it is appropriate to compare the scale score across three or more years to see how an EB is doing on English proficiency (as defined by the test). The drawback is that scaled scores cannot be compared across content areas or subjects. If you are interpreting a scale score from the ACCESS for English language learners (ELLs) language proficiency test from WIDA, there are separate scale scores for reading, writing, speaking and listening; a 380 in speaking does not necessarily mean the same thing as a 380 in writing. Of all the scores, scale scores are the best interpretation to show growth over time within the same area.

Proficiency Levels

Proficiency level scores are an interpretation of scale scores and they are a result of choosing a cut score for each level. Remember that proficiency levels are not set in stone; it is up to the test developers to determine them, which sometimes can be an arbitrary process. This is why proficiency levels for different tests are not comparable. For any test, you have to dig deep to find out how proficiency levels are determined; sometimes, this is too time-consuming and frustrating for EB educators. But for those who really want to know what proficiency levels mean, test companies must give an answer about what theory or conceptual framework was used to develop standards or proficiency levels and how cutoffs for levels were determined. Some companies are more forthcoming than others.

One issue of accessing this important information can be the denseness of reports. For example, the WIDA Technical Report #1 (185 pages total) on the development and field test of ACCESS for ELLs (2006) provides extensive information on the conceptualization of the assessment from standards to development. This report shows how standards were set (remember that proficiency levels are anchored in standards). Technical Report #4 (404 pages total) shows the background information about the cut scores that informed proficiency levels. The total number of pages in the technical reports is enough to scare any educator away because they usually run from 100-350 pages in length and as the name implies, are very technical. If persistent, you can find technical reports by visiting a website or calling a publishing company; according to the *Standards* (AERA, APA, NCME, 2014) technical reports should be accessible. WIDA makes their technical reports available online and annually. Just go to the WIDA website and type in technical report in the search engine https://www.wida.us/index.aspx.

If your state participates in WIDA (35 do), then the six WIDA language proficiency levels are important to you: (1) entering, (2) beginning, (3) developing, (4) expanding, (5) bridging and (6) reaching. As the results of testing, both parents and teachers receive bar graphs showing proficiency scores. Proficiency level scores for the ACCESS for ELLs test also have decimal points to show the proportion within that proficiency level. For example, 3.9 shows the student is almost a level 4; be aware, however, that these proportions are not equal from level to level because different levels of scale scores make up different levels. Therefore, a scale score for 350 in writing may be a performance level of 4.8 for writing, but a scale score of 350 in speaking may be 4.2. Unlike scale scores, proficiency levels may be used to make comparisons between domains. As you can see, with each interpretation, we get further away from the raw score.

Composite Scores

As the name implies, this is a score that combines the scale score of several domains, but with a weight to adjust for the difference in scaling by domain. The proficiency levels of composite scales are determined when scale scores from relevant domains are combined and weighted, then the scores are added together. On the ACCESS for ELLs test by WIDA, the comprehension score is calculated by 70% reading and 30% listening according to the following formula: (reading scale score×0.7)+(listening scale score×0.3)=comprehension scale score. Like non-composite domains, the scale score can lead to a proficiency level. They are intended to offer a variety of perspectives on student language development, but they may make test score interpretation more complicated than it needs to be. This author prefers not to use composite scores much because the results are too aggregated (combined).

Grade Level Equivalent

GEs are often misinterpreted, but are being used less and less. If a sixth grade student is learning English as her second language and she scores 3.5 GE on an NRT that was given to her in English, this could be interpreted in a variety of ways. First, the student may have systematic error caused by not fully knowing the language of the test. Therefore, it is difficult to make any judgments about how much content she actually knows. In this case, alternative assessments should be used to make educational and instructional decisions about the student.

Gerald Bracey (2002), in his book *Put to the Test*, decoded some of the myths around grade level equivalents:

Mischief often occurs when a child in, say, the fourth grade, brings home a test report declaring that she has a grade-equivalent in reading of 7. Why, the parents are likely to wonder, is my child not in seventh grade, at least for her reading, since she is reading at seventh-grade level. But she is *not* reading at seventh-grade level. The seventh-grade level for seventh-graders is the score that the average seventh-grader would score in seventh-grade material. When a fourth-grader gets a grade equivalent of 7 on a test, it represents what the average seventh-grader would score on fourth-grade reading material. Of course this would be true only if any seventh-graders had ever taken the fourth-grade test. But they haven't. Test publishers cannot afford too much out-of-grade testing, such as giving the fourth-grade test to seventh-graders. Mostly, they give the fourth-grade test to some sample of third-graders and fifth-graders. The projection of how a typical seventh-grader would score is a statistical extrapolation based on the scores of third-, fourth- and fifth-graders. We have no idea how valid it might be in reality.

In addition, GEs do not hold equal intervals – the distance between ranks can vary widely. A student who was ranked with a PR of 95 may have scored 625, whereas a student who ranked 94 may have scored 595 (a difference of 30). This will not hold equal interval because a student who scored a PR of 49 may have scored 450 and someone who was ranked 48 may have scored 449 (a difference of 1). Bracey (2002) uses the analogy of house addresses. In a rural area there might be long distances, perhaps a half-mile, between houses, yet the house numbers may be 6005 and 6007. In an urban area, however, house numbers 6005 and 6007 may be only a few feet apart. These house numbers (ordinal) do not hold equal interval and it would make no sense to average them or add them for any reason. Because GEs do not hold equal intervals, it is not appropriate to average them; newspaper writers sometimes do this and it can be very misleading. The GE test score is more misunderstood than it is useful, and therefore it is discouraged for use with students in general.

Percentile Rank (PR)

PR tells where a student stands in regard to other students. PR is similar to GE because PRs are related to the normal curve and NRTs. Most people think that if a student learning English as his or her second language receives a PR of 51, he or she performed better than 51% of the students at his or her school or the students in the nation who took the test that year. However, this is not correct. The norming group is ranked from 1 to 100, and the student is compared to the norming group. Since most norming groups are made up of native English-speaking students, who have the advantage of knowing the language of the test, EBs will almost always rank low. Like GEs above, PRs do not hold equal intervals and because of that should not be averaged.

Normal Curve Equivalents (NCE)

Like the GE and the PR, the NCE is related to the normal curve and NRTs and it carries with it the same inherent concerns. This score was designed to correct for the lack of equal intervals in GE and PR, but the only way to interpret NCE in a meaningful way is to have a normal curve line graph accessible and compare the PR scale to the NCE scale. Rarely do EB educators have the chart in front of them to use this test score. Conceptually, this score can be used to average and often researchers will use NCEs in effectiveness studies.

Are Tests Objective?

Standardized tests are typically promoted as more objective than classroom assessments, but there are many aspects of standardized tests subject to human error aside from scoring, when done by a programmed machine. How to use test results, how items are worded, what items to include on the test, which answers are correct and how the test is administered are all susceptible to human subjectivity as well as human error.

In addition, the increased demand for and quantity of testing required under No Child Left Behind (NCLB) placed an unprecedented strain on the capacity of testing manufacturers. This at times led to an increase in the number of wide-scale errors affecting the lives of hundreds of thousands of children (Torrent of Testing Errors, www.fairtest.org/torrent-testing-errors). In 2003, the Harcourt Assessment Company had to apologize for 45 flaws on the Hawaii state test, which was given to thousands of Hawaiian students. That same year, Harcourt made a series of expensive mistakes in Nevada (including mistakenly informing 736 high school sophomores that they had failed the math test) for which the state fined Harcourt $425,000. In Connecticut, CTB/McGraw Hill needed to hire additional workers to re-score student writing on the Connecticut mastery test to rescue their $48 million contract with the state department of education. There's more. Minnesota denied diplomas to 8000 students based on testing errors. In Illinois, 400 public schools were labeled as failures when they actually had met federal standards in 2003. Table 6.2 shows a sample of newspaper headlines regarding test construction error, as found on FairTest.org.

Table 6.2 A sample of news headlines about widespread test error

$3 Million Settlement for SAT Scoring Error
Florida Test Scoring Error Highlights Exam Flaws
Suits Filed over Teacher Test Scoring Error
GMAT Error Hurts Applicants: Test Takers Not Told of Mistake for 10 Months
Minnesota Students Win Lawsuit
ETS Pays $11.1 Million to Settle Teacher Test Lawsuit
N.C. Lawsuit Charges Test
Seventy Percent of Schools to Fail

(Headlines from FairTest.org)

Snapshot: Hasty Mistakes Erode Public Trust

In New York State, after complaints about the spring 2012 tests, Pearson deleted at least 29 items due to errors such as confusing terminology (such as 'median' confused with 'mean'), negative signs becoming positive signs and so forth. In addition to fundamental errors, many typos were found. Needless to say, this experience eroded public support for using test scores for accountability and cast severe doubt on using test scores to evaluate teachers. However, a panel of experts deemed that using these test scores was still valid. Negative public response, as reflected in many blogs, was directed at Pearson for being so careless and at New York State for contracting with Pearson and using test scores with known flaws to evaluate teachers. One blog response to an article about the errors read, 'You mean to tell me you make $32 million dollars on New York tests, and you can't afford to hire a proofreader?' As a consequence, in 2015, New York cancelled its contract with Pearson, as did many other states.

Discussion questions

- Why do you think large publishing companies such as Pearson made mistakes such as these?
- What are the consequences of these mistakes?
- What can educators do to protect against these types of errors?

Snapshot: The Pineapple Debacle

In an Old Danish fairy tale, an emperor is duped into buying 'magic' cloth that only some people can see. Believing the cloth to be real, the emperor marches in a procession completely naked; but only a small child has the courage to state that the emperor has no clothes. The phrase has come to symbolize an obvious political truth that is still denied by a majority of people. In the world of high-stakes testing, the phrase 'a pineapple has no sleeves' has much of the same meaning and is now used as a rallying cry by the anti-testing movement to symbolize the over-reliance on high-stakes tests.

The roots of the phrase date back to roughly 2007, when a nonsensical passage written by the author Daniel Pinkwater began to appear on English language arts (ELA) tests from the Pearson Corporation. Because test items were withheld from the public and researchers, backlash was restricted to word of mouth. This changed in 2012 when New York State students began to discuss the ELA passage on Facebook and Twitter and almost overnight the news went viral. Teachers and parents were outraged; student reaction ranged from laughter to anger to disbelief and the whole affair came to be known as 'Pineapplegate'. Years later, it still serves as an embarrassment to Pearson and New York State education officials.

The passage itself is a parody of Aesop's famous 'Tortoise and the Hare' fable, but this time the hare races a pineapple. Other animals are worried that the pineapple might have a trick up its sleeve to win, but predictably the pineapple cannot move and the hare wins the race. The animals then eat the pineapple. Students were required to answer six follow-up questions, two of which were impossible to answer correctly based solely on the given passage. Those two questions were:

(1) The animals ate the pineapple most likely because they were: (a) hungry; (b) excited; (c) annoyed; (d) amused.
(2) Which animal spoke the wisest words? (a) the hare; (b) the moose; (c) the crow; (d) the owl.

The story went viral and was covered by national news outlets such as the *Washington Post*, the *New York Times* and the *Wall Street Journal*. Pinkwater, the person who wrote the passage, was 'baffled' that his passage was used in such a way, telling the *Wall Street Journal* that his story was 'nonsense on top of nonsense on top of nonsense'.

(Continued)

Pearson refused to comment on the item, citing company policy. In the wake of the controversy, then New York Education Commissioner John King decided to exclude the item from the test results; he stated that the passage was reviewed by a committee of teachers and was chosen to compare New York students to students in other states who were presented with the same item. He argued that the test itself was still valid, despite the discarded item. Teachers and administrators grew more alarmed and frightened that 20% of their effectiveness would be judged on such tests and test items with little regard for checks and balances. Parents were dismayed that an item such as the pineapple question could be used to make important educational decisions about their child. The fact that the item had appeared on high-stakes tests dating back at least five years seemed to be a stunning indictment of the entire test development system.

Discussion questions

- Why didn't the committee of reviewers catch this item?
- What sort of checks and balances are in place to ensure high-quality items for high-stakes tests?
- How do you think EBs negotiate items such as the pineapple item?
- How can EB educators be assured that the test scores being used for high stakes, such as promotions or determining teacher effectiveness, are valid data?

End-of-Chapter Activities (Instructors: see advice at the end of the book)

After completing Activities 1 and 2, the reader will be able to:

(1) Interpret test scores from language proficiency test results.
(2) Identify nine key terms in psychometrics.

Activity 1

Interpret test scores from language proficiency test results.
Read the chapter and interpret Table 6.3 to answer the following questions.

(1) What are scale scores?
(2) What are proficiency levels?
(3) Which scores are composite and which are not? What are the composite scores made of? What are composite scores? Do you think composite scores help or hinder what you know about a student's language proficiency? How might you use composite scores?
(4) What are some overall trends you see in the data?
(5) How is Orlanny doing?
(6) How is Edwin doing?
(7) How is Leomar doing?

(Continued)

Table 6.3 Simulated 2012 student roster report from ACCESS for ELLs[1] English language proficiency test

Student, year	Tier	Cluster	Listening		Speaking		Reading		Writing		Oral language[2]		Literacy[3]		Comprehension[4]		Overall[5]	
			Scale score	Prof level	Scale score	Prof level	Scale score	Prof level	Scale score	Prof level	Scale score	Prof level	Scale score	Prof level	Scale score	Prof level	Scale score	Prof level
Orlanny 2017	B	9-12	373	3.4	326	2.2	341	1.9	376	3.2	351	2.8	359	2.5	351	2.3	356	2.6
Orlanny 2016	A	9-12	266	1.7	347	2.8	384	4.0	375	3.2	307	1.9	380	3.4	349	2.3	358	2.7
Orlanny 2015	B	9-12	383	3.2	182	1.0	336	1.9	367	3.1	273	1.7	352	2.5	344	2.3	328	1.9
Edwin 2017	B	9-12	406	4.6	370	3.7	350	2.1	402	3.9	383	4.2	378	3.2	367	2.9	379	3.5
Edwin 2016	A	9-12	356	2.8	358	3.2	371	2.9	370	3.0	357	2.9	371	2.9	367	2.9	366	2.9
Edwin 2015	B	9-12	354	2.9	328	2.2	331	1.9	374	3.3	341	2.6	353	2.5	338	2.1	349	2.6
Leomar 2017	B	9-12	416	5.0	406	5.4	392	5.0	417	4.6	411	5.2	405	4.7	389	5.0	406	4.9
Leomar 2016	B	9-12	397	4.4	337	2.6	390	5.6	387	3.7	367	3.5	389	3.9	392	4.7	384	3.8
Leomar 2015	C	9-12	397	4.4	358	3.4	378	3.7	337	2.0	378	3.9	358	2.7	384	4.0	364	3.0

[1] ACCESS for ELLs® stands for *Assessing Comprehension and Communication in English State-to-State for English Language Learners*. It is a large-scale test that first and foremost addresses the English language development **standards** that form the core of the WIDA Consortium's approach to instructing and testing English language learners. **31 US states and territories** now belong to the WIDA Consortium.
[2] Oral language=50% listening+50% speaking.
[3] Literacy=50% reading+50% writing.
[4] Comprehension=30% listening+70% reading.
[5] Overall=15% listening, 15% speaking, 35% reading, 35% writing.

Activity 2

Identify nine key terms.

This is a game of bingo using key vocabulary words from the chapter. Please fold a piece of paper into nine equal parts (fold it into thirds, then fold it into thirds again). The instructor will write nine key vocabulary words on the board. Please write them in any of the squares (one word per square). After this, students should have different bingo boards. The difference between this bingo and traditional bingo is that the instructor will read the clue and students will have to find the key vocabulary word that matches it. After a match is found, cross out the whole square. Once a student has bingo (three across, down or diagonal), he or she shouts 'Bingo!' and the instructor will check the work.

References

AERA, APA, NCME (2014) *Standards for Educational and Psychological Testing.* Washington, DC: American Educational Research Association.

Bracey, G. (2002) *Put to the Test: An Educator's and Consumer's Guide to Standardized Testing.* Bloomington, IN: Phi Delta Kappa Intl Inc.

FairTest: The National Center for Fair and Open Testing (2004) Torrent of testing errors. See http://www.fairtest.org/torrent-testing-errors (accessed 13 October 2016).

WIDA ACCESS for ELLs interpretive guide for score reports: spring 2011. See www.wida.us/

WIDA technical reports. See www.wida.us

Zieky, M. (2006) Fairness review in assessment. In S. Downing and T. Haladyna (eds) *Handbook of Test Development* (pp. 359–376). Mahwah, NJ: Lawrence Erlbaum Associates.

Recommended reading

Copeland, G., Finley, S., Ferguson, C. and Alderete, K. (2000) *A Collection of Tools to Promote Instructional Coherence.* Activity 3: Clapping hands (pp. 22–28). Austin, TX: Southwest Educational Development Laboratory (SEDL).

This activity deepens understanding of psychometrics through participation in a simulation that physically demonstrates the difference between NRT and CRT and other unintended consequences of assessment. The author highly recommends administering the clapping hands activity on the first night of class. Whole-group activity.

MacSwan, J. and Mahoney, K. (2008) Academic bias in language testing: A construct validity critique of the OPT I Oral Grades K-6 Spanish Second Edition (IPT Spanish). *Journal of Educational Research and Policy Studies (JERPS)* 8 (2), 86–101.

Mahoney, K., Haladyna, T. and MacSwan, J. (2009) The need for multiple measures in reclassification decisions: A validity study of the Stanford English Language Proficiency Test (SELP). In J.S. Lee, T.G. Wiley and R.W. Rumberger (eds) *The Education of Language Minority Immigrants in the United States* (pp. 263–294). Bristol: Multilingual Matters.

7 Accommodations

Themes from Chapter 7

(1) We don't need accommodations if we create better assessments for emergent bilingual (EB) students.
(2) Many accommodations are permitted for EBs, but few of them have research to support that they work.
(3) Linguistic simplification is a promising accommodation.

Key Vocabulary

- Accommodations
- Direct linguistic support
- Error
- Indirect linguistic support
- Large-scale assessments
- Reliability
- Reliability coefficient
- Standard error of measurement (SEM)

PUMI Connection

This chapter questions the very foundation of PUMI. The reader is guided to question the concept of accommodations in general and, based on PUMI critical questions, especially in the area of U (Use), whether it is appropriate to even have accommodations. Students first – our students deserve better than tests that have been 'patched' in a wide variety and relatively inconsistent ways and then results are used as if they were 'valid'. The stakes are high for schools and teachers, and every aspect of PUMI, when it comes to accommodations, should be questioned.

This chapter also comes with a warning. Despite some high-quality research conducted on accommodations for EBs, EB educators and policymakers should be aware that accommodations alone cannot eliminate the gaps in achievement between EBs and non-EBs. We need to advocate for better assessments of EBs, not try to find ways to fix bad ones. The problem of less reliable test scores for EBs can be addressed if two things are done: (1) state departments of education specify, as part of their contracts with testing companies, that large numbers of EBs be included in any test blueprint; and (2) a large-scale reliability study proving an acceptable level of reliability (similar to that for native English speakers) be presented *before* any test is used to make important education decisions about EBs. Nobody wants to make educational decisions with unreliable data, and accommodations don't 'fix' reliability issues. The Standards for Educational and Psychological Testing (AERA, APA, NCME, 2014: 45) include important standards for test design related to reliability and EBs. Standard 2.11 states that 'Test publishers should provide estimates of reliability/precision as soon as feasible for each relevant subgroup for which the test is recommended'.

Two states have challenged the idea of using unreliable test scores for EBs in state-level courts, but without much success. In Pennsylvania, *Reading School District v. PA Department of Education* upheld the determination that it is not practical to administer tests in a child's native language (Elliot, 2011). In California (*Coachella Valley v. California*, 2007), a request by nine school districts to not use unreliable tests (Gándara & Baca, 2008) was denied because the state court said it did not have the authority to require the state education department to change its testing policy for EBs. Despite testimony from those who constructed the test saying that the test should NOT be used with EBs, the court still chose not to overrule the 'expertise' of the state department of education.

What Are Accommodations and Why Do We Have Them?

Accommodations are changes in the test process, in the test itself or in the test–response format. The goal of accommodations for EBs is to provide a fair opportunity for them to demonstrate what they know and what they can do and to make tests as fair for them as they are for native English-speaking students, but without giving EBs an advantage over students who do not receive accommodations. Accommodations are sometimes referred to as adaptations or modifications. Accommodations for EBs exist because large-scale assessments[1] were designed for English-speaking students and most often do not yield valid results for EBs.

It is important not to lose sight of this as we move through this chapter, because accommodations may not be able to 'fix', 'patch' or 'make up' for this fact.

Let's use the analogy of applying a small bandage to fix a very large wound. The bandage might cover the wound and make those at stake feel better – at least temporarily – but it will do very little to heal the wound. The best solution to the problem is to prevent future wounds from happening.

If EBs were invited to participate in larger numbers and during the initial stages of test design, there would be less need for accommodations. The usual approach in test development is to develop and field-test items for the intended audience. In the US, tests are mostly piloted with English-speaking students for whom language is less of a problem or no problem at all. Because the field tests of these items are usually done with small numbers of EBs, the items that become part of the blueprint are naturally above their language level, making it more difficult for them to access the content of the achievement test.

Large-scale assessments yield less valid results for EBs than they do for native English-speaking students for a variety of reasons. The first and easiest reason to understand is that access to meaning and understanding is dependent on knowledge of English. Thus, low language proficiency levels in English yield little access to meaning and understanding when only English is used.

Second, as mentioned above, EBs are typically not included or are underrepresented in pilot studies during test design. Pressure has escalated over the past two decades to make tests fairer and pilot studies have begun to include more culturally and linguistically diverse students; however, they still do not have enough EB representation, especially across proficiency levels. This matters because test items are designed and modified by the test makers based on the responses given during the pilot study. If the pilot study is conducted with *all* EBs, they will not respond well to items that do not meet their linguistic and cultural needs and those items will likely be thrown away, resulting in more appropriate instrumentation for EBs.

Finally, test-item writers typically do not take into account what is known about second language acquisition, especially language differentiation. To yield more valid results, assessments should include test items with language complexity appropriate to the student's level of second language acquisition. If you (a monolingual English speaker) take a mathematics test administered in Mandarin but do not speak or write Mandarin fluently, you likely will not be able to show what you know in mathematics; in fact, it will appear you know very little. Having the questions read to you (in Mandarin), giving you extra time or taking the test in a separate location will not make up for your lack of knowledge of Mandarin. Many accommodations are administered – like a bandage – to give the perception of test fairness. The commonly used accommodations just mentioned are not specifically designed for EBs with language needs; instead, many are borrowed from the field of special education.

Linguistic Modifications

A very promising accommodation thus far has been the *linguistic modification* of test items – simplifying or modifying the language of a test without changing the intended construct of the item. By reducing the language barriers to content-area tests, such as mathematics, both reliability and validity can increase. According to Abedi (2006), some linguistic features that may interfere with comprehension include word frequency and familiarity, word length, sentence length, voice of the verb phrase, length of the nominal and complex question phrases. These linguistic features may slow down the reader, make misinterpretation more likely and add to his or her cognitive load. Other linguistic features that may affect comprehension include comparative structures, prepositional phrases, sentence and discourse structure, subordinate clauses, conditional clauses, relative clauses, concrete versus abstract or impersonal presentations and negation (Table 7.1).

Table 7.1 demonstrates how to simplify the linguistic features of a test item without simplifying its content. To begin with, it is important to have a clear understanding of what part of the test item is content and what part is language (Chapter 5 showed an example of this). The accommodation should not make the content of the item any less challenging; a content-area teacher should review the item to assess whether the content has been changed. The list in Table 7.2 comes from a 1997 study conducted by Abedi and colleagues, which evaluated the linguistic complexity of 69 NAEP math items for 8th-grade students. Of the 69, some items were flagged as being potentially difficult for students to understand, and their linguistic features were analyzed (Abedi *et al.*, 1997). The list is original, and not exhaustive, as newer test items are analyzed, linguistic features may be added.

Table 7.1 Linguistic features that may affect comprehension

Linguistic feature	Short explanation*
Word frequency and familiarity	Words that are encountered more often are interpreted quickly and correctly
Word length	Longer words are more likely to be morphologically complex
Sentence length	Sentence length serves as an index for syntactic complexity
Voice of verb phrase	People find passive voice constructions more difficult to process than active
Length of nominals	Noun phrases with several modifiers are difficult
Complex question phrases	Potential source of difficulty
Comparative structures	Potential source of difficulty
Prepositional phrases	Interpretation of prepositions is difficult
Sentence and discourse structure	Some sentence structures are more syntactically complex
Subordinate, conditional and relative clauses	Contributes to complexity
Concrete vs. abstract or impersonal presentations	Better performance when problem statements are concrete
Negation	Terms like *no, not, none, never* are difficult to comprehend

*See Abedi (2006) for more in-depth explanation.

Table 7.2 Original and revised test items based on linguistic complexity

	Original	Revised
Familiarity/frequency of non-math vocabulary	A certain reference file contains approximately 6 billion facts.	Mack's company sold 6 billion hamburgers.
	Census	*Video game*
Voice of verb phrase	A sample of 25 was selected.	He selected a sample of 25.
	The weight of three objects was compared.	Sandra compared the weights of three rabbits.
Length of nominals	Last year's class vice president.	Vice president.
	The pattern of puppy's weight gain.	The pattern above.
Clauses	A report that contains 64 sheets of paper for each report.	He needs 64 sheets of paper for each report.
	If two batteries in the sample were found to be dead.	He found three broken pencils in the sample.
Complex question phrases	At which of the following times	When
	Which is the best approximation of the number	Approximately how many
Concrete vs. abstract or impersonal presentations	The weights of three objects were compared using a pan balance. Two comparisons were made.	Sandra compared the weights of three objects using a pan balance. She made two comparisons.

From Abedi *et al.* (1997) and Abedi (2006).

Solano-Flores (2010) investigated using a sociolinguistic approach to linguistic modification of tests and reported positive findings. Solano-Flores approaches the topic of assessment through a culturally relevant lens, much like culturally relevant instruction. Culturally relevant assessment is viewed by some as a promising assessment accommodation. Strategies include incorporating the characteristics of how languages are used at school sites and also adopting local dialects for use in tests. This approach takes into account the variation in language use across groups of EBs.

State Assessment Policies Addressing Accommodations

According to No Child Left Behind (NCLB) and the current Every Student Succeeds Act (ESSA), EBs must be assessed in a 'valid and reliable' manner and through the use of 'reasonable accommodations'. These accommodations could include 'to the extent practicable, assessments in the language and form most likely to yield accurate data on what students know and can do in academic content areas, until such students have achieved English language proficiency'.

Around the time NCLB was passed, Rivera and Collum (2004) launched a research study to investigate policies related to testing accommodations across the US. They found that in most cases, policies focused on two student groups, EBs and students with disabilities (SWD), with some states treating the two groups together. Of the 75 accommodations listed in state policies, 44 of them were relevant to EBs and 31 relevant only to SWDs. After analyzing 51[2] state policies, Rivera and Collum identified the ways in which states determine whether an EB was eligible for accommodations: level of language proficiency (language related), length of time in English-medium academic environment (time related), achievement and prior schooling level (academic related) and judgment of school personnel and/or family (opinion related) (Rivera & Collum, 2004). This flexibility, of course, was changed upon the implementation of NCLB.

The borrowing of accommodations from the field of special education led Rivera and Collum to suggest linking accommodations more closely with the actual linguistic needs of EBs and the available research on second language acquisition. To articulate the accommodations further, they also suggested placing the 75 accommodations in two categories: *direct linguistic support* and *indirect linguistic support*. Linguistic support includes accommodations such as translation of the test into the native language, simplification of the English language or test language and repetition of the test language; indirect linguistic support includes accommodations such as adjustments to time, schedules or environment.

In 2008, Shafer Willner *et al.* published a descriptive report identifying the 10 most commonly used test accommodations for EBs as recommended by state policies (Table 7.3). Shortly afterward, these authors published a guide for states to provide general guidance on state accommodation policies and how to make them more responsive to EBs. For example, they distinguished between accommodations for EBs and those for SWDs (Rivera *et al.*, 2008).

Table 7.3 Ten most commonly used test accommodations for EBs as recommended by state policy

Use of dual-language dictionary
Extended time
Reading items aloud
Translating direction orally into native language
Clarifying/explaining directions in English
Repeating directions
Reading direction aloud
Allowing student to respond orally in English and describing responses
Clarifying/explaining directions in the native language
Simplifying directions

Shafer Willner *et al.* (2008).

What Does the Research Say?

As mentioned above, states' policies list 75 accommodations to be used with EBs. What we don't know is whether these accommodations actually work, with which students and under what conditions. The larger question is: do accommodations adequately satisfy the legal demands of ESSA to provide valid and reliable assessments for EBs?

The most credible results dealing with accommodations for EBs come from research studies that examine the effects of accommodations one at a time, set up the study as an intentional experiment (as opposed to studying existing data from mandatory testing and looking for trends) and experiment with both EBs and non-EBs to help pinpoint the accommodations that will actually level the playing field between the two groups instead of increasing scores for everyone.[3] Although 75 accommodations are represented in policy, only a few are often studied: (1) testing in the native language or in English with translation (Abedi et al., 1998; Miller et al., 1999); (2) testing in modified English (Abedi & Lord, 2001; Abedi et al., 1998, 2000a; Miller et al., 1999); (3) providing published dictionaries (Miller et al., 1999); and (4) providing a glossary and/or custom dictionary (Abedi et al., 2000a, 2000b).

Jamal Abedi, a US leader in accommodation research, has dedicated much of his career to designing empirical studies with large samples of students to investigate the validity, effectiveness and feasibility of the growing number of accommodations, many of which are already written into state policies. His research studies usually offer the accommodation to both EB and non-EB subgroups in a randomized sample (Abedi et al., 2004). Abedi's research differs from many accommodation studies due to the experimental nature of his research designs. Other studies have investigated the effectiveness of accommodations using large-scale databases, but their research design does not randomly assign EBs to different forms of accommodation and the non-EB group does not receive an accommodation. If the non-EB group does not receive an accommodation as treatment in an experimental research design, we will never know how the accommodation may have affected them. The experimental nature of Abedi's research designs gives his studies an edge over other studies in drawing significant conclusions about the effectiveness of accommodations.

For an accommodation to 'work' for EBs, some would say that it should increase the validity of the test scores for EBs while not affecting the scores for non-EBs. It should not be forgotten, though, that language can be an issue for non-EBs as well. Since Abedi's studies are largely experimental research designs, they usually include a non-EB comparison group. For some non-EBs – for example, native English speakers who struggle with literacy – reducing the linguistic complexity or using other language-based accommodations may work equally well. Technically, if an accommodation increases scores for non-EB and EB groups alike, it is not an effective accommodation for EBs but it is an effective accommodation for all students. Most EB educators, and members of the general public for that matter, would not argue with increasing the validity of test scores for all students.

Around the time NCLB was proposed, Abedi and his colleagues were conducting research at the National Center for Research on Evaluation, Standards and Student Testing (NCCREST) to investigate the validity and reliability of test scores for EBs and the hypothesis that the linguistic complexity of test items may introduce error to test scores, thus decreasing their validity. These studies (Abedi, 2002; Abedi & Lord, 2001; Abedi *et al.*, 2000a) concluded that test scores for EBs are substantially lower than the scores for native English-speaking students in all subject areas; the linguistic complexity of test items may threaten the validity of test scores; and as the language demands of individual test items decrease, the performance gap between EBs and native English-speaking students diminishes. In test items where the language demands were minimal, the gap between native English-speaking students and EBs essentially disappeared.

Several large evaluative studies have been conducted on this topic. Rivera and Collum (2004) reviewed 15 high-quality research studies and concluded that two accommodations hold promise for EBs: *native-language versions of assessments* and *linguistic simplification*[4] *of English versions,* along with combining some indirect and direct linguistic support accommodations such as bilingual glossaries and extra time. Francis *et al.* (2006) outlined best practice, and Pennock-Roman and Rivera (2011) conducted a meta-analysis of 14 studies showing large effect sizes for extra time and computer-administered glossaries, smaller effects for plain English and very sizable effects (1.45) for Spanish test versions. A recent Smarter Balanced Assessment Consortium report led by Abedi and Ewers (2013) recommended several accommodations for EBs based on its research results[5] (Table 7.4). All the accommodations listed met five conditions (effective, valid, differential impact, relevance and feasible).

Table 7.4 Recommended accommodations based on research results

Read-aloud of test directions in student's native language
Picture dictionary (alone, combined with oral reading of test items in English and combined with bilingual glossary)
Test in a familiar environment with other EBs
Traditional glossary with Spanish translations and extra time (content-related terms removed)
Bilingual dictionary

Abedi and Ewers (2013).

Additional accommodations that work for both EBs and non-EBs are not shown in Table 7.4. For example, computer testing shows evidence of validity and effectiveness but may not be feasible for most schools due to the need for one computer per student during large-scale testing time. Abedi (2009) conducted a study that tested the computerized administration of a math test with a pop-up glossary. This feature provided a simple gloss of a word with the touch of a mouse, thereby providing access to non-math words that EBs typically struggle with. Abedi was able to document that EBs spent more time glossing. Therefore, an appropriate accommodation – should your school have computer-testing capabilities for EBs – is to provide the computer-based pop-up glossary combined with extra time.

A recent report from the Center on Instruction (Kieffer *et al.*, 2012) is a refreshing alternative to the laundry list of accommodations that work with EBs. It provides recommendations for accommodations practice based on the results of research; these are shown, in order of importance, in Table 7.5.

Table 7.5 Recommendations for using accommodations for EBs

(1)	Use simplified English in test design, eliminating irrelevant language demands for all students.
(2)	Provide English dictionaries/glossaries to EBs.
(3)	Match the language of tests and accommodations to the language of instruction.
(4)	Provide extended time to EBs or use untimed tests for all students.

Kieffer *et al.* (2012).

A State Example

Each state in the US also has its own list of acceptable accommodations. For example, the New York State Policy on Accommodations guides schools to use 'testing accommodations that may be provided to Limited English Proficient / English Language Learners (LEP/ELLs)'. Note that this appears to be a suggestion and not a directive because of the phrase 'may be provided'. This allows individual school principals and teachers to decide which acceptable accommodations, if any, should be used; the result is a wide variety being employed across districts and schools. In my experience with schools in New York, when I ask about their use of accommodations for EBs, some schools are unaware of the list, some decide to use no accommodations and some use accommodations in different ways. Acceptable accommodations in New York State include time extension, separate location, third reading of listening selection, bilingual dictionaries and glossaries (definitions or explanations not permitted), simultaneous use of English and alternative-language editions, oral translation for lower-incidence languages and writing responses in the EB's native language (Table 7.6).

Nearly all of the research on accommodations focuses exclusively on what works (generalized broadly), but other important questions are ignored. Should we spend time and money researching what accommodations work best instead of using the money to improve the design of tests for EBs? Are all these accommodations equally comparable? How do we control for or even determine whether popular accommodations have parallel effects and are interchangeable in test use?

Despite what looks like a lot of research, even simple questions about accommodations remain unanswered. Should states even use accommodated test scores before we know more answers? Is it legal/ethical to use accommodated test scores to satisfy the accountability policies and laws? Should accommodated test scores be used to evaluate teachers? Even before NCLB was written, Shepard *et al.* (1998) raised a number of similar important questions: Can accommodated test results be combined with non-accommodated test results, or should the test score be flagged as 'accommodated'? Will accommodated test scores be used differently from non-accommodated scores? Does the use of accommodations imply a breakdown of the concept of standardization? How does the use of accommodations affect the construct being measured? With a higher-stakes environment currently in place for the assessment of EBs, these questions have become even more important. A concern among EB educators is whether the test scores for EBs are less reliable than those of non-EBs. The next section discusses the topic of reliability in detail.

Table 7.6 New York state policy on accommodations

The following accommodations are acceptable to the New York State Department of Education and may be provided to EBs.

Accommodation	NYS policy	Considerations for implementation
Time extension	Schools may extend the test time for EBs taking state examinations. Principals may use any reasonable extensions, such as 'time and a half' (the required testing time plus half that amount), in accordance with their best judgment about the needs of the EBs. Principals should consult with the student's classroom teacher in making these determinations.	Inexpensive. No changes to test necessary. Doesn't close gap because all students do better with extra time.
Separate location	Schools are required to provide optimal testing environments and facilities for all students. They may administer examinations to EBs individually or in small groups in a separate location.	
Third reading of listening selection	Proctors may read the listening passage of the Grades 3–8 English Language Arts Tests or the Regents Comprehensive Examination in English a third time to EBs. This accommodation is not permitted in state examinations in foreign languages such as the Regents Comprehensive Examination in Spanish.	
Bilingual dictionaries and glossaries	EBs may use bilingual dictionaries and glossaries when taking all state examinations with the exception of the Second Language Proficiency Examinations, Regents Comprehensive Examinations in foreign languages and the Regents Competency Tests (RCTs) in Reading and Writing. The bilingual dictionaries and glossaries may provide only direct translations of words; definitions or explanations are *not* permitted. No student may use an English-language dictionary when taking any state examination.	If this includes definitions or simple paraphrases of potentially unfamiliar or difficult words, it is effective for EBs. If it does not, then it is not effective.
Simultaneous use of English and alternative-language editions	When taking state examinations for which the department provides written translations, EBs may use both English and an alternative-language edition of the test simultaneously. However, they must be instructed to record all of their responses in only one of the two editions. The alternative-language edition used by the student should be so indicated on the student's answer sheet. Because the alternative-language editions of the RCTs are not direct translations of the English-language editions, students *may not* be given both.	Difficulty maintaining construct equivalence. Often misaligned with language of instruction. Expensive.

Oral translation for lower-incidence languages	Schools may provide EBs with an oral translation of a state examination when there is no translated edition provided by the department. This accommodation is permitted for state examinations in all subjects except English and foreign languages. All translations must be oral, direct translations of the English editions; written translations are *not* allowed. No clarifications or explanations may be provided. Translators may be provided with copies of the English edition of the tests no earlier than one hour prior to administration to become familiar with the material. Translators who also serve as proctors must be familiar with the procedures for administering state examinations. Principals must take the necessary precautions to ensure that the examinations are properly administered and that the students receiving translation services are not given an unfair advantage.
Writing responses in the native language	EBs making use of alternative-language editions or oral translations of state examinations may write their responses to the open-ended questions in their native language. Scoring the tests is the responsibility of the school.

What is Reliability?

Reliability is measured as a coefficient (a number between 0 and 1), which informs us empirically of how much contamination (or error) is part of the overall test score. No test is 100% reliable, but technically sound tests have a reliability coefficient of 0.85 or higher, indicating that at least 85% of the test score is due to actual achievement (for example); the other 15% is due to measurement errors, which for EBs usually take the form of language factors. For example, in one large study (sample size approximately 200,000) conducted by Abedi, reliability coefficients were consistently higher for fluent English proficient (FEP) students than for limited English proficient (LEP) students. In reading, the coefficient was 0.86 for FEPs and 0.75 for LEPs; in math, 0.90 for FEPs and 0.80 for LEPs; in language, 0.80 for FEPs and 0.68 for LEPs; and in science, 0.78 for FEPs and 0.53 for LEPs (Abedi *et al.*, 2004). This means, for example, that 22% of the science test score for FEPS is due to error and 47% of the test score for EBs is due to error! These coefficients are very revealing about how (un)reliable the data really are.

Contamination or error in test scores can be caused by guessing, subjective scoring of essays, unnecessarily complex language, fatigue, nervousness and other factors. Figure 7.1 shows drawings by two EB elementary students illustrating how they felt about the AIMS (an Arizona high-stakes test). The first drawing shows how nervous the student was; the second shows other negative factors known to not only affect the test score but also the student's attitude toward school in general (stressed out, bored, sleepy, being punished). These negative experiences are typically associated with deficit-oriented assessments and not with assessments that lead to promise (see Chapter 1 for this discussion).

Snapshot: How Far Can Clarissa Throw?

The track and field team has an event called the softball throw in which competitors throw a softball as far as they can. Clarissa feels she may be strong in this event; she doesn't really know how far she can throw, so she practices throwing 100 times. Since she consistently throws the softball between 80 and 90 feet, she knows that her true ability lies somewhere between these two distances. During one throw, her hands become sweaty, and the softball slips as she throws it. This causes her distance to be only 50 feet, clearly not her true ability. If Clarissa throws the ball 100 times and takes the average distance, then we can find out a very close estimate to her 'true' distance. If the softball slips, this is not a good measure of the 'true' distance she can throw. If she only throws once, it may not be a reliable (or consistent measure). The same applies to test scores. We would never ask a child to take a test 100 times, but if we did, we could take the average and find out a very good estimate of his or her 'true' score. Test scores are never 100% reliable, and the test scores for EBs are much less reliable than those for non-EBs.

Discussion questions

*   How does throwing a softball relate to taking a test?
*   Why are EB test scores less reliable than those for non-EBs?

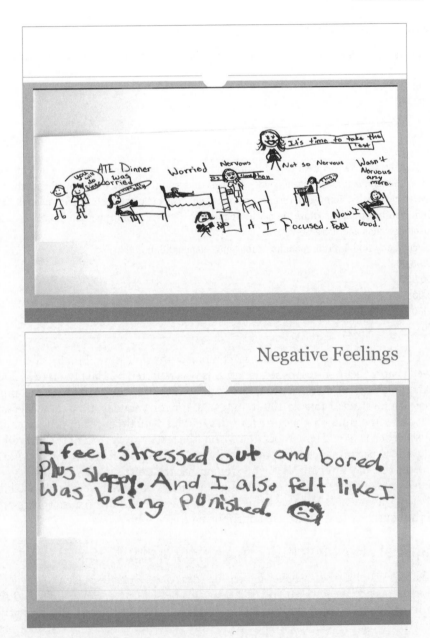

Figure 7.1 Two drawings by EB elementary students[6] in response to a high-stakes test

A topic almost never mentioned by researchers but well known by EB educators is the fact that EBs omit items and 'give up' toward the end of the test more than non-EBs. Those omissions are counted as incorrect answers, but in reality they are signs of difficulty in understanding the language of a test, lack of time to take a test or fatigue

Table 7.7 Unnecessary linguistic complexity in a mathematics item

A certain reference file contains approximately 6 billion facts. About how many millions is that?
A. 6,000,000
B. 600,000
C. 60,000
D. 6,000
E. 600

The test makers chose this item to see if the student knows how many millions are in 6 billion. However, the language of the item is very complex and may cause EBs who know the math to answer incorrectly. Terms like *certain, reference, approximately* and *facts* are not needed to measure whether students know the math. Abedi *et al.* (2003) reword the math item to reduce language demands and increase validity.

Mack's company sold 6 billion pencils. About how many million is that?
A. 6,000,000
B. 600,000
C. 60,000
D. 6,000
E. 600

from cognitive and linguistic overload combined with pressure. Empirical evidence showed that higher non-response rate for EBs was reported by Haladyna *et al.* (2003).

The reliability of a test score refers to how *consistent* the score is. For example, suppose an EB student takes a 100-item test at 1pm on Monday, then takes the same test at the same time for the next four days. (This would never happen, of course, because he or she would remember items from the test or grow tired of the test, which would affect performance.) Hypothetically, no learning or forgetting has occurred during the one-day intervals. If the EB student has the exact same score each day, this score *is* very consistent or very reliable and as such will have a very high reliability coefficient – close to 1. However, this rarely happens with EBs because things other than the construct (e.g. math) are contributing to the score.

Snapshot: How Much Do You Really Weigh?

Rose is watching her weight, and she decides to weigh herself often to see if she loses or gains any weight. On Friday, she weighs herself on her home scale, and she weighs 143 pounds. While visiting her mother later that day, she weighs herself on her mother's scale and she weighs 139. Before swimming laps at the school pool the next morning, she weighs herself on the locker room scale and she weighs 140. Although Rose prefers the results of her mother's scale, she wonders how much she really weighs. The scale in this analogy is like an achievement test, or instrument. The instrument intends to measure the construct – in this case, 'weight' or with a test in school, 'achievement'. Like tests used in schools, no scale is perfectly reliable; if Rose averages all three weights, she may have a closer idea of what her 'true' weight is.

Discussion questions

- How does weighing yourself relate to taking a test?
- Why would different tests (measuring the same thing) produce different results?

Standard Error of Measurement (SEM)

SEM represents the range of a test's accuracy. A standard procedure for testing companies is to include empirical evidence about the reliability coefficient and the SEM in the technical manual. However, technical manuals are difficult to obtain and difficult to read; therefore, the reliability coefficient for EBs remains largely unknown among educators.

End-of-Chapter Activities (Instructors: see advice at the end of the book)

After completing Activities 1–3, the reader will be able to:

(1) Identify nine commonly used accommodations for EBs.
(2) Answer essential questions about reliability.
(3) Apply the concept of linguistic simplification (an effective accommodation) to an item.

Activity 1

Identify nine commonly used accommodations for EBs.

This is a game of bingo using 9 of the 10 most commonly used accommodations in state policies learned in this chapter. Fold a piece of paper into nine equal parts (fold it into thirds, then fold it into thirds again). The instructor writes nine commonly used accommodations on the board. Write them in any of the squares – one word per square. After this, each student should have a different bingo board. The instructor 'performs' the accommodations so the class can guess what each one is. After a match is found, cross out the whole square. Once a student has bingo (three across, down or diagonal), he or she shouts 'bingo!' and the instructor checks the work, and asks for a student explanation.

Activity 2

Answer essential questions about reliability.

Do Inside/Outside Circle. Half of the students are given an index card with one of the questions below written on it and the answer written on the back. Students with the questions form a small circle facing outward, and those without index cards form a circle facing the inner circle. Each student must face another student to state the definition of the term *or* the term when the definition is given. The outside circle rotates clockwise until each student has had a chance to go. After every student in the outside circle has had a chance, the outside circle switches with the inside circle (which always has the card) and the activity is repeated.

(Continued)

---

(1) What is reliability?
(2) How is reliability connected to accommodations?
(3) If a reliability coefficient is 0.70, what does that mean?
(4) Can accommodations close the achievement gap?
(5) What does it mean if a test has an SEM of 3 points?
(6) What is linguistic simplification?
(7) Give two other names for test score error.
(8) Name three common causes of error for EBs.

Activity 3

Take a math test item and simplify it linguistically.

In small groups (four or fewer), students rewrite the following math item using simplified English. They should focus on how they can simplify the language without affecting the math. Each group names three linguistic features of the changes that they made. After 20 minutes, the groups post their new items in front of the room and prepare to make a short presentation to the class. (This activity is adapted from Abedi et al., 2004)

If __ represents the number of newspapers that Lee delivers each day, which of the following represents the total number of newspapers that Lee delivers in 5 days?

a.   5+__
b.   5×__
c.   __+5
d.   (__+__)×5

Notes

(1) In general, this chapter discusses accommodations for achievement tests given to EBs, not including English language arts (ELA) or other language-related tests which typically do not allow for these types of accommodations. Most state policies prohibit the use of accommodations on ELA tests because they would jeopardize the construct.
(2) Washington, DC was treated as a state for the purposes of this analysis.
(3) Most educators do not oppose making tests fairer for everyone and welcome suggestions in how to do so. However, the quest to find a valid, effective and feasible accommodation for EBs dictates that the performance of non-EBs should be relatively unaffected by the accommodation while improving the performance (and reliability) of the scores of EBs.
(4) After reviewing the idea of linguistic simplification at a teacher workshop in Buffalo, my colleague Dr Erin Kearney introduced a term to describe what is happening in this process which this author likes better, linguistic clarification. Linguistic clarification does not indicate simplifying anything but rather clarifying a rather uncommon register, otherwise known as the language of testing.
(5) 'Recommended based on research results' refers to the results of several studies, plus a thorough review from experts in this field which has deemed the accommodation promising with little or no risk of altering the construct.

(6)   These drawings are part of an unpublished study to explore the feelings of EBs taking achievement tests in English in a restricted language policy state (Arizona). Mahoney, K., Mahoney, A., and Rossi, R. (unpublished).

References

Abedi, J. (2002) Standardized achievement tests and English language learners: Psychometric issues. *Educational Assessment* 8 (3), 231–257.

Abedi, J. (2006) Language issues in item development. In T. Haladyna and S. Downing (eds) *Handbook of Test Development* (pp. 377–398). New York: Routledge.

Abedi, J. (2009) Computer testing as a form of accommodation for English language learners. *Educational Assessment* 14 (3–4), 195–211.

Abedi, J. and Lord, C. (2001) The language factor in mathematics tests. *Applied Measurement in Education* 14 (3), 219–234.

Abedi, J. and Ewers, N. (2013) *Accommodations for English Language Learners and Students with Disabilities: A Research-Based Decision Algorithm*. Davis, CA: University of California, Smarter Balanced Assessment Consortium.

Abedi, J., Lord, C. and Plummer, J. (1997) Language Background as a Variable in NAEP Mathematics Performance (CSE Tech. Rep. No. 429). Los Angeles, CA: University of California, Center for the Study of Evaluation/National Center for Research on Evaluation, Standards, and Student Testing.

Abedi, J., Lord, C. and Hofstetter, C. (1998) Impact of Selected Background Variables on Students' NAEP Math Performance (CSE Tech. Rep. No. 478). Los Angeles, CA: University of California, Center for the Study of Evaluation/National Center for Research on Evaluation, Standards, and Student Testing.

Abedi, J., Lord, C., Hofstetter, C. and Baker, E. (2000a) Impact of accommodations strategies on English language learners' test performance. *Educational Measurement: Issues and Practice* 19 (3), 16–26.

Abedi, J., Lord, C., Kim, C. and Miyoshi, J. (2000b) The Effects of Accommodations on the Assessment of LEP Student in NAEP (CSE Tech. Rep. No. 537). Los Angeles, CA: University of California, Center for the Study of Evaluation/National Center for Research on Evaluation, Standards, and Student Testing.

Abedi, J., Hofstetter, C. and Lord, C. (2004) Assessment accommodations for English language learners: Implications for policy based empirical research. *Review of Educational Research* 74 (1), 1–28.

American Educational Research Association (AERA), American Psychological Association (APA) and the National Council on Measurement in Education (2014) *Standards for Educational and Psychological Testing*. Washington, DC: AERA.

Elliot, S. (2011) US legal issues in educational testing of special populations. In S.N. Elliott, R.J. Kettler, P.A. Beddow and A. Kurz (eds) *Handbook of Accessible Achievement Tests for All Students: Bridging the Gaps between Research, Practice, and Policy* (pp. 33–68). New York: Springer.

Francis, D.J., Rivera, M., Lesaux, N., Kieffer, M.J. and Rivera, H. (2007) *Practical Guidelines for the Education of English Language Learners: Research-Based Recommendations for the Use of Accommodations in Large-scale Assessments*. Portsmouth, NH: RMC Research Corporation. Center on Instruction. See http://www.centeroninstruction.org/practical-guidelines-for-the-education-of-english-language-learners-research-based-recommendations-for-the-use-of-accommodations-in-large-scale-assessments (accessed 13 October 2016).

Gándara, P. and Baca, G. (2008) NCLB and California's English language learners: The perfect storm. *Language Policy* 7, 201–216.

Haladyna, T.M., Osborn Popp, S. and Weiss, M. (2003) Non-response in large-scale assessment. Paper presented at the annual meeting of the American Educational Research Association, Montreal, Canada.

Kieffer, M., Rivera, M. and Francis, D. (2012) *Practical Guidelines for the Education of English Language Learners: Research-Based Recommendations for the Use of Accommodations in Large-Scale Assessments*. Portsmouth, NH: RMC Research Corporation. Center on Instruction. See http://

www.centeroninstruction.org/practical-guidelines-for-the-education-of-english-language-learners-research-based-recommendations-for-the-use-of-accommodations-in-large-scale-a-ssessments2012-update (accessed 13 October 2016).

Miller, E.R., Okum, I., Sinai, R. and Miller, K.S. (1999, April) A study of the English language readiness of limited English language readiness of limited English proficient students to participate in New Jersey's statewide assessment system. Paper presented at the annual meeting of the National Council on Measurement in Education, Montreal, Canada.

Pennock-Roman, M. and Rivera, C. (2011) Mean effects of test accommodations for ELLs and non-ELLs: A meta-analysis of experimental studies. *Educational Measurement: Issues and Practice* 30 (3), 10–28.

Rivera, C. and Collum, E. (2004) An analysis of state assessment policies addressing the accommodation of English language learners. Commissioned paper synopsis for the NAGB Conference on Increasing the Participation of SD and LEP Students in NAEP. Washington, DC: The George Washington University Center for Equity and Excellence in Education.

Rivera, C., Acosta, B. and Willner, L. (2008) *Guide for Refining State Assessment Policies for Accommodating EBs*. Washington, DC: The George Washington University Center for Equity and Excellence in Education.

Shafer Willner, L.S., Rivera, C. and Acosta, B.D. (2008) *Descriptive Study of State Assessment Policies for Accommodating English Language Learners*. Arlington, VA: The George Washington University Center for Equity and Excellence in Education. See http://files.eric.ed.gov/fulltext/ED539753.pdf (accessed 13 October 2016).

Shepard, L., Grace, T. and Betebenner, B. (1998) Inclusion of Limited-English-Proficient Students in Rhode Island's Grade 4 Mathematics Performance Assessment (CSE Tech. Rep. No. 486). Los Angeles, CA: University of California, Center for the Study of Evaluation/National Center for Research on Evaluation, Standards, and Student Testing.

Solano-Flores, G. (2010) Introduction and assessing the cultural validity of assessment practices. In M. Baserra, E. Trumbull and G. Solano-Flores (eds) *Cultural Validity in Assessment: Addressing Linguistic and Cultural Diversity* (pp. 3–21) (Language, Culture and Teaching Series). New York: Routledge.

Recommended reading

Zhao, Y. (2009) *Catching Up or Leading the Way: American Education in the Age of Globalization*. Alexandria, VA: ASCD.
Yong Zhao argues that more standardization, increased outcome-based accountability and testing only a few subjects will not prepare American youth for success in an age of globalization. The author does, however, recognize the strengths of American education, and thus puts forth a vision for American schools to promote creativity, talent and diversity, plus global and digital competencies. American schools should continue to lead the way, Zhao says, not play catch-up with other countries.

8 Special Education

Laura M. Geraci and Kate Mahoney

Themes from Chapter 8

(1) There is significant federal and state policy governing the assessment of students who may have special learning needs.

(2) Many challenges regarding the education of emergent bilinguals (EBs) with special needs hinge on assessment.

(3) It's difficult to disentangle speech or language impairment (SLI) from learning disabilities (LD) from second language acquisition (SLA).

(4) The dominant practice of assessment in special education supports a fractional view of EBs.

Key Vocabulary

- CLD (culturally and linguistically diverse)
- High incidence disabilities
- Curriculum-based measure (CBM)
- Disproportional representation

- Least restrictive environment
- Pre-referral
- Response to intervention (RtI)
- Special education
- Speech or language impairment (SLI)
- Learning disability (LD)

This chapter is included for teacher candidates who want to improve their knowledge of policies and practice in the field of special education. This chapter is included to serve as an introduction to assessment and policy related to special education. A large number of students are classified both as an EB and as a student with a disability (SWD). One of the biggest concerns in this field is whether some EBs are classified but shouldn't be (overrepresentation), or whether some EBs should be classified but are not (underrepresentation). Students who are both EBs and SWDs are entitled to the services mandated by law from both the EB classification and the special education classification. Some of the challenges professionals in this field face include (1) ensuring an accurate diagnosis, (2) determining eligibility for special education services, (3) encouraging unbiased assessment procedures and (4) making appropriate educational placements.

There is a large amount of literature available to document the overrepresentation of CLD students in special education programs. CLD students are those students different from dominant culture and language (in the US, non-white or not English dominant). Because most of the literature on this topic addresses CLD students, the authors of this chapter use the term CLD for information pertinent to CLD students (more general group) and EB when targeting students learning English as an additional language (more narrow group). EB students and CLD students are different in the sense that you can think of EBs as a subgroup of CLD students, but CLD students are not necessarily EBs. Unlike EBs, many CLD students are already proficient in English and may have English as their home language as well as being culturally different from the dominant culture (for example African American, Native American or Latino).

The first half of the chapter presents introductory ideas about process, identification and legislation governing services and assessments for students receiving special education services in US public schools. The second half of the chapter focuses on SLI,[1] a category of special education that is oftentimes confused with regular SLA (which does not require special education services). The chapter ends with an overview of research on SLI among bilingual children and suggestions for determining special education needs for EBs.

The reason for the inclusion of this chapter in an assessment textbook focusing on EBs is because assessment methods and the policies that govern assessment practice play a central role in determining appropriate services and advocating for needed services. Of special importance is the need to appropriately identify and discern between those EBs who have special learning needs and those who do not. For instance, some of behaviors associated with SLI are also associated with LD. Therefore, trained professionals should use assessment methods to discern whether the behaviors are due to SLI or SLA. And when assessing language, it is important to assess it in a natural context and over time.

The obvious concern for educators is how to determine the SLI versus SLA distinction, effectively meet the cultural and linguistic needs of EBs and at the same time address English proficiency, along with the issues posed by the disability, for those having both classifications. The merging of special education with CLD individuals requires a unique collaboration – one that includes educational planning that is focused on language proficiency as well as individualized learning plans (Gargiulo, 2012). The following sections give an overview of the legislation that governs this collaboration.

Federal Policy on Special Education in the United States

Individuals with Disabilities Education Act (IDEA)

In the US, the most notable piece of legislation for individuals, families and educators involved in special education is IDEA, passed in 1975. IDEA is viewed as a 'Bill of Rights' for those involved in special education (Gargiulo, 2012). At its inception in 1975, IDEA was named the Education of All Handicapped Children Act (EHA) or Public Law 94-142 and quickly became the most important piece of legislation in the field of special education. Before the passage of this act, children with disabilities were often denied an education or placed in inappropriate settings such as institutions or segregated facilities and parents were often forced to pay high tuition rates for private schooling. In addition, many states passed laws barring children with certain types of disabilities from attending school (e.g. children who were blind or labeled mentally retarded). Therefore, the main premise of Public Law 94-142 was to ensure that students with disabilities received an appropriate and free public education. The law laid out the entire foundation upon which special education focuses today and continues to drive current practice (Pierangelo & Giuliani, 2012). The six major tenets of IDEA are listed in Table 8.1. The tenet most closely related to the direction of this chapter is 'non-discriminatory assessment' practices.

IDEA is inarguably the most important piece of legislation to protect students with disabilities. IDEA has been revised and sometimes reauthorized approximately every five years since its inception. The most recent amended version is titled the Individuals with Disabilities Education Improvement Act of 2004 (IDEA, 2004). Unlike previous amendments, the 2004 amendment strongly focuses on assessment and accountability and is closely aligned with No Child Left Behind (NCLB, Tables 8.2 and 8.3).

Focus on CLD Students

When evaluating for a disability, IDEA 2004 is clear on the need to ensure an unbiased process. Specifically, IDEA 2004 states that all assessments and evaluation instruments are selected and administered so as not to be discriminatory on a racial or cultural basis. This means that the assessments and instruments are to be provided and administered in the child's home language and/or other mode of communication to provide information on what the student knows and can do academically, developmentally and functionally.

Table 8.1 Six components of IDEA (1975)

Component	Description
Free and appropriate education (FAPE)	This is the 'zero reject' philosophy. Any student, regardless of the severity of his or her disability, must be provided with an education at no cost to the parent. This also includes other services that a student may require (e.g. speech therapy).
Least restrictive environment (LRE)	Students with disabilities are to be educated to the maximum extent possible with students without disabilities.
Individual education program (IEP)	This document works like a contract and is individually developed to articulate the specific needs of the student. The IEP includes a description of the educational plan's specific services to meet individual needs.
Procedural due process	This is a safeguard measure for parents. It includes confidentiality, native language requirements, evaluation rights and written notice procedures.
Non-discriminatory assessment	Evaluation conducted by a multidisciplinary team that covers all areas in which the student is suspected of having a disability. Assessment measures cannot be racially or culturally biased.
Parental participation	Parents participate fully in all aspects of the decision-making process.

Table 8.2 The purpose and focus of IDEA 2004

(1A)	To ensure that all children with disabilities are provided a free and appropriate public education that specifically provides special education services and related services that are designed to meet their unique needs and prepare them for life after graduation (employment, college and/or independent living).
(1B)	To ensure that the rights of children identified with a disability (and their parents) are protected.
(2)	To assist all those involved in the education of students with disabilities (government and local school systems).
(3)	To ensure that educators and parents have what they need to improve educational results for children with disabilities (e.g. research, technical assistance, technology).
(4)	To assess the effectiveness of the education of students with disabilities.

Disproportionate Representation of CLD Students in Special Education

In regard to initial evaluations and subsequent assessment measures for EBs, it is imperative that all protocols be closely followed. Disproportionate representation – defined by de Valenzuela *et al.* (2006) as either a higher or lower percentage of students from a particular ethnic group in special education than is found in the overall student population of a particular school district – is a growing concern for educators. An often cited metric to quantify this disproportion is called the relative

Table 8.3 Main tenets of IDEA 2004

Parental informed consent	Informed consent is defined as: The parent has been fully informed of all information to which consent is being sought. Consent must be provided in the parent's native language and/or current mode of communication. Parent needs to agree in writing. The consent form describes the specific activity for which the school is requesting consent. The consent form lists any records that will be forwarded and to whom. The parent understands that his or her permission is voluntary and can be revoked at their request at any time.
Least restrictive environment (LRE)	Students must be placed in the setting (classroom) that will best meet their educational needs. Students with disabilities are placed with students without disabilities whenever deemed appropriate. Placement decisions begin with full general education consideration and then move through a continuum as deemed appropriate by the academic and behavioral achievement of the student. A guiding matrix is applied for how successful the student is learning in his or her current setting. Decisions are made following a least restrictive to most restrictive continuum.
Individualized education plan (IEP)	The IEP is the cornerstone of special education. This document is often referred to as the legal document that drives the education and planning of students with disabilities. The IEP includes all vital information to ensure success (e.g. goals, assessment and progress monitoring).
Evaluation must be non-discriminatory	In order for an evaluation to be non-discriminatory, the following requirements must be adhered to: • Bias-free instruments. • Multidisciplinary team. A multidisciplinary team is defined as a team composed of professionals from different disciplines. • Assessment materials and assessment procedures selected and administered without racial or cultural discrimination. • Validation of all assessment materials. • Administered by trained professionals. • Must use more than one assessment measure to determine eligibility and/or placement decisions.

Table 8.3 (Continued)

Assessed in all areas related to disability	This includes the following (as needed):
	• Health • Vision • Hearing • Social condition • Emotional condition • Intelligence • Academic achievement • Communication • Motor abilities
All tests and reports must be in child's native language	Employing a variety of sound evaluation materials and procedures selected and administered so as not to be racially or culturally discriminatory.
Parents and due process	If a parent disagrees on any part of the process, no change can be made until the issue has been resolved through due-process procedures.
Zero reject	Simply put, all children with a disability have a right to free public school education and cannot be denied this education because of a disability.

Adapted from Gargiulo (2012) and Pierangelo and Giuliani (2012)

risk ratio. The relative risk ratio compares the risk (of overrepresentation) for different racial and ethnic groups. Basically, if the relative risk ratio is 1.0, then this indicates equal representation between two racial/ethnic groups (for example comparing Mexican American to white rates of classification). Any value greater than 1 indicates overrepresentation. For example, if 20% of all Mexican-American students are in special education and only 10% of white students are in special education, then the relative risk ratio is 20/10 or 2.0, indicating that Mexican-American students are two times as likely as white students to be in special education. In the US, when disproportionate representation is documented (using relative risk ratio or some other metric), this is viewed as potential discriminatory practice and monitored by the office of civil rights (OCR). Many times, OCR requires states or regions to develop a correction plan – a plan to correct the perceived discriminatory problem and equalize representation in special education.

Bicard and Heward (2010) fittingly summarize this critical issue:

> ... the fact that culturally (and linguistically) diverse students are identified as having disabilities is not in itself a problem... Disproportionate representation isproblematic, however, if students have been wrongly placed in special education, if they are segregated and stigmatized or are denied access to special education because their disabilities are overlooked as a result of their membership in a racial or ethnic minority group. (Bicard & Heward, 2010: 333–334)

Students who are found eligible for disability categories are sometimes diagnosed through methods requiring judgment or non-standardized evaluations. Assessment methods, when used without rubrics or criteria such as observations and/or interviews, may introduce judgment and de-emphasize objectivity into the process of identification. These types of methods (of diagnosis) are typically found in high-incidence disabilities – those disabilities that are most likely to appear in school for initial evaluation, for example learning disabilities and emotional disturbance (Klingner et al., 2005).

Other Federal Legislation That May Impact SWD in the United States

Section 504 of the Rehabilitation Act of 1973

Section 504 differs from IDEA in the following ways: (1) Section 504 reaches beyond the school setting, (2) schools do not receive funding for students covered under Section 504 and (3) students are found eligible for Section 504 through professional judgment as opposed to test scores. In short, Section 504 is a civil rights law that prevents discrimination against individuals with disabilities by any agency or institution that receives federal monies. It is possible that a student may not quality for services under IDEA but could be considered for services under Section 504. For example, a student who has severe asthma may qualify for modifications under 504 but not IDEA. A student who needs an IEP and qualifies for special education in essence needs specially designed instruction in order to achieve success; a student with a 504 plan only needs accommodations and/or modifications. They do not require the specially designed instruction or the services of a special education teacher.

Americans with Disabilities Act (ADA)

This law reaches beyond the school setting with a focus on the workplace. ADA is important because it provides for the protection of students with disabilities attending college. It is often viewed as an extension of IDEA because it provides for reasonable accommodations and non-discriminatory treatment beyond the school years (Mastropieri & Scruggs, 2014).

The Special Education Process in the United States

The special education process is also regulated at the federal level, where all states are mandated to align state policy with federal regulation. What is special education? In its simplest form, special education is specially designed instruction, at no cost to the parent, to meet the unique needs of a child with a disability. IDEA 2004 defines special education:

(1) Special education means specially designed instruction, at no cost to the parents, to meet the unique needs of a child with a disability, including –

(i) Instruction conducted in the classroom, in the home, in hospitals and institutions, and in other settings; and (ii) Instruction in physical education.

(2) Special education includes each of the following, if the services otherwise meet the requirements of paragraph (a)(1) of this section of IDEA – (i) Speech-language pathology services, or any other related service, if the service is considered special education rather than a related service under State standards; (ii) Travel training; and (iii) Vocational education. (IDEA, 2004)

Federal legislation in the United States requires six steps that schools in all states must follow to identify and provide services to students with a disability (Table 8.1). The following section articulates each of the six steps.

Step one: Pre-referral

This section will begin with a discussion on pre-referral, including RtI, and will then walk through the remaining steps of the process. RtI is going to be a part of pre-referral strategies and intervention for many students (obviously not for students with visual, hearing or orthopedic impairments or traumatic brain injury for example). RtI is only specific to LDs and does not pertain to other categories. All other categories require different processes for identification. In other words, RtI is used for all students, but will only lead to referral for students with a learning disability. Pre-referral interventions are designed to assist a student who is struggling academically or behaviorally in order to improve learning before a referral for a special education evaluation. These interventions are designed to provide supports to students and to be delivered inside the student's regular classroom. This is usually the first step toward improving the student's school performance (NCLD, 2013).

School districts will typically have a school-based team. These teams go by various names, such as child study team (CST), student assistant team (SAT) or pupil personnel team (PPT). The team may include the following members: the child's classroom teacher, principal, school psychologist, special education teacher, school nurse, social worker, speech/language therapist or guidance counselor (Pierangelo & Giuliani, 2012). The team's main objective is to use a data-based decision-making model that will review the student's progress and suggest interventions and supports; they then make decisions based on progress monitoring of the interventions and supports. The data-based decision-making model will be used to determine whether to continue with current interventions (that is, interventions outside of special education) or to move forward for a special education referral.

In an attempt to deter unnecessary referrals, IDEA promotes the idea of detecting and solving learning issues early in what is called a pre-referral stage. IDEA 2004 thus added a new provision entitled Early Intervening Services. This provision is designed for a school to use its special education funds (up to 15%) to design and implement pre-referral interventions for students who are not currently identified with a disability. There is also a strong focus on the need for school personnel to use scientifically based academic and behavioral interventions as well as scientifically based literacy instruction. For example, school districts may send teachers for professional development or provide a direct service to a student such as remedial reading instruction. The goal is to assist students as early as possible in order to reduce the number of unnecessary referrals to special education.

Owing to the high number of CLD students in special education, pre-referral strategies are an important way to focus on CLD students who may not have a need for special education. Pre-referral strategies and teams aim to reduce the number of students from CLD backgrounds that are inappropriately referred to special education. Examples of pre-referral strategies include (1) team meeting with teachers and parents, (2) parent interviews, (3) medical exam, (4) hearing test, (5) vision test, (6) classroom management techniques, (7) counseling and (8) progress reports sent to parents.

Pre-referral interventions have been found to exhibit several advantages. First, data used during the initial stages of pre-referral can be used to recommend alternative programs or instructional strategies. Second, the nature of pre-referral allows for an increased amount of collaboration with other professionals as well as with the student's family. This collaboration can strengthen the family relationship and trust with the school and student's teachers. In addition, the initial data and collaboration serve as a gateway to ensure that additional supports will occur within the general education setting. Finally, and perhaps most importantly, if a referral to special education is deemed appropriate, the student is more than likely to have a 'true' disability (Pierangelo & Giuliani, 2012).

RtI

Every time IDEA is reauthorized, there are changes in the newer policy that try to correct for practices we know are not best. Many educators were relieved when RtI replaced the discrepancy model to determine the existence of a learning disability. The discrepancy model is described below. RtI can function as an alternative for learning disability evaluations. In practice, IDEA 2004 eliminated the requirement for schools to show a severe discrepancy between intellectual ability and academic achievement in order for a student to be found eligible for a learning disability (NCLD, 2013). Before IDEA 2004, discrepancies were 'proven' by comparing two test scores, which were intelligence-test and achievement-test scores. IDEA 2004's main premise was that by using RtI, school districts can identify students early and reduce referral bias (Pierangelo & Giuliani, 2012).

RtI is an assessment and intervention process for systematically monitoring student progress and making decisions about the need for instructional modifications or increasingly intensified services using progress-monitoring data (NRCLD, 2007). Both NCLB and IDEA 2004 encouraged school districts to implement a system to support students who were struggling within the general education setting. In addition, the NRCLD (2007) identified the following components of RtI:

- Progress monitoring in the general education setting using appropriate assessment materials.
- Choosing and implementing scientifically proven interventions (interventions that are research based and have been proved to be effective for most students).
- Following a problem-solving model – use of formal guidelines – to make decisions on a student's progress or the student's response to interventions.
- Monitoring the student at least weekly or once every two weeks.
- Ensuring the intervention is provided accurately and consistently.
- Determining the level of support a student needs to be successful.
- Giving parents notice of the need for a formal referral to special education if a disability is suspected.

RtI is most often carried out within a three-tiered model that includes:

- Tier 1: Screening and group intervention.
- Tier 2: Targeted interventions.
- Tier 3: Intensive interventions and comprehensive evaluation.

See Figure 8.1 for further tier details. It is important to note that at any time during the RtI process, parents may request a formal evaluation to determine if their child is eligible for special education services. Also, school districts cannot use the RtI process to deny or delay a formal referral to special education. RtI is also unique in its use of CBM and progress monitoring to make decisions on a student's progress. CBM is used to track and record a student's progress in the specific learning areas (NCLD). Pierangelo and Giuliani (2012) describe RtI in the following manner:

> RtI is an integrated approach to service delivery that encompasses general, remedial and special education through a multitier service-delivery model. It utilizes a problem-solving framework to identify and assess academic and behavioral difficulties for all students using scientific, research-based instruction. (Pierangelo & Giuliani, 2012: 78)

RtI is a three-tiered approach that is used to provide academic and behavioral interventions to students while collecting data to make data-based decisions on the effectiveness of the interventions. In Figure 8.1, the left side of the pyramid focuses on academic tiered interventions. For example, typically all students in a classroom begin in Tier 1; universal or whole class interventions are provided with a strategic approach on prevention and proactive strategies. As students move up the tiers, interventions become more individualized and target specific learning needs. The same occurs on the right side of the pyramid; interventions and instruction are behavioral in nature and increase in individualization as a student moves up the tiers. In Figure 8.1, the percentages indicate the percentage of students typically in each tiered level in an average classroom. Keep in mind that RtI is not used to make final recommendations about SLI. RtI is primarily used to collect data around potential LDs. This is only 1 of the 13 official categories of special education.

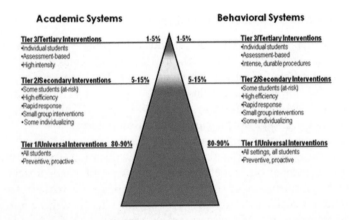

Figure 8.1 An RtI model (http://rtinetwork.org/)

RtI is not without its challenges and criticism. Initially meant to provide early intervention, at times RtI can prolong the evaluation process. As described above, one of the intents of RtI was to reduce the number of unnecessary referrals to special education. Although there are concerns about the overrepresentation of minority students in special education, RtI has quickly become a promising strategy to reduce the number of referrals to special education and to provide culturally appropriate instruction (Mastropieri & Scruggs, 2014).

RtI has the potential to screen learning and behavior problems early to prevent academic difficulties and/or failure of all students, including CLD students with disabilities. RtI also has the potential to bring together professionals from different fields (such as Gen Ed, Special Ed, English as a new language [ENL], speech, etc.) even though these fields are typically bound by isolated practices. If RtI is used with culturally relevant practices and prevention, with early intervention and support that views culture and language in a promising way, then it has great potential. Klingner and Edwards (2006) recommend the culturally responsive interventions shown in Table 8.4 to support students from diverse backgrounds. The bottom line about RtI: The RtI process is only as strong as its strongest assessment method.

Table 8.4 Cultural response interventions for CLD students

Tier 1	Interventions should be implemented by teachers who are familiar with culturally relevant teaching.
Tier 2	Progress monitoring should be carefully tracked and culturally relevant. Tier 2 teams should also be composed of individuals with expertise in working with diverse students.
Tier 3	Focus is on ensuring that assessment and evaluation measures have been conducted with cultural fairness and use of unbiased measures prior to special education referral.

Step two: Referral or request for evaluation

The second major step in the special education process is a formal referral to special education. This occurs after both pre-referral strategies and RtI have proved to be ineffective for the student. At this stage, either the parent or the school district will request a formal evaluation that must be in writing and requires informed consent from the parent (Pierangelo & Giuliani, 2012). This request will set in motion the remaining steps of the special education process.

Note that although informed consent is required, such a requirement does not give permission for the school district to begin special education; the informed consent step is solely for evaluation to determine if the student needs special education. What's more, when the parent or the school district makes the request, the evaluation is conducted at no cost to the parent. This initial referral will be processed by a multidisciplinary team (MDT). This team is responsible for beginning the formal assessment process and working through the remaining steps with parents and students (Pierangelo & Giuliani, 2012).

The evaluation process begins with a review of the pre-referral data. The direction of the assessment process will be aligned with pre-referral information as well as any specific concerns expressed by the referring party. IDEA (2004) defines the evaluation process as follows:

(1) Use a variety of assessment tools and strategies to gather relevant functional, developmental and academic information about the child, including information provided by the parent, that may assist in determining (i) whether the child is a child with a disability under Sec. 300.8; and ... (2) Not use any single measure or assessment as the sole criterion for determining whether a child is a child with a disability and for determining an appropriate educational program for the child; and (3) Use technically sound instruments that may assess the relative contribution of cognitive and behavioral factors, in addition to physical or developmental factors. (Sec. 300.304: Evaluation procedures). (IDEA, 2004)

Step three: Eligibility determination

Once the student has been formally evaluated for special education services, the next step is to determine, based on all of the completed evaluations, whether the student is eligible for services as required by IDEA. At this time, the school district will convene a team, often called the eligibility committee (IEP team), committee on special education or IEP committee. The main focus of the IEP team is to review the assessment results, determine eligibility and make recommendations for classification and placement.

During the eligibility meeting, after the evaluation results have been discussed and the team has determined eligibility, the student will be classified under 1 of 13 disability categories defined by IDEA.

Instead of reviewing all 13 categories, the authors of this chapter decided to define the 3 categories that are known to have overrepresentation of EB students (ED, LD and SLI).

(1) **ED**. A condition exhibiting one or more of the following characteristics over a long period of time and to a marked degree that adversely affects a child's educational performance:

   (a) An inability to learn that cannot be explained by intellectual, sensory or health factors.
   (b) An inability to build or maintain satisfactory interpersonal relationships with peers and teachers.
   (c) Inappropriate types of behavior or feelings under normal circumstances.
   (d) A general pervasive mood of unhappiness or depression.
   (e) A tendency to develop physical symptoms or fears associated with personal or school problems.
   (f) The term includes schizophrenia.

   ED does not apply to children who are socially maladjusted, unless it is determined that they have an emotional disturbance.

(2) **LD**. A disorder in one or more of the basic psychological processes involved in understanding or in using language, spoken or written, that may manifest itself in the imperfect ability to listen, think, speak, read, write, spell or do mathematical calculations. The term includes such conditions as perceptual disabilities, brain injury, minimal brain dysfunction, dyslexia and developmental aphasia. The term does not include learning problems that are primarily the result of visual, hearing or motor disabilities; of intellectual disability; of emotional disturbance; or of environmental, cultural or economic disadvantage.

(3) **SLI**. A communication disorder such as stuttering, impaired articulation, a language impairment or a voice impairment that adversely affects a child's educational performance.

A final note on eligibility: IDEA established a two-pronged process to determine special education services. Prong one states that the student must have 1 (or more) of the 13 categories listed in IDEA. Prong two states that the student must need special education services in order to be successful in school and to make progress in the general education setting (NCLD, 2013).

IDEA 2004 includes special rules for eligibility to prevent the inappropriate identification of a student as having a disability under any category. The team must therefore ensure that the following factors are not a primary reason for the student's lack of progress in the general education setting:

- Lack of appropriate instruction in reading (per NCLB definition).
- Lack of instruction in math.
- *Limited English proficiency.*

The main idea in regard to math or reading is to demonstrate that the student did not make sufficient progress to meet age- or state-approved or grade-level standards in math or reading while provided instruction in reading and math from a qualified teacher in the general education setting. For CLD students, documentation must support that the lack of success in the general education setting, given appropriate supports and instruction, *is not a result* of the student having limited English proficiency.

Step four: The Individual Education Program (IEP)

At this point, the IEP team has reviewed all relevant information provided in the evaluation process, determined eligibility and determined a student's classification category; it will now develop the student's IEP. Simply stated, it is the student's education plan that explains the goals and objectives, related services and where the student will receive his or her special education series (placement). The IEP is otherwise thought of as the critical link between the student in special education and the special teaching that the student requires (Pierangelo & Giuliani, 2012).

Step five: Special education placement

With the IEP developed and actionable, students with disabilities are then placed in the least restrictive environment (see Table 8.3). The *placement* is where the student will receive his or her special education services. This is the next step in the special education process – determining the environment into which the student will be placed. Again, this decision is based on the initial evaluation and assessment results. Students are to be placed where they can gain the most without interfering with the learning of others and where they can progress and meet the goals of their IEP. As noted earlier in this chapter and according to IDEA, placements follow a continuum of least restrictive to most restrictive.

Step six: Annual review

The IEP will be reviewed annually and follow the same process as the initial evaluation process, which makes this process cyclical. The annual review meeting will make recommendations to continue, revise, change or end the student's special education services. It is important to note that each component of the IEP is determined through assessment measures and will be amended and reviewed using assessment and data-based decision-making processes. The student will also have a triennial review, which is an evaluation conducted every three years to provide current assessment information. In general, federal law informs the policy and the policy informs the regulation and each policy and regulation needs to be aligned with the law (IDEA). State laws provide the framework for educational policy; regulations lay out how the law will be implemented (Pierangelo & Giuliani, 2012). A good grasp of the laws and regulations will assist teachers in being strong and knowledgeable advocates for their students and students' parents.

Obstacles and Challenges with Addressing Special Needs of CLD Students

Sometimes, myths and past practice can be difficult to overcome when it comes to schooling issues. Hamayan *et al.* (2013) identified the following three *myths* or misconceptions that prevail in schools about EBs and special education. For more detail, or for a continuum of services framework, please read Hamayan *et al.* (2013).

(1) **If we label an EB as having special education needs, at least he or she gets some help.** Response in short: Not true. The stigma related to the label combined with interventions targeting the wrong needs will lead to more harm than benefit.

(2) **We have to wait three to seven years for EBs to develop their English language skills before we can rule out language as a cause of the student's difficulty.** Response in short: Not true. If a student truly has an intrinsic difficulty, then it exists in the student's entire language repertoire and in most use contexts. The sooner these exceptionalities are identified and supported, the better (Hamayan *et al.*, 2013).

(3) **When an EB is identified as having special education needs, instruction should be only in English, so as not to confuse the student.** Response in short: Not true. Students with speech, language or learning impairments can become bilingual and bilingual instruction provides a more culturally relevant environment.

There is a long list of challenges that current schools experience in the area of educating CLD students. There is a pervasive and historical achievement gap between CLD and non-CLD students. There is an overrepresentation of certain CLD students in special education, especially in high-incidence disabilities. Compared to low-incidence disabilities, high has more CLD students represented. The assessments associated with high-incidence disabilities tend to be subjective and ambiguous in nature, leaving room for bias. This subjectivity, in combination with a historical devaluation of CLD students in US schools, has opened the door to much of the overrepresentation seen today (Zhang & Cho, 2010). There is also an underrepresentation of CLD students in gifted education. Even though schools that receive federal or state funding must provide unbiased and non-discriminatory assessments, including administering assessments in the home language, this goal has been difficult to achieve. Teacher bias may also result in the misidentification or over-identification of CLD with special needs. African-American students in particular have been disproportionately diagnosed with intellectual disabilities, as have Native Americans (Zhang & Cho, 2010).

Although it is unclear exactly what shapes the overrepresentation of certain racial groups in categories of special education, it is likely that many systemic and historical factors contribute, but most people believe that assessment practices are one of the main sources for the overrepresentation. In particular, the use of culturally and linguistically biased assessments is majorly contributing to the collection of invalid data for CLD students. Despite policies mandating fair assessments (NCLB) as well as court decisions mandating fair assessments (*Diana v. State Board of Education*, 1970), the use of biased assessments still happens regularly.

In addition to the problem of using biased assessments, the next prominent obstacle is the shortage of speech and educational professionals who share the same cultural and linguistic background to their students being assessed. Since the early 1980s in the US, training programs have been funded to try to eradicate the shortage of professionals trained in bilingual education and special education.

Despite this, four decades later the US still has a shortage of bilingual special educators and bilingual speech pathologists. This shortage is one of the major challenges facing the service delivery model to EBs with disabilities. Because of a shortage of bilingual teachers in general, many EBs are often served in English-only settings with relatively few modifications to the instruction/assessment. The shortage of bilingual educators and speech pathologists also causes the problem of not having qualified personnel to administer the assessments (for example in the child's home language). These shortages can lead to the practice of assessing only a fraction of a child, or the fractional view, underestimating what students know and can do.

Some of these challenges are superficial, while others are more deeply rooted, such as general diversity issues. To add to this list of challenges, Martin (2009) writes about the many discourses that construct diversity as a problem. These discourses present diversity and difference as interfering with the smooth running aspects of mainstream society and services. Disruptions caused to mainstream life are seen as the fault of individuals who are diverse or different. The author (Martin, 2009) calls this blaming diversity and disabling diversity.

Supporting these discourses is a prevailing amount of research about speech and language difficulties constructed around monolingual children, but very little about bilingual children. Therefore, most of our theories, empirical evidence, assessment methods and interventions are drawn from research on monolinguals. The three categories of language difficulties that have been researched cross-linguistically and in bilingual children are language delay, grammar difficulties and speech difficulties (Martin, 2009). Martin reminds us that having typical overall development except in regard to language learning is what identifies children with SLI. Both monolingual and bilingual children have problems, varying in severity, with speech and/or grammar – both understanding and producing language. They have smaller vocabularies and often atypical patterns in understanding and expressing speech and grammar in comparison with their typically developing peers. These patterns may appear similar to patterns of second language acquisition (Martin, 2009). Martin (2009) also reminds us that bilingualism does not cause speech and language difficulties.

A Review of *Assessing Multilingual Children: Disentangling Bilingualism from Language Impairment*[2] (Armon-Lotem *et al.*, 2015)

This summary section takes the reader out of the US context and examines a non-US context with an emphasis on assessment methods of bilingual children who potentially have SLI. The problem of overrepresentation of bilingual children with SLI across the Western world led to the funding of the European Cooperation in Science and Technology (COST) and in particular, *Language Impairment in a Multilingual Society: Linguistic Patterns and the Road to Assessment*. Researchers in the Armon-Lotem *et al.* 2005 book come from Israel, the Netherlands, Lithuania,

Sweden, the UK, Iceland, Malta, Poland, Denmark, South Africa, Finland, Ireland, France, Germany and Greece. Researchers Armon-Lotem and de Jong (2015) provide the following four guidelines that hold promise for future research and practice in SLI for bilingual children:

(1) Bilingualism and SLI are not the same and can be disentangled.
(2) Bilingual children with SLI show error patterns similar to monolingual children with SLI.
(3) Bilingualism and SLI seem *not* to show a cumulative effect. Therefore, one factor does not increase the other factor; because of this, we should **not** see more cases of SLI in bilingual children than monolingual children.
(4) Bilingualism might sometimes offer a partial compensatory mechanism for language and cognitive development in children with SLI.

There is a problem across the Western world among bilingual children with disentangling SLI from SLA for a variety of reasons. It is believed that the number one reason contributing to this problem of overrepresentation (of bilingual children having SLI) is the types of assessments being used.

In general, the assessments used are designed for monolingual children and have not been normed for bilingual children, who in general do not conform to monolingual norms. For example, many assessments count vocabulary size (lexicon) in one language which lends itself to a fractional view of bilingual children. It only makes sense that if vocabulary is measured in one language only (fractional view), then the bilingual child will appear to have a smaller vocabulary than he or she does if vocabulary is measured in both languages in tandem (holistic view). Even though the holistic assessment makes more sense for a bilingual child, the fractional practice is dominant in schools across the Western world.

One of the difficulties of disentangling bilingualism from SLI stems from the many similarities in the linguistic manifestations of SLA and of SLI. This in combination with the fact that there are a limited number of diagnostic instruments to appropriately distinguish between SLI and SLA; more EB children are diagnosed with SLI than should be. If there were no misdiagnoses, then the percentage of bilingual children with SLI should be similar or equal to that of monolingual children (for example the relative risk ratio of bilingual children to monolingual children with SLI should be 1.0), but it's not. It is believed that inappropriate assessment methods are one reason for the overrepresentation of EBs with SLI. The following sections provide a more detailed sample of some of the ways in which SLI is being assessed across contexts, languages and countries.

Lexical (Vocabulary) Deficits

Despite vocabulary being a very narrow view of a child's speech repertoire, measuring lexicon (counting vocabulary) is often the focus of much of the assessment in this area. Lexical deficits are among the earliest indicators of SLI (Leonard, 1998), partly because they appear early and partly because they are relatively easy to assess.

Bilingual children often exhibit smaller vocabularies in *each* of their languages even though the number of words put together in their two languages may be larger than monolingual norms. Also, delayed lexical development is an early sign of SLI. Perhaps the overuse and fractional use (measuring languages separately) of lexical assessments play a role in the mis- and overrepresentation of bilinguals with SLI.

The following section reviews some methods of assessment in use with bilingual children suspected of SLI. Drawing from Armon-Lotem *et al.* (2015), some assessment methods (this does not include a full review of methods) are reviewed to give the reader an idea about assessment methods used to diagnose SLI. There is no one assessment used to diagnose SLI; therefore, any of these can be used alone or in combination to provide evidence for or against SLI. There is a wide range of ways to assess speech and an even wider range of methods used.

Sentence Repetition Tasks

One assessment method is called sentence repetition tasks. Sentence repetition tasks (Marinis & Armon-Lotem, 2015) are exactly what they sound like. For example, a sentence is spoken to the child, then the child has to repeat the sentence. The child receives a score of 0–3 based on how he or she responds, where the child scores a 3 if he or she repeats the sentence verbatim. Sometimes, sentences are presented to students through a PowerPoint and the sentences are pre-recorded by a native speaker. Sometimes, students are given incentives, such as rewards, to continue repeating sentences throughout the assessment. These tasks measure a part of language called lexical (vocabulary) and morphosyntactic (the study of words and grammar combined) knowledge. These have been shown to identify SLI among monolingual, children but show less promise with bilingual children (Marinis & Armon-Lotem, 2015).

Picture Prompts to Elicit a Response

It has often been shown that shortcomings in verbal morphology (analyzing spoken words) is typical of monolingual and bilingual children (de Jong, 2015). It shows promise that assessing verbal morphology (basically subject and verb agreement) can help diagnose SLI. To assess this, the administrator might present a picture description task testing subject–verb agreement. For example and in short, the child is given a picture of one boy pinching another and the child is asked 'What is happening in this picture?' to hopefully elicit a response that will show whether the child has subject and verb agreement, such as 'I pinch him' or 'He pinches me'. There are concerns about the validity of assessing verbal morphology using picture prompts to elicit response – namely, verbal morphology may be a predictor of SLI in some languages but not others (de Jong, 2015).

Even though an analysis of the cultural relevance in picture prompts was not conducted, some photos that appear not culturally relevant (for example a picture of an adult washing a child in a bathtub) can generate utterances (like 'I wash you', 'You wash me' or 'He washes you'). Perhaps culturally irrelevant picture prompts may introduce error into results for some children but not others. In fact, many of them include pictures that may be difficult to interpret or that are detached from any real-life experience, such as a girl washing a giraffe or an elephant that flies, or that use words that don't really exist.

Storytelling

One promising assessment method for bilingual children that is more contextualized (natural setting) than the aforementioned methods, is storytelling. Telling a story, even from pictures, is a difficult task for a child with SLI. Storytelling methods are holistic in that they allow for a look at multiple linguistic levels in one single task, such as lexis (the vocabulary of a language), morphosyntax (the study of words and grammar combined), discourse structure and fluency. Because the bilingual child tells the story, a cultural expert (the child) determines the content, as opposed to a preselected picture or sentence created by someone not likely to share the home language and culture.

Background Questionnaire

Another contextualized (questions about natural language use) and very important assessment is a background questionnaire completed by parents that includes questions about language use with siblings, birth weight, parent concerns, etc. The most promising practice at this point is to use a combination of many of these assessments to understand the unique profile of bilingual children.

Assessment Suggestions

This chapter ends with Table 8.5, which gives 11 suggestions surrounding the assessment of bilingual students who are under consideration as having special learning needs.

Table 8.5 Suggestions for assessment practice surrounding EB students potentially having special needs

(1)	Answer this critical question: Are the difficulties present in both the child's home language and the new language? Is his or her communication impaired with family members or others who speak the same language? Remember: A child's developmental delay or disability will be observable in both languages and across multiple settings.
(2)	Make all comparisons to 'peer cohorts' or 'true peers' to avoid invalid conclusions. Peer cohorts are groups of children who are bilingual, share the same home language and have similar life experiences.
(3)	Educators who value and reinforce the student's home language in assessment will experience more success with CLD students (and vice versa).

Table 8.5 (Continued)

(4)	Use culturally relevant pedagogy (CRP) in all three tiers of RtI. See Gloria Ladson-Billings' work on a theory of CRP. Combine with Funds of Knowledge (Louis Moll's work) to capitalize on family/home 'funds' in school. This will create a culturally relevant environment.
(5)	Use translanguaging as pedagogy in all three tiers of RtI to promote a holistic view of a child's language and academic ability (as opposed to a fractional view). See Ofelia Garcia's work on translanguaging pedagogy. This will create a culturally relevant multilingual environment.
(6)	Ask PUMI questions whenever an assessment is used with EBs. Only use instruments normed on bilingual children. Do not use instruments normed on monolingual children. You can read the blueprint of the test to find out how the instrument was normed or piloted.
(7)	When selecting assessment methods for language, choose methods in context (natural setting, real authentic language use) and over time. Avoid pre-made stories, sentences and other pre-made language tasks. These may be culturally incongruent or make no sense to the child. Choose holistic and open-ended language assessments to allow the child to construct language that makes sense to him or her.
(8)	Choose assessment methods that include a holistic perspective (both languages, translanguaging), not a fractional one (one language or the other).
(9)	Ask a cultural expert (preferably someone who shares home language and culture with the bilingual child being assessed) to analyze pictures and pre-made sentences for cultural relevance and appropriateness.
(10)	Seek information from families about language practice at home. Use questionnaires or interviews, preferably administer in the home.
(11)	Interviews and observations are assessment methods that lend themselves to culturally relevant assessment; they take more time and more trained professionals.

End-of-Chapter Activities (Instructors: see advice at the end of the book)

By doing Activities 1–3, the reader will be able to:

(1) Orally or in writing, define each tenet of IDEA and provide evidence to support tenet choice.
(2) Discuss the special education process.
(3) Organize and map the three disability categories (ED, LD and SLI).

Activity 1

Orally or in writing, define each tenet of IDEA and provide evidence to support tenet choice.

Activity 2

Participate in a gallery walk and discussion of the special education process.

Activity 3

Develop a mind map of the three disability categories relevant to EBs (ED, LD and SLI).

Notes

(1)   IDEA uses this acronym for SLI (speech or language impairments). There are many terms used to describe language and communication difficulties. Most terms are deficit focused and specific to one language level (Martin, 2009). For example, specific language impairment (SLI), specific speech impairment, language impairment (LI), specific speech and language difficulties, semantic and pragmatic impairment and pragmatic impairment (Martin, 2009).

(2)   In the book *Assessing Multilingual Children: Disentangling Bilingualism from Language Impairment*, the authors refer to SLI as specific language impairment. This is also used in the current chapter.

References

Armon-Lotem, S., de Jong, J. and Meir, N. (2015) *Assessing Multilingual Children: Disentangling Bilingualism from Language Impairment*. Bristol: Multilingual Matters.

Bicard, S. and Heward, W. (2010) Educational equity for students with disabilities. In J. Banks and C. Banks (eds) *Multicultural Education: Issues and Perspectives* (7th edn; pp. 315–341). Hoboken, NJ: Wiley.

de Jong, J. (2015) Elicitation task for subject–verb agreement. In S. Armon-Lotem, J. de Jong and N. Meir (eds) *Assessing Multilingual Children: Disentangling Bilingualism from Language Impairment* (pp. 25–37). Bristol: Multilingual Matters.

De Valenzuela, J.S., Copeland, S.R., Huaqing Qi, C. and Park, M. (2006) Examining educational equity: Revisiting the disproportionate representation of minority students in special education. *Council for Exceptional Children* 73 (4), 425–441.

Gargiulo, R. (2012) *Special Education in Contemporary Society* (4th edn). Thousand Oaks, CA: Sage Publications.

Hamayan, E., Marler, B., Sánchez-López, C. and Damico, J. (2013) *Special Education Considerations for English Language Learners: Delivering a Continuum of Services*. Philadelphia, PA: Caslon Publishing.

IDEA 2004 Regulations: Subpart E – Procedural Safeguards. See http://www.wrightslaw.com/idea/law/idea.regs.subparte.pdf (accessed February 2013).

Klingner, J.K. and Edwards, P.A. (2006) Cultural considerations with response to intervention models. *Reading Research Quarterly* 41, 108–117.

Klingner, J.K., Artiles, A.J., Kozleski, E., Harry, B., Zion, S., Tate, W., Duran, G.Z. and Riley, D. (2005) Addressing the disproportionate representation of culturally and linguistically diverse students in special education through culturally responsive educational systems. *Education Policy Analysis Archives* 13 (38). See http://dx.doi.org/10.14507/epaa.v13n38.2005 (accessed 19 October 2016).

Leonard, L. (1998) *Children with Specific Language Impairment*. Cambridge, MA: MIT Press.

Marinis, T. and Armon-Lotem, S. (2015) Sentence repetition. In S. Armon-Lotem, J. de Jong and N. Meir (eds) *Assessing Multilingual Children: Disentangling Bilingualism from Language Impairment* (pp. 95–121). Bristol: Multilingual Matters.

Martin, D. (2009) *Language Disabilities in Cultural and Linguistic Diversity*. Bristol: Multilingual Matters.

Mastropieri, M.A. and Scruggs, T.E. (2014) *The Inclusive Classroom: Strategies for Effective Differentiated Instruction*. Boston, MA: Pearson.

NASP IDEA Information Page. See https://www.nasponline.org/ (accssed 20 October 2016).

NCLD (n.d.) IDEA parent guide. See www.ncld.org (accessed February 2013).

NICHCY: 1.800.695.0285 4 Categories of disability under IDEA. See http://nichcy.org/schoolage/iep/iepcontents#contents (accessed 19 October 2016).

NRCLD (2007) Responsiveness to Intervention in Conjunction with Learning Disability Determination. Lawrence, KS: NRCLD.

Pierangelo, R. and Giuliani, G. (2012) *Assessment in Special Education: A Practical Approach* (4th edn). New York: Pearson.

US Department of Education (n.d.) Building the legacy: IDEA 2004. See http://idea.ed.gov/explore/view/p/,root,regs,300,D,300%252E304

Zhang, C. and Cho, S.J. (2010) The development of the bilingual special education field: Major issues, accomplishments, future directions, and recommendations. *Journal of Multilingual Education Research* 1 (1), 45–61.

Recommended reading

Abedi, J. (2009) English language learners with disabilities: Classification, assessment, and accommodation issues. *Journal of Applied Testing Technology* 10(3).

In this paper, Abedi discusses issues concerning accessibility of assessment classification and accommodations for English language learners with disabilities (ELLWD). Abedi presents recommendations for more accessible assessments.

Abedi, J. and Faltis, C. (2015) Review of research in education: Teacher assessment and the assessment of students with diverse learning needs. *AERA* 39. See http://rre.aera.net

The purpose of this volume is to bring awareness to specific considerations necessary in the use of high-stakes tests with teachers, ELLs and students with special needs.

Artiles, A., Rueda, R., Salazar, J. and Higareda, I. (2005) Within-group diversity in minority disproportionate representation: English language learners in urban school districts. *Exceptional Children* 71 (3), 283–300.

The authors examine EB placement patterns in California urban districts. Disproportionate representation patterns were found to relate to grade level, language proficiency level, disability category, type of special education program and type of language program.

Burr, E., Haas E. and Ferriere, K. (July 2015) Identifying and Supporting English Learner Students with Learning Disabilities: Key Issues in the Literature and State Practice. Report from Regional Educational Laboratory (REL) at WestEd.

This report reviews research and policy in the 20 US states with the largest populations of EBs. It is deemed helpful for education leaders who are setting up processes to determine which EB students may need placement in special education.

Harry, B. and Klingner, J. (2005) *Why Are So Many Minority Students in Special Education? Understanding Race and Disability in Schools*. New York: Teachers College Press.

Harry and Klingner examine disproportionate placement of black and Hispanic students in special education. The authors examine the experience of children, family interactions with school personnel, the school's estimate of child and family and the school climate that leads to decisions about referrals.

The Iris Center (funded by the US Department of Education's Office of Special Education Programs – OSEP) Dual language learners with disabilities: Supporting young children in the classroom. See http://iris.peabody.vanderbilt.edu/module/dll (accessed 19 October 2016).

These modules provide resources about evidence-based practices for use in pre-service preparation and professional development programs. In addition to this 1 module, there are 15 modules to better understand RtI.

MacSwan, J. and Rolstad, K. (2006) How language proficiency tests mislead us about ability: Implications for English language learner placement in special education. *Teachers College Record* 108 (11), 2304–2328.

The authors argue that EB language assessment policy and poor language tests partly account for EBs' disproportionate representation in special education. They present empirical evidence to support this claim.

Paradis, J., Genessee, F. and Crago, M. (2011) *Dual Language Development & Disorders: A Handbook on Bilingualism and Second Language Learning*. Baltimore, MD: Brookes Publishing. This textbook is designed to prepare SLPs to work with bilingual children.

9 Accountability

Source: Gary Huck and Mike Konopacki Labor Cartoons Collection; WAG 264; Box 23; Folder 5; Tamiment Library/Robert F. Wagner Labor Archives, New York University. Reproduced with permission.

Themes from Chapter 9

(1) Accountability related to assessment has come to the forefront of education in the last 10 years.
(2) Accountability based on student assessment results has never been more intense and directly tied to assessment.
(3) Accountability without validity isn't meaningful (see Chapter 2).

Key Vocabulary

- Annual professional performance review (APPR)
- Growth model
- Multiple measures
- Status model
- Student learning objective (SLO)
- Title III

- Value-added assessment
- Data-driven instruction (DDI)

PUMI Connection: Use

This chapter focuses on the U (Use) in PUMI. Test score results are being used like never before for accountability purposes. After reading this chapter, new teachers will have a clearer understanding of what's behind the accountability terms and from where they are derived.

What is Adequate Yearly Progress (AYP)?

A key covenant of the No Child Left Behind (NCLB) Act (2002–2015) was to ensure AYP for all students. Schools and districts had to demonstrate AYP to their state departments of education, and in turn state departments had to demonstrate to the federal Department of Education that *all* students were showing adequate progress. Schools could not submit test scores as an average achievement score of the whole school because this might 'hide' the low performance for a specific group of children, like emergent bilinguals (EBs). Such an increase in state- and federal-level accountability was unprecedented and many believed that the emphasis on accountability for EBs was much needed in US schools. The federal government outlined the process that individual states must follow to develop systems that measure the progress of all students, but the way to best measure AYP for EBs was left unspecified (as is often the case with federal direction for EBs). The general process for 'all students' included setting challenging academic standards, developing annual state-level assessments that address state learning standards, setting an initial starting point, specifying successive targets for AYP and providing increased support to schools that consistently fail to meet AYP.

When NCLB was first passed in 2002, it required each state to set its own AYP targets the same for all students, regardless of the educational challenges that some students face (because of this idea, the cartoon showing a race track with different 'challenges' was selected to introduce this chapter). Each state has its own system of accountability, which is separate and sometimes strikingly different from the federal school accountability system. It is possible for a school to be 'passing' according to the state system but 'failing' under the federal system. The EBs at a school form a subgroup of students who are examined; if the school does not show AYP for this subgroup, the entire school 'fails' (in theory leaving no child behind, even EBs). However, shortly after the Bush administration passed the NCLB law, it quickly became apparent that AYP for EBs contained fundamental flaws. Schools with large numbers of EBs were behind because the subgroup of EBs always had lower proficiency in English (hence their English language learners/limited English proficient [ELL/LEP] label) and tended to score low on tests in English partly due to their status as EBs (not knowing enough English to participate meaningfully). Because of this catch-22 situation (Wright, 2006), the Bush administration announced more flexibility in the law for the EB subgroup, allowing former EBs to be included in the EB subgroup for up to two years. Also, newly arrived EBs were allowed a 12-month exemption from English language arts (ELA) assessments. However, anyone familiar with second language acquisition (SLA) knows that newly arrived EBs cannot reach the required level of proficiency needed to garner valid results in a single year – another fundamental flaw that undermines the accountability of schools for EBs.

The law overlooked EBs in many ways; therefore, amendments were introduced to try to 'fix' things. Another amendment soon expanded the subgroup of EBs to include fluent English proficients (FEPs). In the few years immediately following passage and amendments, the US Government Accountability Office (GAO) conducted a study that focused on the 2003–2004 school year. The GAO asked several questions: To what extent were EBs meeting academic progress goals? What were states doing to ensure the validity of their English language proficiency (ELP) tests? How was the Department of Education supporting state-level efforts to meet the 'valid and reliable' requirement? In the study, which was published in 2006, the GAO found that 25 states did not provide adequate evidence to ensure the validity or reliability of academic test results for EBs. Moreover, a 2005 Department of Education-funded technical review of the available documentation for 17 ELP tests found insufficient documentation of the validity of these assessment results (GAO, 2006).

One example of the use of AYP is a set of statistics published on the New York State Education Department website: 'The Good News: Approximately 64% of schools make AYP for EBs in ELA and 98% in math. The Bad News: The failure rate for EBs in ELA is by far the highest of any group–almost twice the rate of Students with Disabilities (SWD)'. This result is not surprising for teachers who understand that it takes 4–9 years to learn academic language, otherwise known as language used for academic purposes, which is a partial prerequisite for scoring high on the ELA exam. For policymakers unfamiliar with the length of time it takes to learn a language, however, it might sound alarming. Keep in mind that the same students who cannot pass the ELA test may be progressing very well in their second language development according to more authentic measures of English. Because AYP has been so problematic, it is no longer a federal requirement. With the passage of the Every Student Succeeds Act (ESSA) (Public Law 114-95) in 2015, AYP is no longer a federal requirement; however, individual states may choose to continue to require AYP. Table 9.1 outlines the pros and cons of applying AYP to EBs.

Table 9.1 Pros and cons of AYP for EBs

Pros	Cons
Increase accountability for EBs.	Assumptions underlying AYP are too simple (don't account for complexity of second language acquisition [SLA]).
Focusing on progress is a positive thing.	EBs likely can't read the test very well that is used to measure AYP; therefore, test scores don't really show what they know.
	EBs were an afterthought to the AYP concept (as shown by two amendments published shortly after the law passed).

What is an Annual Measurable Achievement Objective (AMAO)?

AMAOs are objectives that states must meet to prove to the federal government that they are providing a good educational environment for EBs in their districts. Between the years 2002 and 2015 (NCLB), states received money if they reported AMAOs each year. Title III awards were granted to states who met the set requirements; the funds were targeted to help EBs meet English and content standards (Title III replaced the Bilingual Education Act, otherwise known as Title VII). The first requirement of Title III of the NCLB Act was to establish ELP standards aligned to state academic-content standards, which must be appropriate for students learning content in their second language. The second requirement of Title III was to annually assess the ELP of each EB using one valid and reliable assessment of English that is aligned to the ELP state standards. Because there are no national achievement standards (in theory at least), each state is entitled to its own state standards. The third requirement of Title III was to define, measure and report on the AMAOs annually. Because NCLB was introduced in 2002/2003, that year was considered the baseline year; districts must meet AMAOs from that point forward. With the passage of ESSA, there is no annual measurable objective (AMO) (or AMAO)[1] requirement as there was under NCLB. However, ESSA does require states to 'establish ambitious State-designed long term goals...for all students and separately for each subgroup of students'.

Under NCLB, for a school to receive Title III money, the state was accountable to three AMAOs. AMAO 1 focused on *progress* in English language acquisition and specifies that schools/districts must show an annual increase in the percentage of EBs making progress in English. AMAO 2 focused on reaching ELP or being *reclassified* out of ELL/LEP status, and states that schools/districts must demonstrate that there is an increase in the percentage of ELL/LEP reaching ELP. AMAO 3 concerned AYP, whereby schools/districts had to demonstrate the subgroup of EBs that met grade-level academic achievement standards in ELA and mathematics. In general, the minimum subgroup size was 30. That means that schools (mostly rural) having fewer than 30 EBs did not have to report data for the purpose of AMAO accountability.

Because no test is perfectly reliable and all test scores contain 'error' – otherwise known as 'test pollution' – the measurement community has long stood by the idea that no one test score should inform a high-stakes decision (such as AMAOs and AYP); using multiple methods is the best approach. The American Educational Research Association (AERA) (2000) recommended that any high-stakes decision be based on more than one source of valid data. Yet, most states do the opposite with AMAOs and AYPs or other annual goals.

Snapshot: Do the Consequences of 'Inadequate Progress' Help Schools?

A K-8 inner-city school has 250 out of 500 students learning English as their second language. Students in Grades 3–8 who are classified as EB do not know enough English yet to participate meaningfully in non-differentiated instruction or assessment. They struggle with the language demands of the mathematics and ELA exam; for EBs, these are tests of language before mathematics. It may take them longer to read, they may mix up the directions or they may misread an item or a response. As might be expected, their performance in mathematics as measured by this test in English is lower and therefore contributes to inadequate yearly progress. As a consequence of not meeting annual goals, the school is placed on probation for several years, given the label 'persistently low achieving' and the principal is removed. A new principal arrives, but just when teachers and students get to know her new style, she volunteers to leave because she realizes that with so many EBs (and the low test scores they typically receive), the school will never reach annual targets and it is unlikely for her to achieve tenure in this context. She leaves and another new principal starts the following year. The same pattern persists each year, and there are four principals within five years.[2]

By removing and driving away principals (and teachers), the consequences of not meeting annual set goals caused this school to experience even more serious unrest. This is an example whereby AMAOs – designed to raise schools to higher levels – in reality caused the school to become more disenfranchised.

Discussion questions

* How is accountability using annual goals like AMAOs supposed to improve schools?
* How did this concept backfire in this case?

What is a 'Growth Model' for Accountability?

Growth models grew out of a general frustration from working with what are called status models. Status models take a snapshot of a subgroup, such as EBs, at one point in time and compare it to an established target. In the status model, growth may not be rewarded – a fact that frustrated schools with high numbers of EBs. Status models do not work well with EBs learning English because not all EBs – nor all children, for that matter – start at a similar place and grow at the same rate. SLA rates of growth rely heavily on many factors that vary from student to student. Stated plainly, you can set high standards for all students, but this does not remove the many obstacles that get in the way of some students. In the cartoon at the beginning of this chapter, on the track, some children have a clear path toward the goal with very few obstacles in their way while others have to overcome nails, potholes and barbed wire.

In general, growth models for accountability refer to models that evaluate the progress of a group of individual students over time. This is much like a longitudinal research study in which individual students are tracked over time instead of being evaluated on the snapshot of their achievement in a single year. Growth models also control for transiency and reclassified students; this means that students are tracked

Table 9.2 Growth versus status models of accountability

Growth model	Status model
Recognizes growth in achievement or language proficiency	Recognizes how far a student is from a final goal
Tracks one student or cohort from year to year	Snapshot of students in one year; usually a different group of students is compared from year to year
Controls for individual differences (e.g. SES [socioeconomic], OSF [out of school factors])	Does not control for individual differences (e.g. SES, OSF)
Rewards growth	Highlights deficits
Used in many states now as a reaction to the status model	Aligned with original conception of NCLB

by growth from year to year. If Mrs Smith receives 10 new beginner students from refugee camps in Indonesia in one year, her average won't 'go down'. Therefore, an increase in English proficiency is rewarded, not punished, regardless of the endpoint – or the beginning point, for that matter. Table 9.2 outlines the differences between the status and growth models.

What is Value-Added Assessment?

Most authors consider a value-added assessment model to be a type of growth model, because one of the main assumptions behind the value-added assessment model is to measure change over time in student test scores. In a value-added model (VAM), changes are mostly attributed to the teacher. (Note that this ignores out-of-school factors [OSFs].) Value-added assessment models follow individual student achievement over time, and they also intend to show the specific effects of programs and other relevant factors; in practice, however, they mostly target a teacher's instruction. Basically, a student's test score from last year (for example, 3rd grade) is compared to the current year's (4th grade); if the 4th-grade test score is higher than that for the 3rd grade, the teacher is 'adding value' to the child's education. If a child's test scores decrease from year to year, the teacher is not contributing value to the child's education. This model is considered fairer than simply measuring a teacher's value by looking at current 4th-grade test scores (which would be a status model, not a growth model) because the multi-year approach does take into account some background variables. But it also has many identified flaws and the measurement community warns against using it. In November 2015, the AERA issued a statement on the use of VAM. The statement notes that there are potentially serious negative consequences in the context of evaluation that can result from the use of VAM based on incomplete or flawed data, as well as from the misinterpretation and misuse of the VAM results. See http://www.aera.net/Newsroom/NewsReleasesandStatements/AERAIssuesStatementontheUseofValueAddedModelsinEvaluationofEducatorsandEducatorPreparationPrograms/tabid/16120/Default.aspx.[3]

What is Annual Professional Performance Review (APPR)?

The annual professional performance review (APPR) takes the idea of evaluating students through standardized test scores and applies it (in principle) to teachers. It is a way to give teachers and principals a 'grade', or an effectiveness rating. This new teacher and principal rating system is governed by rules set by the state. For many states, this is the first time ever that a portion of the teacher evaluation is directly tied to student performance on standardized tests. APPR is cast as an educational reform put in place to improve student learning, but many perceive it as a way for states to place the blame for achievement gaps on teachers without accounting for factors outside teachers' control that affect learning. Using test scores for APPR has caused a lot of controversy across the US. The need for school districts to adopt local APPRs, and have them approved by state departments, was directly tied to the need for states to receive Race to the Top (RTTT)[4] federal money. Approved APPR plans were directly tied to states that want to receive RTTT money.

The results of APPR evaluations may rate teachers as highly effective, effective, developing or ineffective. In New York, for example, 60% of APPR is based on observations of teachers. Other factors (20%–25%) come from student growth based on state tests or progress made toward meeting student learning targets called student learning objectives (SLOs). The final 15%–20% is based on a measure of student achievement selected by each school district. Administration, scoring and the most critical parts of the APPR are governed by state-department regulations. Teachers in New York, for example, will be observed at least twice a year by the building principal or a trained administrator; one of these observations must be unannounced. These are state regulations, but much of the APPR is bargained locally — such as the classroom observation procedures, the appeals process and what to do when a teacher is ineffective. When a teacher is ineffective, a teacher improvement plan (TIP) is designed to remediate his or her ineffectiveness.

SLOs are used to gauge student growth in areas such as art, PE or those areas for which student achievement tests are not given (pre-K through 2). They must be aligned with the state standards (for most states these are the Common Core Learning Standards [CCLS]) and be written as measurable and observable objectives. The teacher will be accountable for these objectives through APPR. There are many points of debate in using the APPR for accountability as described above, but one major point of contention is the release of the ratings to students' parents.

How Do I Ensure I'm Following National and State Requirements?

This question and its possible answers continue to evolve. Owing to high-stakes testing, the unspoken answer is: The only standards that matter are the ones that are tested. One way to ensure that the standards are followed is to conduct a standards crosswalk – an analysis comparing the curriculum and instruction in your class with the CCLS. This is a time-consuming task; usually, the results of the analysis are presented in table format where one cell shows the intersection of two standards. This is also very effective in showing gaps or areas that need to be developed. Thus, it is advantageous to conduct a similar crosswalk with grade-level teachers to produce a horizontal crosswalk. Ideally, the entire school participates in the crosswalk to produce a vertical crosswalk.

How Do I Identify, Monitor and Reclassify EBs?

In larger, mostly urban school districts, the process of identification may be completed before you meet your students, depending on which grades you teach. However, it is likely that you will be called upon to administer the identification process and/or score the state's language proficiency test on an annual basis. The process is governed by the state department of education, including in most cases exactly what instrumentation you will use. Figure 9.1 shows the process of identification for EBs in New York State. This process is governed in New York by Commissioner Regulation (CR) Part 154, and all schools in New York State are expected to identify EBs in the same way with the same instruments. Each state has a different identification process, but all must meet minimum federal guidelines.

Each state has a law that governs the identification and reclassification process, which also satisfies federal guidelines for identification/reclassification. In New York and most states, the process of identifying, monitoring and reclassifying EBs over-relies on one standardized test that may or may not have evidence of validity for these particular purposes. The data needed to conduct a validity study of the use of the high-stakes test and its cutoff scores for the purpose of identification, monitoring and reclassification are unavailable due to 'test security'.

What is the Appropriate Use of Norm- and Criterion-Referenced Assessments?

When determining the appropriate use of any assessment, one must consider the four-step process called PUMI (see Chapter 1). In general, norm-referenced assessments have fallen out of favor due to their inherent unfairness to groups not represented in the norming sample (such as EBs) and because of the way that the norm referenced are designed to compare test-takers to a 'normal group of children', usually not including EBs learning English. Many times when using norm-referenced assessments, test-design concepts override content-validity considerations. This means that more importance may be put on test design and the precision of response rates than on whether the items and their responses actually make sense and are used appropriately (validity). Although criterion-referenced tests are more popular now, they too have problems – mostly in regard to the cutoff score. Who is to determine the difference between proficient and not proficient? Upon what evidence will the determination be based? As always, though, neither a norm- nor a criterion-referenced test will be 'valid and reliable' with EBs if they cannot read it.

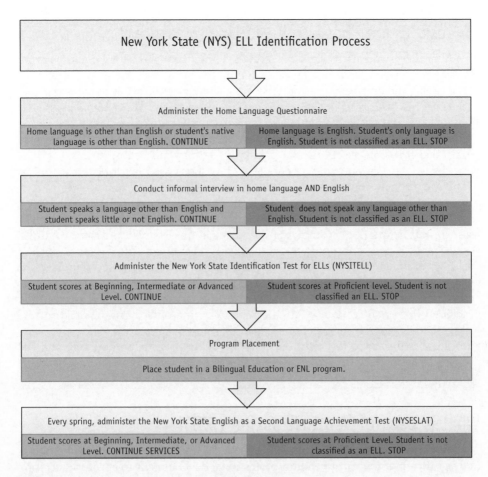

Figure 9.1 The process of identification for EBs in New York State

What is Meant by Multiple Measures?

The concept of multiple measures is a longstanding and important one to practice good assessment. It is similar to the concept of triangulation in radio telemetry, wherein multiple directional references are used to confirm location. Multiple measures are also used to increase validity within research studies. For example, a student survey shows that a student perceives himself as a strong reader, he scores high on reading achievement tests and the teacher observes him reading often during his free time. Through the process of triangulation, we can say with confidence that this child is a strong reader. If you measure a construct three different ways and they all point toward the same result, your results are good. Multiple measures, in other words, are different methods of assessment, which allow us to know that a result is near true, and not due to method or format.

Snapshot: Are These Truly Multiple Measures?

A mother is confused when she receives a note from the school indicating that her son Victor will be receiving academic intervention support (AIS) in reading, because she thought he was a good reader. She observes Victor at home reading all the time; his favorite books are fishing encyclopedias and Hardy Boys mysteries. The teacher and the principal assure his parents that Victor indeed has a deficit in reading, and if he doesn't attend intervention classes (where they seldom read but rather focus on phonics and vocabulary), he may fall behind even more. The principal further assures the parents that the school used 'multiple measures' to draw these conclusions.

However, upon closer inspection, this was not true. The school used three views of the *same* method (as opposed to three *different* methods of assessment) – the ELA state test, benchmark to ELA and the district reading assessment. All these measures used standardized, criterion-referenced, highly decontextualized assessments of reading; so similar, they were really one measure, not multiple. They all missed the fact that Victor not only reads but reads a lot, by choice – which to many educators are important indicators of being a good reader. The parents became frustrated and exercised their right to waive AIS, ultimately opting out of standardized testing altogether (an option for parents in New York and other states). The parents are not anti-testing; they feel that the tests are being used inappropriately and the consequences of how the scores are used (multiple hours a day of phonics practice) could potentially deter their child from enjoying reading overall.

What is Data-Driven Instruction (DDI)?

The current test-based accountability has led schools to implement DDI programs and significant amounts of funding/professional development to ensure all decisions regarding curriculum, instruction and assessment are using data. Using data to inform instruction in a cyclical and reflective way is not new and is very similar to many other education initiatives in the past. The decision cycle is one that all teachers have used before, albeit often in different forms. What is new for teachers is the emphasis on standardized test scores in the decision-making process and the heightened level of accountability and consequences attached to test results that we see in schools today. What is also new for veteran teachers is using standardized test results that are directly aligned to state content and language development standards.

DDI is generally understood in practice to be the use of quantifiable data (numbers) obtained from measuring articulated goals to determine if a student is improving his or her academic skills or remaining at the same level. The EB educator analyzes the data, which serve as a guide to determine how to modify or design the next steps for instruction. This section draws on the preceding discussion of promising assessment practices and on the PUMI framework to help educators look critically at what DDI for EBs means in their district and schools. This section also introduces the theme of authentic DDI for EBs put forward in this book.

Many new teachers today are given the message that DDI is 'the way' to increase student achievement. Statements such as 'Everything we do is data driven' or 'All instruction is driven by data' are often heard in conversations with school leaders. What do such statements really mean? More and more, data are available in schools each year, but the question about what to do with the data remains primarily unanswered. Not a new idea, DDI can be traced back to 1970s-era debates about *measurement-driven instruction* whereby some states required the use of *outcome data* in school-improvement planning and strategic planning. These debates continued through the 1980s and 1990s.

Unlike the previous models of DDI, the current model of school reform, however, narrowly interprets the definition of data and places a greater emphasis and value on the results of standardized-achievement and language-proficiency tests designed and scored outside a school – usually at the state or commercial level. Schools are drowning in these test data, and at the cost of oftentimes more valid data. As a result, other forms of data such as the results of portfolios, parent surveys, interviews and oral presentations are used less and less. In fact, most schools spend more time collecting, documenting and organizing data than on processing and reflecting on what the data mean, which data are meaningful and which are appropriate for EBs.

The consequences of drowning in 'one type' of data (standardized test results) include loss of instructional time, diversion away from subjects such as science and social studies (tested less), testing saturation (testing students too much) and rerouting of funding toward data initiatives and away from classroom- and school-level initiatives. Stephen Krashen recommends reducing or eliminating testing to increase instructional time and save money for buying books and hiring more teachers. According to Krashen, we only need a sample of test results, such as the National Assessment of Educational Progress (NAEP)[5] test, a test we've had for many decades. To use a funny analogy, Krashen (2011) says that doctors only take a *sample* of someone's blood to measure their health; they don't draw all the blood. He promotes the principle of NUT – No Unnecessary Testing. Despite the warnings of excessive testing, all states are full steam ahead in promoting more and more testing and using DDI based on standardized test results.

It is important to recognize that DDI means different things to different people. For some schools, DDI means simply printing out state test scores to determine areas of weakness and then targeting instruction toward those weaknesses. A more complex model of DDI might use multiple measures (use at least three different types of data to draw inferences) and look for patterns to decide what the underlying causes might be. Some schools have hired more administrators or data coaches (at times at the expense of other teaching budget lines) to help manage and coach data-uses at the school, grade and classroom levels. Data teams might also include experts such as English as a new/native language (ENL)/bilingual teachers, mathematics teacher-leaders who sift through the data to determine what is worthy of becoming 'actionable knowledge' – in other words, data interpretations worthy of instructional time. After all, not all data and data interpretations should initiate action, especially with EBs. Using the PUMI framework will give EB educators the questions that they need to ask to determine what data are actionable and what data should be abandoned.

Nobody says that data has to equal the results of standardized tests. EB educators should use the results of performance assessments, one-on-one communication and other methods to inform their instruction. Teachers have always used data in the form of the results of essays, multiple-choice quizzes, interviews, portfolios, responses to questioning and parent surveys – using multiple measures – to make instructional decisions. In addition to using the results of assessments, teachers relied on their *experience* with students to help meet the needs of students. Using multiple measures is best practice.

The picture of DDI shown in Figure 9.2 (Institute of Education Sciences [IES], 2009) may lead teachers to believe that DDI involves linear and continuous processes. In real settings, however, educators often skip steps, rely on intuition or hesitate to collect more (or more meaningful) data. Proponents of DDI favor the objective (without judgment) aspect of DDI; however, DDI may involve more judgment (less objective, more subjective) than many realize. The first judgment occurs when the people who make the tests judge whether a test item truly measures the intended construct. The second judgment takes place when school leadership prioritizes data based on what is meaningful and appropriate (e.g. state, district or school requirements/recommendations). Further judgment is needed to decide what actions to take (increase time on task, change or modify the curriculum, institute more professional development). Even though the process of DDI is empirically based (uses data), it turns out to be less objective than most think.

End-of-Chapter Activities (Instructors: see advice at the end of the book)

By completing Activities 1–2, the reader will be able to:

(1) Identify nine key vocabulary terms.
(2) Answer the following guiding questions about assessment:

What are all the buzz words (AYP, AMAO, growth model, value-added, APPR)?

How do I ensure that I'm following national and state requirements?

How do I identify, monitor and reclassify EBs?

What is the appropriate use of norm- and criterion-referenced assessments?

What is meant by multiple measures?

What is meant by DDI?

(*Continued*)

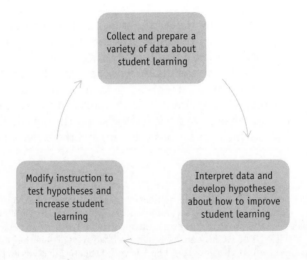

Figure 9.2 Data-use cycle presented by the Institute of Education Sciences (IES)

Activity 1

Identify nine key vocabulary terms.

This is a game of bingo using key vocabulary words from the chapter. Fold a piece of paper into nine equal parts (fold it into thirds, then fold it into thirds again). The instructor writes nine key vocabulary words on the board. Write them in any of the squares – one word per square. After this, students should have different bingo boards. The difference between this game and traditional bingo is that the instructor will read the *clue* and students must find the key vocabulary word that matches it. After a match is found, cross out the whole square. Once a student has bingo (three across, down or diagonal), he or she shouts 'bingo!' and the instructor checks the work. Use the nine clues and terms below.

Activity 2

Answer the following guiding questions about essential assessment:

What are all the buzz words (AYP, AMAO, growth model, value-added, APPR)?

How do I ensure I'm following national and state requirements?

How do I identify, monitor and reclassify EBs?

What is the appropriate use of norm- and criterion-referenced assessments?

What is meant by multiple measures?

(Continued)

Do Inside/Outside Circle. Half of the students are given an index card with one of the above questions written on it and the answer written on the back. Students with the questions form a small circle facing outward, and those without index cards form a circle facing the inner circle. Each student must face another student to state the definition of the term *or* the term when the definition is given. The outside circle rotates clockwise until each student has had a chance to go. After every student in the outside circle has a chance, the outside circle switches with the inside circle (which always has the card) and the activity is repeated.

Notes

(1) AMAO refers to annual measurable achievement objectives and AMO refers to annual measurable objective. They are the same in concept. States and districts need to set annual targets or objectives and prove that they are meeting them in order to receive funding. AMAO was related to Title III of NCLB and AMO was related to AYP. Neither are required by the federal government under the new law, ESSA (Every Student Succeeds Act); however, states still have to set goals for subgroups of students, like EBs.
(2) True story.
(3) See Amrein-Beardsley (2014) in the recommendation section of this chapter for an in-depth and critical view of VAMs.
(4) In the United States, RTTT funding came and went in three phases from 2010 to 2013. This was a 4.35 billion dollar competitive grant, funded as part of the American Recovery and Reinvestment Act of 2009.
(5) The National Assessment of Educational Progress started in 1964 and measures student achievement across topics. Using sophisticated sampling techniques, the NAEP takes samples of groups of students to determine 'the Nation's Report Card'; the NAEP does not test all students in all topics.

References

American Educational Research Association (AERA) (2000) Position statement of the American Educational Research Association concerning high-stakes testing in preK-12 education. *Educational Researcher*, 29 (8), 24–25.

Amrein-Beardsley, A. (2014) *Rethinking Value-Added Models in Education: Critical Perspectives on Tests and Assessment-Based Accountability*. Routledge: New York.

Institute of Education Sciences (IES) (2009) *Using Student Achievement Data to Support Instructional Decision Making: IES Practice Guide*. Washington, DC: US Department of Education.

Krashen, S. (2011) NUT: No Unnecessary Testing. See http://www.sdkrashen.com/content/articles/nut_no_unnecessary_testing.pdf (accessed 25 October 2016).

US Government Accountability Office (GAO) (2006) *No Child Left Behind Act: Assistance from Education Could Help States Better Measure Progress of Students with Limited English Proficiency*. See www.gao.gov/products/GAO-06-815 (accessed 25 October 2016).

Wright, W. (2006) A catch-22 for language learners. *Educational Leadership* 64 (3), 22–27.

Recommended resources

Amrein-Beardsley, A. (2014) *Rethinking Value-Added Models in Education: Critical Perspectives on Tests and Assessment-Based Accountability*. Routledge: New York.

Advice for Instructors on Chapter Activities

Chapter 1: A Decision–Making Process called PUMI

Instructor guidance for Activity 1

Before class, the instructor prints out all 14 clues from Table 1.1 and tapes them to sticky notes. The 14 clues are associated with using the lens of promise or of deficit.

It's not as easy as saying one way is good and the other is bad. Each approach and point on the continuum has strengths and weaknesses. As the name implies, the lens of promise has more strength for assessing emergent bilinguals (EBs), including opportunities to provide assessments that are culturally relevant; it sets students up for success, not failure; it focuses on language as asset, not deficit, of EBs; and it produces more valid results. Weaknesses of the promising practices may be that some of these practices are time-consuming and many times they yield data that are not comparable across districts and states. Weaknesses of the deficit practices include a one-size-fits-all approach that does not account for individual language and culture; decisions on results may not be valid; students have less agency; students may not perform well on test day; and EBs usually are not included in the norm, among others. Strengths of the practices leading to deficit may be that comparison of results can be made across school, district and state. Some might choose deficit approaches (they won't call it that) because large numbers of students can be assessed at the same time and therefore they can be more efficient or there is a need for baseline data. Explore other strengths and weaknesses.

A way to negotiate both views is to make sure you use many assessment methods, including as many promising assessment practices as possible. Teachers tend to use promising methods when there is a choice and yield to deficit assessment practices when mandated. For example, use observation and checklists (more promising) during class to document academic language proficiency and compare those results to state-mandated tests (more deficit). Include a balance of data to use as a profile of learning in addition to results from state tests. Analyze how checklists, portfolio results, etc., align with state test results. Make collective decisions about EBs using both models; never use the result of one assessment to make a big decision. And use PUMI (Purpose, Use, Method and Instrument) with all assessments so that you can understand them better and raise critical questions when the time is appropriate.

Instructor guidance for Activity 2

Bring to class four index cards labeled P, U, M and I for each pair of students in your class. If you have 20 students, bring 10 sets. Collect sets at the end of class to use in the future. After discussing PUMI and giving the students examples, ask them to complete Activity 2. If you are in a WIDA Consortium member state, give students general information about ACCESS for English language learners (ELLs; https://www.wida.us/assessment/access/) and ask students to complete a PUMI table (Table 1 shows an example) to better understand the English proficiency test used in your area.

Table 1 PUMI chart for ACCESS* for ELLs

P	U	M	I
Purpose	Use	Method	Instrument
To measure English language proficiency (ELP) (reading, writing, speaking, listening)	To monitor student progress every year To help determine when EBs have gained full proficiency	Criterion-referenced** test (CRT)	Pre-ordered printed tests from WIDA

* ACCESS for ELLs (Assessing Comprehension and Communication in English State-to-State for English Language Learners) is a secure large-scale ELP assessment given to kindergarten through twelfth graders who have been identified as ELLs. It is given annually in WIDA Consortium member states to monitor students' progress in acquiring academic English.

** Because this is a criterion-referenced test, it is not intended or appropriate to compare student to student or grade level to grade level (that would be more like norm referencing). It is intended to compare student performance on this test to the set of ELP standards published by WIDA.

Chapter 2: History: How Did We Get Here?

Instructor guidance for Activity 1

Purchase a roll of adding machine paper in advance. A roll of adding machine paper (the paper used for older adding machines – great for creating timelines) can be purchased in paper supply stores. Split adding machine paper so that each pair of students can have one strip to fit across their desks or table. Ask students to pair up and give each pair 10 sticky notes; then ask them to copy 10 events from the board and order them on their 'timeline'. Ask students to post their timeline in the front of the class upon completion. Use Table 2.1 to verify the order of events after students have finished their timelines.

To open and close Activity 1 as a whole group and to integrate movement into the activity, the instructor might model the timeline by asking 10 students to stand in front of the class, facing the class. For this whole group activity, the instructor might have 10 sticky notes prepared with a historical event (not date) written on the sticky note; then, the instructor 'sticks' one on each student out of order. The instructor then calls on two students at a time to come up and reorders the students until the order is correct. The instructor should ask students to explain why they reordered and what the event means. The instructor clarifies and adds details.

Instructor guidance for Activity 2

The instructor prepares a blank word web (a diagram with the question *Why do some students succeed and others don't?* in the middle, from which branches extend with different arguments) and projects it in front of the class. (See Figure 7.2, designed in less than one minute using MS Word SmartArt.) The instructor comes to class familiar with arguments for school failure as described in the introduction of Guadalupe Valdés's (1996) book *Con respeto* or another framework for understanding school success/failure.

Ask students why some students succeed and others don't. Categorize the reasons students say on a whiteboard according to arguments presented in this chapter (Valdés, 1996) – genetic, cultural or class analysis or another framework of your choice. Construct the word web in front of students as they each give one reason for school success/failure. Identify the categories *after* the students brainstorm and discuss findings. Ask the students to guess the categories before you name them (cultural, difference and deficit, genetic or class analysis).

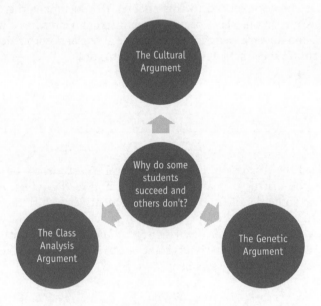

Figure 7.2 Example of a word web, designed using MS Word SmartArt

The instructor listens to students' comments and decides where they belong in the word web. The instructor leads a whole-group discussion: How does testing and assessment play a role in answering this question? What does testing and assessment have to do with this? This should lead to a thoughtful open discussion.

Instructor guidance for Activity 3

(1)   The two main accountability validity scenarios discussed in this chapter are less accountability/more validity and more accountability/less validity. Less accountability/more validity describes the pre-No Child Left Behind (NCLB) climate, wherein EBs were largely exempt from large-scale testing and its consequences, which led to less accountability. More accountability/less validity describes the climate after NCLB, wherein all EBs must take tests even though they don't know English yet; a consequence of higher accountability is less valid test results that misrepresent what EBs really know.

(2)   Two examples of less accountability/more validity could include a state law that exempts EBs from achievement testing for three years and teachers using portfolios to show how EBs are meeting English and language arts (ELA) standards. Two examples of more accountability/less validity could include NCLB allowing no exemptions from achievement testing in English – even for non-English speakers – and a river project cancelled to spend more time on test preparation for EBs.

Instructor guidance for Activity 4

The instructor comes to the academic discussion prepared with open-ended questions about themes explored in this chapter. To document the results of the academic discussion on one sheet of paper, the instructor prepares a class list with three columns, one for each category in the rubric above and with student names in rows. The recording sheet below is for the instructor only.

Student name	Quality of comments	Resource/document reference	Active listening
Student A			
Student B			
Student C			

Students lead the discussion, not the instructor. As students add comments to the discussion, the instructor marks points according to the rubric. All comments should reference some detail from the book. Students can shift the discussion at any time; if students have already contributed twice, they should yield to those who have not contributed to the discussion yet. One discussion with a class of 20 students takes approximately one hour. Point out to students that you are modeling authentic assessments in this assessment.

Chapter 3: Validity

Instructor guidance for Activity 1

The instructor will pass out blank index cards and ask students to discuss the definition of a unified view of validity as a group. After about 20 minutes of discussion, the instructor will call on one person per group to write on the board and share the group's definition. At the end of the activity, students submit their own definition on an index card with their name to the instructor for review; the instructor returns the cards at the end of class or the next class.

The instructor stresses that each student should have a unique definition that makes sense not only to them, but also to others around the table and in the classroom. They should also feel comfortable saying their definition of unified validity at school faculty meetings and in discussions with administrators and parents in the context of discussions of test scores for EBs. Be sure to do this in a constructive way so that each student's definition is unique and accurate.

Example definitions: (1) *Validity as a unified concept takes into account all aspects of traditional validity, plus new ideas like test interpretation, test use and social consequences.* (2) *Validity is a very complicated topic that includes both science and ethics and should be considered each time schools use test scores for EBs in different ways.* (3) *Validity as a unified concept advocates for validating test use for EBs on a case-by-case basis, not just validating the test.*

Instructor guidance for Activity 2

The instructor comes to class prepared with a marker, sticky notes and a list of key vocabulary words related to the unified view of validity (use the list at the beginning of the chapter) and provides a brief review. It is suggested that the instructor always be the model for this activity. Model for your students how to play vo-back-ulary so they can see what you want them to do. Use the following key vocabulary terms and suggested definitions in a sentence related to EBs. Possible hints, answers and use in a sentence with EBs are given below for six key unified validity vocabulary words.

- Example Hint #1: This describes the way we use test scores for EBs. This is different from the purpose and is an important idea in the unified view of validity. *Answer: test score use.* It is important to pay attention to test score use for EBs because many times test scores may be used in questionable ways.
- Example Hint #2: This is a difficult part of validity to study because it involves making judgments to some degree. This is the part of validity that involves ethics, values and ideologies. *Answer: test score interpretation.* Test score interpretation always involves ideologies such as language ideologies that often do not favor EBs.
- Example Hint #3: These include results such as being retained in a grade, when parents feel that their child is not smart or when a teacher doesn't get tenure.

Answer: social consequences of test score use. One factor that makes unified validity different from most definitions of validity is that it includes social consequences. When a note is sent home saying that an EB is a limited speaker of Spanish and English, it affects the child and family's social identity and is a social consequence of test score use.

Instructor guidance for Activity 3

The instructor comes to class with five or six printed copies of your state accountability law regarding teacher and principal evaluation and highlighter pens. Together, find the areas that discuss teacher–principal–school accountability and test scores. Split the class into small groups by counting (to mix up students), then review the above assignment.

Possible advocacy statements could include some of the following: *It is important to examine the intended use for a test. The tests used by this state for accountability were not designed (as articulated in the technical manual) to evaluate teachers, but rather were designed to measure achievement among dominant English speakers. Teachers with high numbers of EBs are evaluated unfairly compared to teachers with few or no EBs because many EBs cannot fluently read the items on the test; as a result of this, effective teachers of EBs are being evaluated negatively. If test scores increase or decrease, what does this really mean for EBs when they are given a test in English, a language in which they are not yet proficient? Sometimes this means that the test items were practiced over and over, which may not indicate a true increase in true learning. There are better ways to evaluate teachers, principals and schools and it is time to advocate for better use of test scores. It is not enough to say a test is valid; rather, the actual use of a test should be validated.*

Instructor guidance for Activity 4

Students may need some assistance to interpret this statement and feel confident making a decision about whether they agree or disagree with it. The instructor can project the statement onto a screen in front of the class and use the Microsoft highlight feature to highlight key words in order to help students understand what the statement means. Deconstruct the statement with the students before asking them to agree or disagree with it.

Set up a value line (I usually set mine up in the hallway before class starts) where students need to take a stand about whether they agree or disagree with the statement. Allow students in small groups or pairs to discuss the meaning of the statement, their stance and the reasons why they agree or disagree. Draw the numbers 1 (strongly disagree) through 10 (strongly agree) across the whiteboard or use small posters with the numbers 1 through 10 in the hallway. Place the numbers far enough apart to allow enough room for all students to stand near the numbers at the same time. When all students are standing near the number representing their agreement, select three or four to explain why they chose that number and ask the other students whether they disagree or agree and why. As a follow-up question, ask if any students can connect this to the arguments for school success/failure introduced in Chapter 7. This is a whole-group activity.

Chapter 4: Methods

Instructor guidance for Activity 1

Ask students to brainstorm activity and mark on chart paper 10 ways to use multiple languages to create assessment products. To scaffold students, give them the first column and ask them to complete the second column. Think of more...

Final product	Add translanguaging
Write persuasive reviews about local restaurants	Write one in English and one in home language to target more audiences.
Write about cause/effects of WW2	Create a short audio recording summarizing causes/effects of WW2 in home language.
Research a country of their choice	Take notes in home language and English. Read research on internet from home language websites and English websites.
Write a document-based question (DBQ)	Write a DBQ in home language. Include one sentence in English and English key vocabulary words.
Write a story	Use home language and English to write a story.
Create campaign advertisement	Create one advertisement in home language and one in English.
Critique a poem	Choose a poem in the home language and create a PowerPoint in English to explain the poem to peers. Include comparison of English to home language. Give oral presentation in English.

Instructor guidance for Activity 2

See the example checklist and rubrics presented in this chapter. Model how to go through the process of writing language and content objectives to creating a checklist for observation and two rubrics to support the documentation of assessments. In small groups, students should use MS Word, Excel and/or RubiStar to create checklists and rubrics. (Students using RubiStar need to register.) Answers will vary.

Chapter 5: Content and Language

Instructor guidance for Activity 1

Create one set of clue cards per group (six or eight is good, depending on the number of groups you organize) using 3×5 index cards. Do not put the answers anywhere on the clue cards. (Clues and answers are shown below.) Be sure to collect clue cards at the end of this activity, using a paperclip for each set so that you can easily reuse them in a future class. Ask each group to sort them by the five categories and discuss for 15 or so minutes. Come to class with five paper bags lunch sized) labeled with each content target category (knowledge, reasoning, key practices, products and dispositional) and set them in a central location. One by one, a representative from each group will come up and deposit their clue card in the correct bag and explain why. To make it more challenging, the instructor should select the clue card. To make it less challenging, allow the group to select the clue card. Because there are 10 cards, each group will participate twice. The categories of content are not mutually exclusive and therefore may cause confusion or discussion; for example, an act of reasoning could perhaps be classified as reasoning or key practices. Ask the students to go with where they think it fits best. For example, if the learning focuses directly on reasoning, it should be labeled reasoning. If the primary focus of the learning is on *practicing* (usually through written or oral expression), it should be key practices. An extension of this activity could be to have students make their own clue cards and test one another.

Clue	Answer
A square with side length 1 unit, called 'a unit square', is said to have 'one square unit' of area.	Knowledge
Genes are located in the chromosomes of cells, with each chromosome pair containing two variants of each of many distinct genes.	Knowledge
Analyze how two or more texts address similar themes or topics in order to build knowledge or to compare the approaches the authors take.	Reasoning
Compare the interactions between individuals, events and ideas in a text (e.g. how ideas influence individuals or events and how individuals influence ideas or events).	Reasoning
Use tiling to show in a concrete case that the area of a rectangle with whole-number side lengths and $b+c$ is the sum of $a{\times}b$ and $a{\times}c$.	Key practices
Use an oral and written argument supported by evidence to support or refute the idea that a square is also a rectangle.	Key practices
Assessing attitude toward learning English is something many EB educators do.	Dispositional
Shyness, motivation and attitude are all factors in the affective filter hypothesis. EB educators want to keep the affective filter low for EBs.	Dispositional

Instructor guidance for Activity 2

Answer for Table 5.12; answers will vary.

Objectives	Instruction	Assessment
Content: SW be able to compare and contrast the attributes of a square and a rectangle.	Is a square a rectangle? TW model use of blocks to identify characteristics of square and rectangle. SW use a graphic organizer to collect evidence for or against.	Content. Selected response. TW will play Find the Fib* (selected response game where two truths are told about squares/rectangles and one fib).
Language: SW be able to produce a written argument for why a square is a rectangle.	TW model using graphic organizer to write arguments and how to turn those arguments into a short paragraph.	Language. Written response. SW write a short paragraph using supporting evidence to argue why a square is a rectangle.

Source: Adapted from Echevarria et al. (2008).

Answer for Table 5.13; answers will vary.

Objectives	Instruction	Assessment
Content: SW be able to calculate the number of protons, electrons and neutrons in an element, given its atomic number and atomic mass.	TW use clue cards which have a question side and an answer side. SW rotate cards around small circle and practice reading and answering chemistry Q&A.	Content. Selected response. Survey using selected response (yes/no) is given to students to assess whether they met the objective. Modality is self-assessment.
Language: SW be able to listen to a question and tell a partner the number of protons/electrons/ neutrons in an element.	In pairs, each student will listen to their partner read a chemistry clue card and practice answering it.	Language. One-to-one communication. Questioning is used in a peer-to-peer modality.

Instructor guidance for Activity 3

The instructor should model the process of writing language objectives from standards and practicing PUMI at least once before asking students to complete this activity. For the activity listed above, Step 2 might be stated as: Students will follow oral instructions to categorize objects according to their length. A variety of language objectives align with this standard, so perhaps give a few examples. The important thing about language objectives is that they are observable and measurable. Avoid using phrases such as 'students will think' or 'students will know' because these are difficult to observe. If students write objectives using such words, ask them, 'How will they know that?' 'What will they observe the student doing?' This should help articulate language objectives. Remind students that language objectives are narrower than English language development (ELD) standards and they can think of objectives as the little steps students and teachers need to take to 'meet' the standard.

Step 3 is the real assessment piece; if students use PUMI, an appropriate standards-based method can be selected. As shown below, after considering all of PUMI, observation is an appropriate standards-based method for assessing this language standard, with the use of a simple checklist (they followed instructions or they didn't).

P	U	M	I
To measure listening skills in the context of a math lesson	To inform instruction	Observation	Checklist

Instructor guidance for Activity 4

Familiarize your students with MS Word Smart Art if possible; however, this activity can be done without Smart Art. Smart Art is a great tool in general for developing quick and easy graphic organizers for instructional purposes. For this assignment, it is suggested that students review the graphic organizers under the 'list' or 'process' category under the Insert (Smart Art) tab. To warm up for this activity, have students recite the levels of language proficiency used in your state (these will vary) and use movement in some way to physically demonstrate the different level of language proficiency. The purpose of this warm-up is to use creativity and physical movement for instruction, as well as to become very familiar – by memory – with

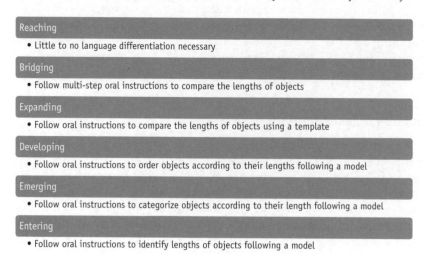

Figure 5.8 Differentiated instruction for EBs (WIDA, 2012: 24)

the language proficiency levels used in your state ELP standards document. For the purposes of this book, the six WIDA levels are used.

Chapter 6: Psychometrics

Instructor guidance for Activity 1

Before interpreting and using data, it is necessary to complete a PUMI table with your students to familiarize them with the most important aspects of the test that produced these results and to make them more aware of what the test company says about this test. In order to complete a PUMI on ACCESS for ELLs, find the ACCESS for ELLs interpretive guide for score reports that was written in spring 2011 (www.wida.us/assessment/access/ScoreReports/ACCESS_Interpretive_Guide11.pdf). It is 67 pages long, but the PUMI parts can be easily located. Complete a table similar to Table 2 with students or have them complete it for homework before class. Note how the test constructors advise using these scores. The two uses mentioned are to monitor student progress annually and to help determine when EBs have gained full proficiency. These are both accountability uses; there is no mention of using these data for instructional purposes[1]. Also note that the scores should be used to *help* determine English proficiency; they should not be the sole decider.

Table 2 PUMI chart for ACCESS for ELLs

P	U	M	I
To measure English language proficiency (ELP) (reading, writing, speaking, listening)	To monitor student progress every year To help determine when EBs have gained full proficiency	CRT*	Pre-ordered tests from WIDA

* Because this is a CRT, it is not intended or appropriate to compare student to student or grade level to grade level (that would be more like norm referencing). It is intended to compare student performance on this test to the set of ELP standards published by WIDA.

Here are answers to the questions posed to students above:

(1) Scale scores are derived from the raw score and they are very useful to show how a student is doing from year to year within *one* language domain. Do not compare scale scores across domains because they are scaled differently.

(2) Proficiency levels are cut scores designed by the test developers based on a set of standards (or theory of language). Because they are derived from the scale score, they also cannot be compared to other domains, but if you stay within one language domain both scale scores and proficiency levels can be compared across years.

(3) The only scores that are *not* composite are listening, speaking, reading and writing. Composite scores in this report add about half of the numbers, which may lead to confusion; you should cross out composite scores when you are

first looking for meaning in the data and stay in the listening, reading and writing domains, the main domains. Composites are a combination of the main domains anyway and you can easily overlook a problem. For example, oral language=listening+speaking; literacy=reading+writing; comprehens ion=listening+reading; and overall=listening+speaking+reading+writing. Don't worry about composite scores until you have studied the main domains thoroughly; domain scores may give you the information you need without the possibility of losing meaning or hiding something. In fact, you may never need composite scores.

(4) Table 6.3 shows data reported for three high school students across three years. It is important to think about what tier the students have taken and, also, who decides what tier they will take. Each form of a test has three tiers (except kindergarten). Within each grade-level cluster, there are three tiers to account for three levels of language proficiency. Tier A is for beginners, tier B is for intermediate and tier C is for advanced. The ACCESS interpretive guide states that tier A is for newcomers, students with limited or interrupted formal schooling, or EBs whose initial literacy development is in their native language. Pay attention to tiers, because tiers A and B have capped scores. In other words, due to the leveled nature of the tiers, students taking tier A cannot score above proficiency level 4 and students taking tier B cannot score above proficiency level 5. Therefore, students taking tiers A and B cannot demonstrate ELP until they take tier C. Equipped with this information about tiers, you can notice two peculiarities when scanning the data. The first is that students A, B and C do not progress through tiers as we would expect them to. Student A takes tier B in 2010, tier A in 2011 and tier B again in 2012. We would expect to see a progression from A to B to C, not from B to A to B. The same pattern shows for student B. Student C progresses from tier C in 2010 to tier B in 2011, then remains in tier B for 2012. The other peculiarity involves the performance level of 5.4 that student C scored in 2012. The WIDA ACCESS interpretation guide states that students taking tier B are capped and cannot score above level 5, yet the data show level 5.4. The simple explanation for this is probably that the tier C students cannot score a 6 or above. The reason for administering the tier B and then regressing to tier A is unknown. Perhaps the different tiered test may have affected student A but not students B and C. In general, proficiency levels can be used to make comparisons between domains and across tiers. However, whenever a different form of a test is used to determine any score, some precision in comparison is lost.

(5) Year 2 (2011) for student A is showing some outlier data, but years 1 and 3 appear to make more sense. For example, it seems strange that second language development in listening would decrease as much as it did in year 2 (2011) and then go back up in year 3. Year 2 was also the only year out of three when student A was given a differently tiered test. Therefore, this analysis will focus

on years 1 (2010) and 3 (2012) and gather other evidence of how the student performed in 2011 instead of ACCESS scores. Student A had very small growth in all areas except for speaking, which showed the most growth. Investigate background and school factors more for this student.

(6) Student B showed a large increase in English language development over the three years, especially in listening and speaking. The ELD growth of this student is aligned with the research showing how long it takes to learn academic language (4–9 years).

(7) Student C is showing large growth across the years in all language domains and is on a similarly positive trajectory as student B.

In short, student A is not doing so well and needs to be treated as a case study; more evidence is needed, along with interviews with his or her teacher. Students B and C are progressing well and current programming or other school factors appear to be supporting ELD.

Instructor guidance for Activity 2

Make your own bingo board (3×3) so that students can see what it looks like. Keep reading the clues until one student shouts 'bingo!' Keep track of the words you called, review the winner's board word by word and discuss each term. Use clues and terms below.

Clue	Term
A measurement scientist.	Psychometrician
By definition, half of all test takers score at or above the 50th percentile.	Norm referenced
Score performance is in reference to criteria.	Criterion referenced
The wrong answers presented in a multiple choice question.	Distracter
No test is perfectly accurate because of this.	Measurement error
A child in fourth grade brings home a test and because of this score her parents think she should be moved to seventh grade.	Grade equivalents
Line all students up from lowest score to highest score. Don't average this score because of unequal intervals.	Percentiles
Was developed to try and remedy the problems concerning grade equivalents and percentile ranks.	Normal curve equivalent (NCE)
This score can be used to show growth within one domain from year to year.	Scale score

Chapter 7: Accommodations

Instructor guidance for Activity 1

From the 10 accommodations listed in Table 7.3, write 9 where the students can see them. Make your own bingo board (3×3) so the students can see what it looks like. Then 'perform' the accommodations so that the class can guess what each one is. Before class, download test item samples from your state content test to help you perform the accommodations. (This is like a role-play activity.) Continue performing clues until one student shouts 'bingo!' Keep track of the words you called, review the winner's board word by word and discuss each term. Ask students which accommodations they have observed in schools during field study.

Instructor guidance for Activity 2

Prepare index cards before class with one of the eight questions on one side and a brief answer on the other. Each question is discussed in this chapter. Try to keep answers to paraphrases. Walk around, listen to the answers and help the students to clarify concepts. Rotate the group every two minutes; after all of the students have had a chance to answer the questions, ask them what needs to be clarified. Modification: Do not put the answer on the cards. The instructor clarifies any confusion at the end. There are eight questions, so this will accommodate a class size of 16. If a class is larger, simply ask new questions. Answers to questions may include the following:

(1) What is reliability? *Reliability has to do with the consistency of a score. Is the score due to chance or error or is it due to true achievement? If a score is reliable, it should have little error.*
(2) How is reliability connected to accommodations? *Accommodations are designed to address the barriers to testing, such as language. If accommodations work, the reliability of a score will increase.*
(3) If a reliability coefficient is 0.70, what does this mean? *It means that roughly 70% of the score is due to true achievement and 30% is due to error.*
(4) Can accommodations close the achievement gap? *No. Accommodations can decrease some of the obstacles to testing experienced by EBs, especially language barriers, but they will never close the achievement gap.*
(5) What does it mean if a test has the standard error of measurement (SEM) at 3 points? *SEM is a range in which the true score is located, but we never really know the true score. This means that if a student scores 68 on a test, the true score is somewhere between 65 and 71.*
(6) What is linguistic simplification? *This is a promising accommodation for EBs in which test items are simplified linguistically without changing the construct of the item.*
(7) Give two other names for test score error. *Test pollution, test contamination, garbage or nuisance variables.*

(8) Name three common causes of error for EBs. *Language of the test, fatigue, nervousness or anxiety.*

Instructor guidance for Activity 3

Bring chart paper to class and distribute one blank piece to each small group. Briefly discuss possible linguistic modifications by drawing the students' attention to Table 7.2 and review line by line with brief explanations. With the revised item, students may employ some of the following linguistic changes to make revisions to the language: conditional clause changed to separate sentence; two relative clauses removed and recast; long nominals shortened; questions phrase changed from 'which of the following' to 'how many'; item length changed from 26 to 13 words; number of clauses changed from 4 to 2.

Chapter 8: Special Education

Instructor guidance for Activity 1

After discussing the six major tenets of IDEA with students, provide brief scenarios that are linked to each tenet. Ask each student to pick which tenet they believe is being described and provide support for their choice. Students can do this individually or in small groups.

Instructor guidance for Activity 2

Label six pieces of chart paper with the following headings: referral, evaluation, eligibility, individualized education plan (IEP), placement and annual review. Have students put one big idea for each heading on chart paper. Circulate until chart paper and/or headings are conclusive. Generate a group discussion on the muddiest points.

Instructor guidance for Activity 3

Provide the following directions to students to complete a mind map. First, explain the concept of mind mapping as a visual representation, similar to a graphic organizer. Offer the opportunity to work in pairs. Have students design their mind maps with the following characteristics: define the category, define the identification and referral process and provide four recommended educational practices. Students can present their mind maps to the whole class and submit a written document that includes: one interesting component, with citation; one thing to learn more about; design rationale; what they learned from the experience; and how the assignment could be used as a resource and in a classroom.

Chapter 9: Accountability

Guidance for Activity 1

Make your own bingo board (3×3) so students can see what it looks like. Keep reading the clues until one student shouts 'bingo!' Keep track of the words you called, review the winner's board word by word and discuss each term.

Clue	Term
Part of the NCBL law that requires EBs to attain English proficiency and meet the same academic standards as English-speaking peers.	Title III
For a school to receive Title III money, the state is accountable to three of these.	AMAO
Schools must demonstrate this to the state and the state must demonstrate this to the federal government.	AYP
This accountability model can track student progress or cohorts of student progress over time. The progress is rewarded.	Growth model
This accountability model takes a snapshot of a subgroup at one point in time. It may not reward growth.	Status model
This model largely attributes changes in test score to the teacher.	Value-added assessment
This is a way to give teachers and principals a 'grade' – an effectiveness rating.	APPR
These are used to gauge student growth in areas such as art, PE or areas in school for which student achievement tests are not given (pre-K through 2).	SLO
The key is using different methods of assessment. This allows us to know that a test result is not due to method or format.	Multiple measures

Instructor guidance for Activity 2

Prepare index cards before class with one of the eight questions on one side and a brief answer on the other. Each question is discussed in this chapter. Try to keep answers to paraphrases. Walk around, listen to the answers and help the students to clarify concepts. Rotate the group every two minutes; after all of the students have had a chance to answer the questions, ask them what needs to be clarified. Modification: Do not put the answer on the cards. The instructor clarifies any confusion at the end. There are eight questions, so this will accommodate a class size of 16. If a class is larger, simply ask new questions.

Notes

(1) The kindergarten form of ACCESS for ELLs includes proficiency levels to be used for instructional purposes and proficiency levels to be used for accountability levels. All other grades levels have accountability only.

Glossary

Accommodations: Changes in the test process, in the test itself or in the test-response format.

Annual Professional Performance Review (APPR): The Annual Professional Performance Review (APPR) takes the idea of evaluating students through standardized test scores and applies it (in principle) to teachers. It is a way to give teachers and principals a 'grade', or an effectiveness rating.

Assessment: A broad term that can be thought of generally as the use of information from various sources to make decisions about a student's future instruction/schooling.

Assessment lens of promise: Highlighting what the student knows, grounded from ideas of dynamic bilingualism and sociocultural assessment, it is used to guide emergent bilingual educators on how to assess and instruct emergent bilinguals within a meaningful and culturally responsive context.

Assessment lens of deficit: Highlighting what the student doesn't know relative to one measure and does not provide a culturally responsive context.

Class analysis argument: Ascribes school failure to the role of education in maintaining class differences (that is, maintaining the power of some over others).

Construct: What the learner is being measured on and these ideas are constructed by experts in the field and informed by a theoretical or conceptual framework chosen to guide the test construction, for example 'language proficiency' and 'academic achievement'.

Construct irrelevant variance: The major threat of validity for using emergent bilingual test scores and the systematic measurement error that reduces the ability to accurately interpret scores or ratings. Otherwise known as bias.

Construct validity: Takes into account how the test will be used, the consequences of using it in those ways and for whom the test was intended.

Content or language target: Knowledge and associated processes such as analyzing, producing, constructing, reasoning, defining, developing, using, etc., that help articulate the purpose (in PUMI).

Criterion referenced: Students' performances are compared to a set of behaviors, usually standards.

Cultural argument: Proposes that children who perform poorly in schools are either culturally deprived or culturally different and therefore mismatched with schools and school personnel, problematic when children and families are identified as having deficits instead of the school.

Culturally and linguistically diverse (CLD): Students who are distinguished from the mainstream culture and language (in the United States, non-white or not English dominant).

Curriculum-based measure (CBM): Assessment derived directly from the curriculum being taught; characterized by frequent, direct measures of school behaviors; formative in nature; allows teachers to make instructional decisions about teaching and curriculum while learning is taking place.

Cut scores: Determine the point between proficient and not proficient, many times problematic.

Data-Driven Instruction (DDI): Using data to inform instruction in a cyclical and reflective way.

Direct linguistic support: Includes accommodations such as translation of the test into the native language, simplifying English language or test language and repetition of test language.

Dispositional: Dispositional targets help EB educators understand factors affecting second language acquisition (SLA) such as motivation, attitude, negative and positive experiences with immigration or English or school and so on.

Disproportional representation: A greater number of students from diverse groups placed in special education programs when compared to mainstream students (such as white middle-class)

Emergent bilingual (EB): The preferred term for students who are in the process of learning English as a new language.

English language learner (ELL): Students who are in the process of learning English as a new language.

Error: When testing, can be caused by guessing, subjective scoring for essays, unnecessarily complex language, fatigue, nervousness and other factors.

Eugenics: The science of improving a human population by controlled breeding to increase the occurrence of desirable heritable characteristics.

Formative assessment: Formative assessments gather information in order to 'form' or shape student learning. This kind of assessment is ongoing and happens most often in classrooms. Benchmarks, which are mini-goals set to scaffold a student to reach an end goal, guide formative assessments. Most assessments used in classrooms are meant to show how students are progressing toward language and content goals throughout the year. The results of formative assessments also help shape and form the teacher's instruction. Good formative assessments should lead to better summative outcomes.

Four categories of methods: Selected response, written response, performance and one-to-one communication.

Four categories of modalities: One-to-group, one-to-one, group-to-group or to-self (examples: teacher-to-student, student-to-student or peer assessment, student to group, student to family or teacher to family).

Genetic argument: The view that some groups are genetically more able than others, and because of these inherent differences, children of different racial and ethnic groups perform differently in schools.

Growth model: In general, growth models for accountability refer to models that evaluate the progress of a group of individual students over time. This is much like a longitudinal research study in which individual students are tracked over time instead of being evaluated on the snapshot of their achievement in a single year.

High incidence disabilities: Those disabilities that are most likely to appear in school for initial evaluation and are usually diagnosed after a student starts school by non-medical personnel (e.g. learning disabilities, emotional disturbance).

Indirect linguistic support: Includes accommodations such as adjustments to time, schedules or environment.

Instrument: The last step in the PUMI process where teachers and administrators decide what instruments will be needed (tests, prompts, realia, rubric, checklist, etc.).

Key practices: Practices or procedures (what we do with content) are sometimes called *key practices*; the idea of key practices within a content area can be thought of as 'things we do with the content' or otherwise thought of as the application of content.

Knowledge: Knowledge can be defined in many ways, but within a school setting it is usually defined as the subject-matter content that teachers want EBs to master.

Large-scale assessments: Assessing large numbers of people on the progress at local, state or national level.

Learning disability (LD): A disorder in one or more of the basic psychological processes involved in understanding or using language, spoken or written, which may manifest itself in an imperfect ability to listen, speak, read, write, spell or do mathematical calculations.

Least restrictive environment: Students with disabilities are to be educated, to the maximum extent appropriate, with students without disabilities.

Method: The third step in the PUMI process where teachers and administrators decide what method is most appropriate for the language or content purpose.

Multiple measures: Multiple measures, in other words, are different methods of assessment, which allow us to know that a result is near true, and not due to method or format.

Normal curve equivalent (NCE): This was designed to correct for the lack of equal intervals in grade equivalent and percentile rank by having a normal curve line graph accessible and compare the percentile rank scale to the NCE.

Norm referenced: Students' performances are compared to another group of students' performances to judge how well they learned.

Oral interview: (one-to-one communication) Emergent bilingual educators can ask questions (input) and evaluate answers from emergent bilinguals (output).

Percentile rank: Tells where a student stands in regard to other students, should be used with caution.

Portfolio: (may include all or a mix of selected response, written response, performance assessment and one-to-one communication) Contains samples of student work, selected by the student and the teacher systematically and purposefully to show evidence that the student is learning core standards

Pre-referral (for consideration in special education): Beginning of the assessment process that gathers data on student academic and behavior progress; reviews strategies and student's response to interventions.

Proficiency level: Scores that are an interpretation of scale scores and are a result of choosing a cut score for each level.

Psychometrics: The science of measuring mental capacities and processes.

Purpose: The first step in the PUMI process where teachers and administrators define what the purpose (or target) of a particular assessment is.

Raw score: A score that is not ranked or compared to groups of children and that nothing has been done to it yet.

Reasoning: Most people think knowledge gives rise to *reasoning,* and some think knowledge and reasoning grow together. Reasoning means that students will think, understand and form judgments using logic.

Reliability: The extent to which a test yields the same results on repeated trials.

Reliability coefficient: How reliability is measured (a number between 0 and 1), which informs us empirically how much contamination (or error) is part of the overall test score.

Response to intervention (RTI): A three-tiered process that determines if a student is responding to empirically validated, scientifically based interventions. In the United States, RTI is required and used with suspected *learning or emotional disabilities only.*

Role play: Invites students to speak or act through the identity of others, provides an authentic context for students to learn language and content and for teachers to assess it.

Rubric: A tool to keep data collection systematic and focused on the same purpose or target and can be used in different modalities, perhaps by the teacher, the student or even a parent.

Scale score: Derived from the raw score, and links together all test forms within one content area.

Special education: A customized instructional program designed to meet the unique needs of an individual learner.

Speech or language impairment (SLI): Impairments in communication and/or language function, which adversely affect a student's educational performance.

Standard error of measurement (SEM): Represents the range of a test's accuracy.

Standard score: A set of scores that have the same mean and standard deviation so that they can be compared.

Standardized: Everything is the same: the items, the amount of time, the responses, the directions, etc. Typically, standardized tests consist of some combination of selected response and open response, and are usually given to a large group of students at the same time.

Stanine: A method of scaling test scores on a nine-point scale with a mean of five and a standard deviation of two.

Status model: Status models take a snapshot of a subgroup, such as EBs, at one point in time and compare it to an established target. In the status model, growth may not be rewarded – a fact that frustrated schools with high numbers of EBs.

Story retelling: (performance assessment) Emergent bilinguals read or listen to text and then retell the main ideas and some details.

Student learning objective (SLO): SLOs are used to gauge student growth in areas such as art, PE or those areas for which student achievement tests are not given (pre-K through 2). They must be aligned to the state standards (for most states these are the Common Core Learning Standards) and be written as measurable and observable objectives.

Summative assessment: Summative assessments are intended to 'summarize' the progress of a program or a child after a long period of time such as a marking period or an academic year. Summative assessments often look like grades, final-exam scores, regents tests, a research project or a language-proficiency test score.

Teacher observation: (performance assessment) The teacher continues to observe and make instructional decisions based on what he or she sees.

Test fairness: Test norms based on native speakers of English either should not be used with individuals whose first language is not English, or such individuals' test results should be interpreted as reflecting, in part, their current level of English proficiency rather than ability, potential, aptitude or personality characteristics or symptomology.

Test interpretation: How the test developers want the test to be interpreted. A rationale should be presented for each intended interpretation of test scores for a given use, together with a summary of the evidence and the theory of bearing on the intended interpretation.

Test misuse: Using tests as gatekeepers to advance some groups over others. State mandates requiring testing students in a language that they do not know yet are increasing. Achievement test scores will not accurately reflect knowledge of a specific subject area if the student is not yet proficient in the language of the test.

Test score use: The way a test developer uses the test results, for example, giving grades, deciding a program, deciding promotion, emergent bilingual classification or SPED certification in some cases.

Testing: One measuring instrument that produces information we use in assessment.

Title III: Title III awards are granted to states who meet the set requirements; the funds are targeted to help EBs meet English and content standards (Title III replaced the Bilingual Education Act, formerly known as Title VII).

Translanguaging: In assessment, students use their home languages and literacies during instruction and assessment to learn content and language in meaningful ways.

Unified view of validity: An integrated evaluative judgment of the degree to which empirical evidence and theoretical rationales support the adequacy and appropriateness of interferences and actions based on test score (Messick).

Use: The second step in the PUMI process where teachers and administrators decide how the results of a particular assessment will be used.

Value-added assessment: In a value-added model, changes are mostly attributed to the teacher. (Note that this ignores out-of-school factors [OSFs].) Value-added assessment models follow individual student achievement over time, and are supposed to show the specific effects of programs and other relevant factors.

Index